THE RELIGIOUS ATTITUDE AND LIFE IN ISLAM

The Religious Attitude and Life in Islam

BEING THE HASKELL LECTURES ON COMPARATIVE RELIGION DELIVERED BEFORE THE UNIVERSITY OF CHICAGO IN 1906

By

DUNCAN BLACK MACDONALD, M.A., B.D.

Sometime Scholar and Fellow of the University of Glasgow; Professor of Semitic Languages in Hartford Theological Seminary; Author of *Development of Muslim Theology, Jurisprudence and Constitutional Theory*, etc.

LONDON
DARF PUBLISHERS LIMITED
1985

First Published February 1909
New Impression 1985

ISBN 978 1 85077 050 3

To

M. L. B. M.

PREFACE

The following lectures are an attempt to outline the religious attitude and life of Muslims, as opposed to the systematic theology of Islām. Of the development of the latter I published a sketch some years ago; to that the present volume may be regarded as a complement.

That its contents will be a surprise to many, I am very conscious. Instead of being an oriental replica, however humble, of Mr. William James's *Varieties of Religious Experience*, as might reasonably be expected, it will probably suggest to most the *Human Personality* of the late F. W. H. Myers. But nothing else was possible. Orientals have never learned the art of ignoring all but the normal, the always renewable; they have kept a mind for infinite possibilities, and the infinite possibilities have continued to come to them. Naturally, then, instead of their religion gradually limiting itself down to emotions quickened by ethical aspirations, it has retained a very lively feeling of contact with an actual spiritual world, self-existent and in no process of dependent becoming.

It was necessary, therefore, in the search for interpretative analogies, to turn, not to our metaphysical systems or to our religious philosophy, but rather to what we call commonly, in jest or earnest, the occult. These analogies, therefore, had to be sought chiefly in the *Proceedings of the Society for Psychical Research* and similar publications. The case of Muhammad himself, for example, can be indefinitely more completely illustrated and explained by the phenomena of so-called trance-mediumship than by any other hypothesis. In the light of what we know now on such matters, even Sprenger's most able and learned investigation has been completely antiquated. And it is noteworthy, further, that the theory of veridical hallucinations worked out by Gurney and Myers is essentially that of al-Ghazzālī and Ibn Khaldūn.

But my use of these analogies has been so extensive that in order to avoid misconceptions, some statement of my own views is necessary. So far, then, as one may who has had no first-hand experience, I am driven to regard telepathy as proved. Again, so far as one may who is neither a physicist nor a conjurer, I regard the proof of what Dr. Maxwell has called telekinesis, movement of objects at a distance without contact, as approaching certainty. Of communications by discarnate spirits, on the other hand, I know of no satisfactory proof. I trust that this personal statement in explanation and defense may be pardoned.

References have been kept to a minimum, but have been given exactly for all the Arabic texts used. Of Ibn Khaldūn's *Prolegomena* I have consulted the Beyrout and Būlāq texts and de Slane's translation. The last, made from Quatremère's text, is fullest of all; that of Beyrout has considerable omissions, intentional and accidental, and some amazing blunders. As it is the most accessible and seemingly usable text, it may be worth while to say that neither as regards its consonants nor its vowels can it be trusted. The other references will explain themselves to the Arabist; for him also I have inserted a number of important words in transliteration; but not, I trust, so many as to annoy the general reader. Of necessity, I have had to reproduce much from Arabic authors. For the most part this is condensed and paraphrased with as faithful rendering of the thought as possible. But, from time to time, sections of simple translation occur; these are always indicated. My own inserted comments will also be recognizable. It is hardly necessary to add that in these ten lectures hardly an entrance has been made into the subject. But I venture to hope that I have sketched the essential outlines, and that future research will bring only additions and corrections in detail. Very little has so far been done in this field; but several articles in Hasting's *Dictionary of Religion*, at present in preparation, will contribute to it; and all signs indicate a renewed general interest in Islām.

I have again to express my indebtedness to my colleague, Professor Gillett, for his counsel in philosophy, and to my wife for much patient labor in copying and for suggestion and criticism in arranging and correcting. Without her comradeship in interest and her knowledge of the general subject this book might never have taken form, and in her hands I now fittingly leave it.

DUNCAN B. MACDONALD

HARTFORD, CONN.,
October, 1908

CONTENTS

PAGE

LECTURE I 1

The religious attitude in Islām; reality of the Unseen to Orientals; its nature; comparison with mediaeval Europe; oriental lack in sense of law; the shell of law and the supernatural behind it; oriental indifference to incompatible facts and devotion to single ideas; prophecy among Hebrews and Arabs; the soil of prophetism; its width and products; Hebrew poets and the Schools of the Prophets; Goldziher's investigation of the ancient Arab poet; poets as soothsayers and leaders; the Jinn; initiation of Ḥassān ibn Thābit; inspiration of Muḥammad; Arab and Hebrew illustrations; inspirational nature of Arab poetry; *shā'ir, kāhin, 'arrāf; hātif, bath qôl,* al-Khaḍir; *shayṭān;* fetish cursing of Arabs and Hebrews; *kāhins* and *saj'; Qur'ān* in *saj';* story of King Hujr; Muḥammad's inspirational seizures; Ibn Ṣayyād; Muḥammad's problem and germinative conceptions; essentially a dualistic mystic.

LECTURE II 41

Ibn Khaldūn, his life, philosophy of history and psychology; his views on inspiration and its place in the world; the five signs of a prophet: (*a*) exhibiting trance conditions; Muḥammad's pathological state; (*b*) a pure disposition; (*c*) summoning to piety and good works; (*d*) in a respected position; (*e*) working miracles; different theories of miracles; the nature of the Muslim universe; the prophet's place in it; the soul that tends upward; the senses and the powers of the mind; the three kinds of souls; (*a*) the learned of this world; (*b*) saints,

PAGE

(*c*) prophets; how prophetic inspiration comes down; its grievousness; soothsayers (*kāhins*) and their inspiration; imperfect prophets; use material inducers and excitants; rhymed prose or *sajᶜ;* Ibn Ṣayyād; do soothsayers cease when prophets are sent? the pelted devils; soothsayers pale in the light of prophecy; astrological doctrine of philosophers on them; their attitude to prophets; the *Qurᵓān* composed in *sajᶜ;* how did Muḥammad bring on his trances? or could he induce them?

LECTURE III 70

Ibn Khaldūn's doctrine of dreaming; its causes and kinds; "one of the six and forty parts of prophecy;" the comforters; how the rational soul apprehends and works; its relation to the animal spirit; the cause of sleep; immediate spiritual perception by the soul; the clothing of its results by the imagination; the three kinds of dreams; methods of inducing dreams; *al-ḥalūmīya;* automatic parallels to these; Muslim oneirocritics; Muḥammad's example; criteria of true dreams; examples; al-Ghazzālī on the nature of the vision of Allāh and Muḥammad; his doctrine of images or symbols; Ibn Khallikān's dreams; al-Bērūnī's dream; Nāsir ibn Khusraw's dream; al-Ashᶜarī's dreams; Burton's anecdote of a vision of ᶜAlī; al-Ghazzālī's dream; Ibn Baṭūṭa.

LECTURE IV 95

The soul of wizards and its place among human souls; the essence and form of the soul; the child soul; the two apprehensions of the soul; apprehension through "scrying;" divination through the insane; "possession;" "automatic speech;" the *ᶜarrāf;* the *kāhins;* the speaking head; artificial death by asceticism; Ibn Baṭūṭa and the *yogis;*

PAGE

attitude of Ṣūfīs; their disapproval of seeking such things; their miracles; idiot saints; their relation to the ritual law and the Unseen; geomancy; mysterious powers of numbers and letters; origin of this idea; difference between magic and the science of talismans; legal status of both; source of their sciences; "Nabataean Agriculture;" Geber; Maslama of Madrid; the true basis of magic according to Ibn Khaldūn; souls of magicians of three kinds: (*a*) working through the will; (*b*) using talismanic help; (*c*) affecting imagination; reality of magic; in the *Qurʾān*, the ancient world, Egypt; Ibn Khaldūn's own experiences; the "slitters;" "amicable numbers;" doctrine of philosophers on these; compare "mental" and "Christian science;" distinction from miracle; Ṣūfī miracles; the Eye; "interest" and "utilitarianism" in Islām; Ibn Khaldūn's position; "interesting" in Arabic and Turkish; Muslim mysticism utilitarian; al-Ghazzālī; two views of Averroes; magic for the modern Muslim; Lane's experiences; Professor E. G. Browne's experiences; the paradox in it all; "God's in his world."

LECTURE V 130

Ibn Khaldūn and the Jinn; his attitude to metaphysics; a Ghazzālian pragmatist and a mystic; his view of "obscure" verses of the *Qurʾān;* the Jinn in old Arabia; Robertson Smith on them; the Jinn in Muḥammad's time; his attitude; later legend and theology on Muḥammad's intercourse with them; their position under the Law; traces of a theological effect of the Fall; Iblīs in Europe and Islām; the Jinn and Hārūn ar-Rashīd; marriage between men and Jinn; the saints and the Jinn; al-Ghazzālī's experience; legend of ʿAbd al-Qādir; tales from Ibn ʿArabī; ash-Shaʿrānī and the Jinn;

PAGE

devotees of the Jinn; attitude of philosophers; al-Fārābī; have the Jinn reason (ʿ*aql*)? Avicenna; Muslim attitude in general; Professor E. G. Browne's story; comment; Bayle St. John's experience; Muslimate westerners.

LECTURE VI 157

Recapitulation; saints and the emotional religious life in Islām; Islām a mystical faith; its varying degrees; saints as teachers; begging friars; darwīsh fraternities; the Qādirites; organization of fraternities; the Sūfī hierarchy; comparison and contrast with organization of Roman Church; Ibn Khaldūn's philosophy of Ṣūfī history; derivation of *Ṣūfī;* the Ṣūfī ladder of "states;" as a written science; rending the veil of sense; transition to metaphysics; relation of God to the world; unity and multiplicity; influence of Ismāʿīlites and Shīʿites; Ṣūfīism under four heads: (*a*) discipline of the soul; (*b*) unveiling of the Unṣeen; (*c*) control of material things; (*d*) wild expressions in ecstasy; al-Ghazzālī as an example; his autobiography; search for ultimate truth; the depths of skepticism; the mercy of God; the seekers of his day; his study of Ṣūfīism; the snares of the world; his conversion; his flight; life as a Ṣūfī religious; experiences; the mystic union with God; the phenomena of the inner life as a proof of the Unseen; his doctrine of man's nature; the "heart" and its sickness; the medicine of the law; anecdotes.

LECTURE VII 195

Hypnotic and antinomian saints; Mollā Shāh; Tawakkul Beg; virtues of *Qur.* cxii; opening the spiritual world by thought transference; colored photisms; case of Dārā Shukōh; of Princess

PAGE

Fāṭima; woman in Islām; Lane's two *walī* friends; the wandering ascetic life; order in the Muslim Unseen; the will and personality of Allāh; pathways to reality; the religious life in general; emotional effects of pilgrimage; Hadgi Khan—a modern instance; Islām and Roman Christendom.

LECTURE VIII 220

The discipline of the traveler on his way through the world; al-Ghazzālī's doctrine of the "heart;" definition of terms: "heart;" "spirit;" exoteric and esoteric; "flesh" or "soul;" "intelligence;" the armies of God, visible and invisible, material and spiritual; the journey to God; the body as a vehicle; its needs; the armies of the heart; al-Ghazzālī's allegories thereof; a king in his kingdom; the leaguer of the City of Mansoul; a hunter with horse and dog; man's knowledge and will; how he comes to them; between the beasts and the angels; under his hide a pig, a dog, a devil, a sage; "our hearts are restless;" the heart as an instrument of knowledge; the mirror of the Unseen and its defects; created for God and containing God; the revelation therein; its degrees; classification of kinds of faith; "Everything is perishing save His Face;" *Allāhu akbar;* the Reality and absorption in it; *ittiḥād; fanā;* kinds of knowledge, all ultimately inspirational.

LECTURE IX 252

Sources of man's knowledge; *ilhām; waḥy;* the mirror and the Preserved Tablet; the veils of sense and their removal; al-Ghazzālī's epistemology; attitude of Ṣūfīs; the method of the seeker; *Allāh! Allāh!* auto-hypnosis; Tennyson; "Kim;" *Lā ilāha illā-llāh; jadhba* versus *sulūk;* darwīshes *bā-sharʿ* and *bī-sharʿ*; the Naqshbandite *Ṭarīqa;* by

the heart; three kinds of hearts; Allāh's absolute guidance aright and astray; "These are in the Fire, and I care not;" the end of the matter; escape of the Muslim mystic from orthodox theology into pantheism.

LECTURE I

THE ATTITUDE OF THE SEMITES TOWARD THE UNSEEN WORLD; PROPHECY AS A SEMITIC PHENOMENON AND ESPECIALLY AMONG THE ARABS

You may remember how Robertson of Brighton used to say, speaking of his sermons and their inspiration, "I cannot light my own fire; I must convey a spark from another's hearth." The same idea and the same expression occur in Islām. Muḥammad, following the usage and speech of the desert, tells (*Qurʾān*, xx, 10; xxvii, 7) how Moses left his family and went aside to the Burning Bush to seek from it a brand, a *qabas*, for their own fire, Thence *iqtibās*, "brand-seeking," persists in the rhetorical language of Islām, for such borrowing of fire from predecessors. Permit me, then, having both Christian and Muslim authority, to quote, by way of text for these lectures, a couple of sentences from Mr. William James's *Varieties of Religious Experience*, that give very precisely the thesis which I propose to set before you as illustrated in Islām. At the beginning of his third lecture, when approaching the broad question of the reality of the Unseen, he says:

Were one asked to characterize the life of religion in the broadest and most general terms possible, one might say that it consists of the belief that there is an unseen order, and that our supreme good lies in harmoniously adjusting ourselves thereto. This belief and this adjustment are the religious attitude in the soul.

This religious attitude, then, as developed in Islām, I desire to put before you now. With some danger of cross-division it can be analyzed into three points: first, the reality of the Unseen, of a background to life, unattainable to our physical senses; second, man's relation to this Unseen as to faith and insight therein; that is, the whole emotional religious life ranging, at the simplest, from a prayerful attitude and a sense of God's presence to the open vision of the mystic with all its complicated theological consequences; and, lastly, the discipline of the traveler on his way to such direct knowledge of the divine, and during his life in it. My training in the schools of philosophy is of the slenderest, but I think I see in these three a metaphysical, a psychological, and an ethical side to our inquiry. Let me beg your indulgence, however, if my philosophical footing ever slips. I am neither metaphysician, psychologist, nor ethicist; I am simply a student of Arabic and of Islām who desires to suggest to those who are metaphysicians, psychologists, and ethicists some of the problems which lie for their science in that vast and so broadly unknown territory. Regard me, then, as a traveler who brings back from far wanderings but partially assorted and understood gatherings, which scientific geographers, botanists, zoölogists, may further examine and classify. That these will repay the trouble may, I think, be taken for granted by those who consider that in them has lain the faith for life and death of millions of the world's best minds during twelve centuries of time and over a quarter of the earth in space. It is surely worth our while to turn some little of our attention from the so often childish speculations of Indian sages, and see what contributions have been made to the final problems of time and eternity by races far more nearly akin to us in thought, if not in language.

But from this *captatio benevolentiae* let me return. What, first, is to be said on the reality of the Unseen in Islām? What part does that world play; how close is it; what is its relationship to the everyday life of Muslims? How do Muslims think of it? Over this, the reality and nature, for Islām, of the Unseen we must spend some little time. The Muslim attitude is so different from our trodden paths of thought and experience that only a patient turning of all its sides and an accumulation of example and illustration can make it real to us. I shall have to ask your indulgence for much simple translating in what follows. You want the views of the Muslim writers and thinkers as they have rendered them, and not any lucubrations of mine.

It is plain, I think, and admitted that the conception of the Unseen is much more immediate and real to the Oriental than to the western peoples. I use these two terms in the broadest fashion. But the cause is by no means so plain, and upon it much shipwreck has been made by ingenious students of race and race characteristics. There are also, on both sides, large modifying elements which seem, from time to time, almost to upset the general law. If we say that the Semitic peoples, as a race, believe in and bow in reverence to an Unseen, we may be met by the curious skepticism of the Arabs themselves, a skepticism which nearly baffled Muḥammad, and which appears at the present day more or less through the entire desert. The Arabs show themselves not as especially easy of belief, but as hard-headed, materialistic, questioning, doubting, scoffing at their own superstitions and usages, fond of tests of the supernatural—tempting God, in a word—and all this in a curiously light-minded, almost childish fashion. They had diviners, it is true, as we shall see hereafter, and were ruled partly by their guidance, but these had always to be prepared to permit tests of their powers and to be regarded with general suspicion. Nothing for the Arab succeeded like success, as Muḥammad discovered, and there was no balance of faith to carry them over the cracks in the supernatural scheme. They demanded of Muḥammad signs, and their ideas of signs were of the crudest, most non-spiritual description; the

Jews, in their most trying days, had not the same blindness as these Arabs for non-material things. On the other side, take Europe and faith as developed there. We find everywhere, and again and again, the possibility and the actuality of just such absolute acquiescence in and acceptance of an immediately impinging unseen world, which we commonly ascribe to the devout East. Hereafter, I shall have to tell you many tales, queer to grotesqueness, simple to childishness, devout to ecstasy, marvelous to madness, of oriental saints and their vicissitudes, but I venture to say that you can parallel them all, down to details, in the *Legenda Aurea* of Jacobus a Voragine, archbishop of Genoa in the late thirteenth century.

Take, for example, the fastidiousness as to their place of burial so often exhibited by saints after their death. The very same trick on their part of making their bier so heavy that it could not be lifted until the bearers had decided to grant them their will is found in the hagiology of both East and West, and several times in the *Legenda Aurea*.[1] And further, it was not the West, but the supposedly devout East, which fell on the cynical counter-trick of spinning the bier round rapidly until the saint had lost his sense of direction and did not know whither he was being carried.

[1] E. g., Vol. IV, p. 170, and Vol. VII, pp. 145, 169, of the edition in "Temple Classics."

Again, take the case of al-Ghazzālī, perhaps the greatest constructive theologian in the Muslim church, who died A. D. 1111. He, as I trust we shall see in more detail hereafter, had to fight against unbelief of the most absolute during his whole life. In his earlier days it was in himself. At one time he touched the depth of complete skepticism and doubted even the operations of his own mind and the axioms of reason. And when, in the light of the mystic, he was able to see his own way again, he found the mass of the people round him slipping into similar unbelief. The creeds had broken down; the law of Islām was no longer respected; its divine origin was criticized or doubted; the nature and reality of prophecy were questioned. It was his work to build up again the breaches in the Muslim Zion, and that Islām exists still is largely due to him. It would be easy to add other testimonies. In Islām, as in Christendom, he who seeks the ages of faith looks ever backward.

The truth is, I am persuaded, that we commonly regard this acknowledged difference between East and West from the wrong point, and are governed by the wrong word. It is not really faith that is in question here, but knowledge; it is not the attitude to God, but the attitude to law. The essential difference in the oriental mind is not credulity as to unseen things, but inability to construct a system as to seen things. It has been well said, that the

Oriental has the most astonishing keenness in viewing, grasping, analyzing a single point, and, when he has finished with that point, can take up a series of others in the same way. But these points remain for him separate; he does not co-ordinate them. They may be contradictory; that does not trouble him. When he constructs systems—as he often does—it is by taking a single point, and spinning everything out of it; not by taking many points and building them up together. Thus, he may criticize one point and be quite indifferent to the consequent necessity, for us, at least, of criticizing other points. A good enough example is the oriental method, which I have just mentioned, of thwarting a saint's caprice as to his place of burial. There is no great devoutness of feeling there; no awe at the breaking in of the Unseen, and at their nearness to the direct working of God. There is simply the fact of this obstinate, if deceased, saint, and, "Well, we'll try to rattle him," as we may imagine them saying in the slang of the bazaar. Familiarity breeds contempt. The supernatural, to them, is the familiar—the usual; only it is not subject to law, and they never dream that it can be. The most they can do is to set their wits against it in detail.

Start, then, with this, that the difference in the Oriental is not essentially religiosity, but the lack of the sense of law. For him, there is no immovable order of nature. "The army of unalterable law" which we see in the heavens for him may change and pass. There is no necessity in themselves why the things that have been should be the things that will be. You will remember that even Ecclesiastes looks beyond them and finds his unchanging circlings fixed by the will of God. So, at every turn, the Oriental is confronted by the possibility of unforetellable, unrationalizable difference. He is like a man who opens his mouth to speak, but utters what he would not, and cannot utter what he would. We would call it aphasia and construct another law. He recognizes that God has created for him other words than he intended, instead of the words he did intend. It would be God's creation in either case. We feel vaguely that there is a divine event and element in the world, but it is far off. A deep, and for our experience, impenetrable shell separates us from that event and element. That shell, we find, is subject to law; we can depend upon its action and reaction. We have never pierced beyond it, and are tolerably sure that we never shall; that we shall always find it, however far we go; that it is all the world for us. But to the Oriental, this shell is the merest film. The strict theologian of Islām would tell him that there was no such shell at all; that all action and reaction spring from the immediate will of God. This, probably, would be too hard a doctrine for the wayfaring man in Islām, but he is very well assured of the thinness of the shell. He knows that the supernatural has often peered through it at him. Our ghost-stories and strange experiences are everyday things for him which he never dreams of investigating, for he never doubts them. Our investigations are really attempts to bring these things under law; at that, he would simply shrug his shoulders.

This being so, it is evident that anything is possible to the Oriental. The supernatural is so near that it may touch him at any moment. There is no surprise; and therefore there is need, in verification, of a small test only. In the case of our investigators of occult phenomena, spiritism and the like, the trouble is that no test, however complete, is really enough. There *must* be something wrong, is our attitude. But even the heathen Arabs, light minded and materialistic as they were, accepted their soothsayer, if he told them any single thing which they were assured he could not know of himself. That he was a soothsayer was not for them a practically unthinkable idea. Give them good evidence, such as they would accept in ordinary life, and they would accept anything. There are some things that we, in the fetters of our sense of law, cannot accept. And when the Oriental has once been thus touched, once had an impulse, however mysterious, in a certain direction, there may be no limits to the results. For example, it has been a favorite subject for argument, about it and about, how much the personality of Muḥammad had to do in the Muslim movement; how much Islām is his individual creation, or merely a product of his times and circumstances. The fact is, I suspect, that the Arabs were just in this state of unstable equilibrium. His personality was strong enough to convince them—a sufficient number, at least, of them—that the shell had broken and the supernatural had come near. Once start, then, the idea that this man is a messenger from God and that his words are the words of God, and the oriental mind would carry it out to its utmost limits. A theory of all things in heaven and earth would be developed from this single idea. Other things might not agree with it; they would simply be left aside. The Oriental feels no need to explain everything; he simply ignores the incompatible; and he does so conscientiously, for he sees only one thing at a time. This is not deduction; it is eduction. The idea is an egg from which a complete explanation of life is hatched. For example, once given the idea of Muḥammad, it was not long before the Muslim mind reached the persuasion that he must have been the first of all creatures, created before all worlds, existent from the beginning of time—we have exactly the Arian doctrine of the person of Christ. Further, the fact of him became so overpowering that in a tradition Allāh is made to declare: "Had it not been for thee, I had not created the worlds."

Inability, then, to see life steadily, and see it whole, to understand that a theory of life must cover all the facts, and *liability* to be stampeded by a single idea and blinded to everything else—therein, I believe, is the difference between the East and the West.

But I have detained you too long over my own speculations, uncertain in much, probably erroneous in much. The certain thing in it all is the thinness of the shell which separates the Oriental from the Unseen. I turn, then, to the standard breakages in that shell, which Islām recognizes.

These may be roughly classified as follows, though the divisions, I fear, will be found often to cross: prophets, diviners, magic and talismans, appearances of the Jinn, dreams, saints.

First, then, prophets and prophecy. Here I can begin on familiar ground. The Hebrews, a Bedawi tribe which abandoned the desert and turned, more or less, to the agricultural life, exhibit the essential characteristics of Arab prophetism. Nowhere does their unity with Arabia come out more strongly, and yet nowhere is the essential difference of the religiosity of the Hebrews more marked. Such a figure as Elijah, so far, at least, as the Old Testament has preserved for us his legend, must have appeared again and again in the earlier desert, and certainly did among the saints of Islām. The schools of Sons of the Prophets of which from time to time we have fleeting glimpses can be exactly paralleled by the darwīsh fraternities of Islām. Their relations to the people, their ceremonies and usages, their mode of life, their ecstasies and religious excitements, were evidently precisely the same. The soil, in a word, from which the great prophets sprang was alike among the Hebrews and the Arabs.

Let me illustrate this vital matter of soil and the growth therefrom by a parallel in creative literature. I take the case of a single poet, though the broad literature of a whole people always exhibits the same phenomena. The mind of Wordsworth was a constant poetic soil, and from it there sprang in luxuriant and bewildering tangle all manner of plants. The most of these were scrub and brush, underwood often commonplace and even grotesque. There only a small coterie of sworn worshipers finds delight. But above that scrub and brush there rise, from time to time, great trees, glorious in their unique and tranquil beauty as any beneath the sky of English letters. What kindly influences there had intervened we cannot tell; the processes of the poet's mind are as mysterious as that spirit of the Lord which leapt upon the Hebrew prophet. But at one time, as one has said, harshly but not untruly, the voice of Wordsworth is that

> of an old half-witted sheep,
> Which bleats articulate monotony
> And indicates that two and one are three.

and at another, and that in a flash, the very heavens are cloven by some clear creative thought clothed in noble words. So after trivialities of college life there suddenly rises the memory of

> Newton with his prism and silent face,
> The marble index of a mind forever
> Voyaging through strange seas of thought, alone.

Or in still stranger context of placid commonplace there is struck, one of the half-dozen times in all English verse, the clear faery note,

> or lady of the mere,
> Lone sitting by the shores of old romance.

What spirit touched Wordsworth then, we know not, but we do know that some relation lay between his painful crawlings and those lofty flights.

So, when we turn from the common soul of prophetism to the great Hebrew prophets, how wide is the difference! Isaiah—any of the Isaiahs—rises from the howling, frenzied mob of *nebhî'îm;* of them and not of them. He could have part in their orgies, yet his head was high above their sensuous fogs, his brain and conscience were never swept away by their gusts of passionate ecstasy. So Samuel moved clear eyed through the turbid airs of the religious life of his fellows. He and his like had seen the Lord, and the beauty of holiness was theirs. In these lectures, I shall not often have opportunity for comparison, still less for apologetics. Let me seize this one to say, as fixedly and broadly as in me is, that, while the soil of Semitic prophecy is one, I know nowhere in the Semitic world any appearance like that of the great prophets of the Hebrews. They stand as clear from their soil as love in Christian marriage from the lust of the flesh, and the relation is much the same.

In Islām some few attempted the same heights, but never reached them. Muḥammad, a figure now strangely sympathetic and attractive, now repellently weak, once and again in his early life, has touches of the ethical glory of Amos, but never saw the vision of love in Hosea. In his later life he fell, and it is not for us to judge him. Perhaps, if Jeremiah had come to rule with absolute sway some small but conquering remnant of Judah, he, too, might have fallen. If Isaiah, from wazīr in Jerusalem, had come to be sulṭān, his robes might have been spotted by the flesh and his soul by ambition. But, apart entirely from the last unhappy ten years of Muḥammad's life, he was not of the goodly fellowship of the Hebrew prophets.

Al-Ghazzālī, I have mentioned already. He was a man of the intellectual rank of Augustine. Yet he was himself a darwīsh, and had part in their religious exercises. These he knew with sympathy, and he has, in a treatise which I have translated elsewhere,[1] applied the methods of science to the

[1] "Emotional Religion in Islam," *Journal of the Royal Asiatic Society*, 1901–2.

analysis of their emotional and theological value. But though his mind was probably keener than that of any Hebrew, and though the root of the matter was in him, yet no one can mistake the difference of atmosphere in his writings and that of the Old Testament. In the latter there is the freshness of life and, in spite of everything, of hope; he is an ascetic scholastic, and all his endeavor is to gain assurance of the world to come. Whatever may have been the cause, it was well for the Hebrews that they were not blinded to the facts and duties of this life by the vision of another. Islām, like mediaeval Europe, could think of nothing but the unending hereafter with its sharply divided weal or woe.

Yet, for all this, the soil was the same, and from it we must start. But here we are landed in another question. How wide was that soil? How much of the life, thought, emotional output and literature, in a sense, of the people, is to be included in this broad prophetism? Let me meet this with another question. How is it that we do not find in the extant remains of Hebrew literature anything but the directly or indirectly religious? Further, and still more incisively, even if, by a strange chance, their profane literature has all been lost—there is some tolerably profane still in the Old Testament—why is there almost no mention of poets among them? I speak subject to correction, but I know in Hebrew no unmistakable word for poet; *môshēl* certainly is not. Did they classify and name poets in some other way? put them in some other category? Further, they did have stories, current among the people, of their heroic age, of their great warriors and deliverers. What were the channels down which these passed? Who played the part of the wandering gleemen, scalds, bards, minstrels of mediaeval Europe? That there were such we cannot doubt. The desert knows them to this day. May I hazard another questioning answer? Was their part taken by *nebhî'îm*, solitary or in bands? Was poetry and legend—production, preservation, transmission—all in the Schools of the Prophets? This, you may say, is as absurd as to bring under one hood the mendicant friars and the gleemen of Europe. Sometimes, even these did come most queerly together, but that in Christendom was exceptional. In the Semitic world, I venture to say, it was the rule, and for the desert it can be proven.

What was the belief of the ancient Arabs as to the nature of poetry, and what their attitude toward the person of the poet? Since Ignaz Goldziher's investigations, published in his *Arabische Philologie*, Part I, there can be no doubt as to the answers to these questions. The answers which the Arabic sources give us are those, too, which the analogy of other primitive peoples would suggest. Poetry is magical utterance, inspired by powers from the Unseen, and the poet is in part a soothsayer, in part an adviser and admonisher, and in part a hurler of magical formulae against his enemies. The most common and primitive word in Arabic for poet is *shāʿir* and that means simply, "he who perceives, knows." In meaning it is parallel to the Hebrew *yiddiʿônî*, but that Hebrew word never passed from the idea of divination to that of poetic utterance. On the other hand, the Hebrew *môshēl*, which in Arabic suggests only proverb, likeness, parable, has passed over to mean a poet of a special type, the utterer of reproach and malediction, whose words bear sure fruit. In Hebrew history, the outstanding example of the *môshēl* and an example of the Arabic *shāʿir*, poet, on this side of his activity, is the remarkable figure of Balaam. So in the Semitic world the bard and the prophet join. Balaam was evidently thought to stand in some very real relation to the unseen world, a relation which gave his words supernatural force—if they were once uttered and not checked on his lips by a higher power; the poet of the Arabs drew his knowledge, wisdom, skill, and destroying utterance from his relationship to the Jinn, those beings which for the heathen Arabs were as the fauns, nymphs, and satyrs of the classical world, which often seem to have been regarded as simple divinities and which Islām has accepted as a class of created beings and pictured to itself partly as Muslim, partly as unbelieving, and partly as diabolic in nature. Such, then, is the situation in a nutshell.

But let me illustrate in detail. A good example is given in the stories told about Ḥassān ibn Thābit, a close personal follower of Muḥammad, and, in a sense, his poet-laureate. Muḥammad in general was opposed to poetry; the poets were mostly opposed to him; but Ḥassān upheld his cause with poetry of a kind, and was especially useful in replying to satirical and abusive attacks. But this Ḥassān, while still a young man in the days before Islām, and before he had made any verses, was initiated into poetry by a female Jinnī. She met him in one of the streets of Medīna, leapt upon him, pressed him down, and compelled him to utter three verses of poetry. Thereafter he was a poet, and his verses came to him as to other Arab poets from the direct inspiration of the Jinn. He refers himself to his "brothers of the Jinn" who weave for him artistic words, and tells how weighty lines have been sent down to him from heaven in the night season. The curious thing is that the expressions he uses are exactly those used of the "sending down," that is, revelation, of the *Qur'ān*. Evidently in his case there was a struggle between the idea of the Jinn—those half or wholly heathen spirits—as inspirers and the divine inspirations of the angels.

Further, the story runs that Muḥammad used to set up for him a pulpit in the mosque and stand by in evident enjoyment, while Hassān hurled from it stinging verses against the enemies of Islām. This was one of the few occasions on which Muḥammad seems to have tolerated poetry, and his reported comment is significant, "Allāh aids Ḥassān with the Holy Spirit so long as he is defending or boasting of the Apostle of God." But by the Holy Spirit here, you must not understand any conception like that of the third person of the Christian trinity. For Muḥammad the phrase referred only to the angel messenger who brought to him his revelations. The theological consequences of the lack of the conception of the Holy Ghost, the Lord and Giver of Life, in Islām were wide, but this is not the place to enter upon them. Here Muḥammad simply ascribed to Ḥassān the same kind of inspiration that he had himself, and that is remarkable enough.

Another point to observe is the close parallel between the terms used in the story of Ḥassān's initiation and that of the first revelation to Muḥammad. Just as Ḥassān was thrown down by the female spirit and had verses pressed out of him, so the first utterances of prophecy were pressed from Muḥammad by the angel Gabriel. And the resemblances go still farther. The angel Gabriel is spoken of as the companion (*qarīn*) of Muḥammad, just as though he were the Jinnī accompanying a poet, and the same word, *nafatha*, "blow upon," is used of an enchanter, of a Jinnī inspiring a poet and of Gabriel revealing to Muḥammad. It was, of course, the nightmare of Muḥammad's earlier years—a fear of his own and an accusation of his enemies—that he was simply a poet possessed by a Jinnī; it dictated his whole attitude to poets and poetry, and it is very plain how near the fact the fear and the accusation lay. He was in truth a poet of the old Arab type, without skill of verse, and with all his being given to the prophetic side of poetry. Add to this a strange jumble of Jewish and Christian conceptions, and you have the key to Muḥammad.

I need not go into detail of the many stories told of the intercourse between poets and their inspiring spirits: how a poet would sit helpless without an idea, until his "comrade" would call to him from the corner of the chamber; how another, in desperate need, saddled his camel, rode off into the desert, and having come to a certain place, alighted and cried out, "Come to the aid of your brother, your brother!" how the aid came swiftly, the poet lay down, and did not rise until he had one hundred and thirteen lines. Of such stories, which later came to be told in jest, there are many.

But can we draw the connection closer between the poet and the prophet; and especially between the Arabs and the Hebrews? You will remember how we are told in Numbers 9:18, 23, that the children of Israel broke up camp and encamped according to the word of Yahwé at the hand of Moses. Through Moses, that is, came the guidance of Yahwé for these significant elements in the nomad life, the right time and place for encamping and departing. Now it is curious that among the old Arab tribes exactly the same place was taken by the poets, the *shāᶜirs*. For instance, of Zuhayr ibn Janāb, the poet, it is narrated:

Whenever Zuhayr said, "Ho, the tribe journeyeth," then it journeyed; and whenever he said, "Ho, the tribe abideth," they alighted and abode.

Similarly we are told of others.

Here are guidances cast in solemn formulas:

When Allah sent the breaking of the dam of ᶜArim on the people of Mārib, which was the tribe of Azd, there arose their leader and said, "Whoever has a sufficient camel and a milk-skin and a strong water skin, let him turn from the herds of cattle, for this is a day of care, and let him betake himself to Ath-thinyu min shann—it is said to be in ash-Sharā, and those who settled there were Azd of Shanūᶜa; then he continued, "And whoever is in misery and poverty and patience against the straits of this world, let him betake himself to Baṭn Marr"—those who dwelt there were the tribe Khuzāᶜa; then he continued, "And who of you desireth wine and leaven, and rule and government and brocade and silk, let him betake himself to Buṣra and al-Ḥufayr"—these are in the land of Syria and those who dwelt there were the tribe of Ghassān; then he continued, "and who of you hath far-aiming purpose and a strong camel and a new provender-sack, let him betake himself to the New Castle of ᶜUmān"—those who settled there were Azd of ᶜUmān; then he continued, "And who desireth things rooted in mud and nourished of dust, let him betake himself to Yathrib, rich in palm trees"—those who settled there were the tribes of Aws and Khazraj.[1]

All this is in the solemn language of rhymed prose, the language of the soothsayers, and the leader divides his people in a scene not unlike that of the blessing of Jacob or of Moses. You will notice, too, how the narrator weaves in notes exactly in the style of Deuteronomy.

Still more in the tone of these Blessings is a narrative that has come down to us of the part played by Sawdā bint Zuhra, the Prophetess, or Kāhina, of her tribe, that of Quraysh, in prophesying the birth of the future warner of his people. She bade them bring to her all their daughters, "For," said she, "one of them is a woman-warner, and will bear a man-warner." As they passed before her, she uttered over each a saying, the truth of which time showed, until Āmina, the future mother of Muḥammad appeared and was shown as the warner spoken of.[2]

But to return—Such a poet as speaks here is called the leader (*qāʾid*) of his tribe. Another boasts himself to Muḥammad as their poet and representative. To another his tribe intrusted all its warlike undertakings. Another tribe rejected the warning of their poet, just as the Hebrews those of their prophets, and repented it. Here is his

[1] *Aghānī*, Vol. XIX, p. 95.

[2] Damīrī, Vol. II, p. 328, edition of Cairo, A. H. 1313.

speech, and you will observe how closely its tone resembles that of a prophecy:

> Go not in against the Banū ᶜĀmir; I of men know best of them. I have fought with them, and they have fought with me; I have overcome them and they have overcome me. I never saw a people more restless in a halting-place than the Banū ᶜĀmir. By Allāh, I can find no likeness to them but Bravery itself, for they abide not in their hole for restlessness, and will surely come out to you. By Allāh, if ye sleep this night, ye will not know when they descend upon you.

Of the poet sitting as judge like Samuel, Dr. Goldziher can quote no case from heathen Arabia. But that certainly is due to our very defective sources. It must be regarded as significant that in very early Muslim times, the poet al-Akhṭal, though a Christian, sat in the mosque of his tribe as judge. Evidently this points at once to old pre-Muslim custom, and to a religious authority and dignity encircling the poet.

We must not, therefore, think of the poet as being given this position by any respect for the beauty or vigor of his verses, or even for his human insight and wisdom in matters of tribal conduct and politics. The idea that the Arab tribes so respected their poets—in the first instance at least—because of their keen artistic sense, their appreciation of the beauties of poetry, must be given up. Their attitude was much more practical. The separateness of the poet from other men had struck them. So, too, had the way in which his verses came to him, out of the sky apparently, apart from his labor and will. We must remember that the Arab poet was a lyrist, first and last; intensely subjective and personal as regarded both himself and his hearers. When he sang before the tribe on the day of battle and onset, it was as though a spirit sang through him. When he brooded in the council and then suddenly arose and flung out his judgment in clanging words and ringing rhymes, it was as the utterance of a god. From time to time, too, in the intense nervous susceptibility of the Arab race in the keen desert air, there fell upon him cataleptic rigors, swoons, and dreams, from which he returned with strange words in his mouth. If any could hear or see the Jinn in the desert stillness and solitude, or in the dark recesses of the mountains, it would be he with his strained nerves and loaded imagination. Often, as to Socrates, his own decision must have come as with a voice from without, and it would take little to add a visible form. This night-side of human nature, in which the nerves and the senses conspire to mislead, is only gradually being cleared to us, but we know enough of its possibilities to see fully how the Arabs thought their poets were illumined from the Unseen, and could make little if any distinction between them and diviners and prophets.

As a matter of fact, the Arabic writers on these old things are put to it to distinguish between the *shāʿir*, "poet," as we have called him, the *kāhin* or diviner, and the *ʿarrāf*, also a kind of diviner. All were supernaturally guided, but the last was on the lowest step. He told—again like Samuel—about stolen things, and where wandered beasts might be found. Curiously enough we find him consulted, too, as a physician; perhaps with thought of the lost or stolen health. The *kāhin* foretold the future and secret things generally. He was limited mostly to a certain sanctuary—you will remember, of course, that *kāhin* is exactly the Hebrew *kôhēn*, "priest"—and there he had to be consulted. He was, as Goldziher, following Wellhausen, well puts it, an institution. The *shāʿir*, on the other hand, was free. He was the counselor of his people, and his counsel was inspired from the Unseen, by the Jinn, exactly as was the case with the others. But he was also a man and a warrior, free as the desert, and bound to no sacred shrine, no Urim and Thummim. Not only wisdom came to him but words, beautiful or fiery and terrible; which could give life or death by a mysterious power in them, but also give delight by their sheer loveliness. And this belief long survived the coming of Islām. The oriental poet cannot rid himself of the faith that verses come from without. His method is inspirational, not that of the labor of the file. If he is a religious man, a *hātif*, a wandering voice, the Hebrew *bath qôl*, will reach him, or he may have an interview even with al-Khaḍir, that undying wandering saint, the most picturesque figure in Muslim mythology, who journeys through the earth, rescuing, guiding, counseling. Even as late as the seventh Muslim century we find a Hanbalite theologian, the narrowest sect of all, arguing that the *Qur'ān* must be uncreated, for otherwise it would be no better than poetry with which God, as is accepted, inspires the poet. But if the poet were not a religious man, or if the attitude to all poetry were hostile, then its inspiration was easy to seek elsewhere. The Jinn and the devils have become hopelessly confused in Islām, and we can never be sure whether with the word *shayṭān*, "devil," an Arabic writer means the personal evil spirit borrowed from Christianity and Judaism, or merely a malignant member of the Jinn. So it was easy to say that the inspiration of poetry was from the devil, and even to brand all poetry as the *Qur'ān* of the devil.

But all that was long after our period, and we must go back to the winged words of the old Arab poets. Our connection with Balaam is not yet absolutely made out, but it must be beginning to sweep before you. It is well known how among primitive peoples there has always been supposed to lie in words a certain fetish-power. Words for them are things; they are strict realists. So the curse once spoken is an existent entity, which must strike and rest somewhere; if not the one against whom it is hurled, then the hurler himself. In Islām this has endured longer than anywhere else. I doubt whether in the scholastic theology of any other people you could find passages like the following:

> When two men curse one another, the curse falls on him who deserves it; if neither deserves it, then it returns and falls upon the Jews, who conceal what God has revealed.

And again:

> When a curse is sent against any one, it goes toward him, and if it finds access to him it goes in unto him. But if it finds no access, it returns to its Lord, whose are Might and Majesty, and says "O my Lord, so and so sent me against so and so, but I find no access to him; so what dost thou command me?" He then says, "Return whither thou camest."

But all this is only a reduction to scheme and method of a belief which Islām, from the first, has held unshaken, and before Islām the earlier Semitic faiths. It meets us amongst the Hebrews; there the story of Balaam is unmistakable. And in early Arabia it was the custom that the poet of a tribe, on the day of battle, should advance and recite satirical and abusive verses against the opponents. This was not simply to hearten his own tribe, or to strike with shame and confusion the other. There was a magical power in his words, and they show the traces often, as preserved in the *dīwāns* of the greater poets, of simple cursing.

Similarly, among the Hebrews, Goliath mocked and ridiculed (*ḥêrēph*) the armies of Israel. In all this it was a spirit which had entered the poet, and which spoke through him. Hence the magical efficacy of his words; he was only the channel of communication along which the unseen world worked. Gestures, too, and symbols often aided. So long as the hands of Moses were upheld, even mechanically, the Israelites prevailed against Amalek. In later Muslim times certain poets came to have the reputation of possessing peculiarly unlucky tongues. Whom they cursed, some misfortune befel; and we have even traces of their using for the purpose certain symbolic actions and methods of dress.

I have now, I think, made tolerably clear the Semitic belief that the poet was inspired—was a *vates*, in short—and that his poem, or rather song, was a *carmen*, a charm. For further details I would refer you to the epoch-making paper of Dr. Goldziher, which I have already used. Whether you will follow me in my further explanation of the absence of definite references to poets and poetry in the Hebrew literature—that they are swept into the general category of prophecy and prophets—does not greatly matter for my present object. That poetry and prophecy, for the early Arabs and Hebrews, both go back to inspiration from the Unseen, and are, for many purposes, a practical unit, I now take for granted.

Before dealing directly with the position of the prophet among the Arabs and in Islām, it may be in place here to take up the *kāhin*, or soothsayer. As I have already said, this word is the exact linguistic equivalent for the Hebrew *kôhēn*, and—without entering on the vexed questions which lie round that word—I would only remind you that Potiphar, Jethro, and David's sons are all called *kôhēns* in the Old Testament. In Arabia the matter is much simpler. The *kāhins* were soothsayers, connected with a sanctuary, or sometimes with a tribe, and played much the same part as Eli and Samuel at Shiloh. All mysterious and obscure things seem to have been referred to them. They were judges, but they also foretold the future and the Unseen. How real this was to the Arabs of Muḥammad's time is evident from the fact that he felt compelled to admit their foreknowledge, if only in part, and to ascribe that part—in agreement, probably, with Arab belief—to the help of the Jinn.

But what in them most claims our attention is the invariable form of their utterance, which was the form of utterance, also, of all mysterious knowledge limited to a narrow circle, and professionally guarded. As the Greek oracles were couched in verse, so the oracles of the Arab *kāhins* were cast in that primitive verse which was called *sajᶜ*, literally "pigeon-cooing." You will remember in Isaiah (8:19) how the *Yiddeᶜônîm* chirp and mutter. The word there for "mutter" (*hāgâ*) is used also of the cooing of the pigeon, and there seems little question that we have an allusion to a similar phenomenon. This *saj*ᶜ, which has now become the normal rhetorical form of language in Islām, consists essentially of a series of short phrases in prose—that is without fixed meter, but it may be with rhythm—all rhyming together. Reduce the rhythm to rule, and monorhymed verse appears; take away the rhymes, and you have more or less rhythmical prose. This rhymed prose, then, was the essential characteristic of the speech of the *kāhins*, and is evidently a very elementary first feeling-out toward verse. You will remember that it appears from time to time in Hebrew. Riddles and the like are cast in it; and some long passages, such as Job, chap. 10, and Proverbs, chap. 31, exhibit monorhyme, though incompletely. But among the Hebrews, there is no such limitation of it to messages dealing with the mysterious and the Unseen, as we find among the Arabs at the time of Muḥammad and immediately before. With the Hebrews it appears to be simply a literary form; if we may speak of literature, where there need not be letters. Among the Arabs poetical form had fully developed, with all its wealth of meters, and the primitive *saj*ᶜ survived as the vehicle of only the most primitive modes of poetry, the shamanistic utterances of the *kāhins*. But that this *saj*ᶜ, in those early days, was fully recognized as a form of poetry (*shiʿr*) and not as such a separate literary form as it came to be in later Islām is perfectly clear.

The reason for this brings us at once to Muḥammad. What are we to think of him as a literary artist? To what form of literary art current in his time did he fall heir? The answer is very simple, and will at once come to any one who reads a few lines of the *Qurʾān*, especially of its older portions. The *Qurʾān* is written in rhymed prose throughout. The portions rhymed, verses as we may call them, vary greatly in length. In the earlier chapters these verses are short, just as the style is living and fiery; in the later chapters they are of lumbering length, prosaic and slow, and the rhyme comes in with often a most absurd effect. It is very plain that Muḥammad's first utterances were in genuine *kāhin* form and *kāhin* spirit; that they boiled forth from him as though under uncontrollable external pressure. Here is a curious narrative from the heathen times which gives an excellent picture of a *kāhin* under prophetic influence.

King Ḥujr, the father of the great pre-Islāmic poet, Imr al-Qays, had grievously oppressed the Banū Asad and driven them from their territory. The author of the *Aghānī*, an immense collection of pre-Islāmic and early post-Islāmic history, legend and song, then goes on thus in his life of Imr al-Qays (Vol. VIII, 66):

Then the Banū Asad advanced until, when they were a

day's journey from Tihāma, their Kāhin, who was ᶜAwf ibn Rabīᶜa, prophesied and said unto them, "O my servants!" They said, "With thee! O our Lord!" He said, "Who is the king, the ruddy one, the all-conqueror, the unconquered, among camels as if they were a herd of gazelles, with no clamor by his head? He! his blood is scattered wide! He, tomorrow, is the first of the stripped and spoiled!" They said, "Who is it, O our Lord?" He said, "If my heaving soul were not disquieted, I would tell you that he is Ḥujr openly." Then they mounted all, every beast broken and unbroken, and the day had not risen upon them when they came upon the army of Ḥujr, and charged upon his tent.

The story goes on how the words of the *kāhin* were fulfilled to the letter, but we have no further interest with that. Our point is the manner and tone of this prophecy. The word which I have rendered, "he prophesied," *takahhana*, means, "a prophetic fit came upon him;" it is evident that he, for the time, was out of himself. The form of his utterance is the rhymed prose (*sajᶜ*) of which I have spoken, the language peculiar to the ecstatic life. He speaks, you will notice, to the people, not as their fellow, but directly as their God; they are his "servants," strictly "slaves." They reply with the formula used only to a God, "With thee! O our Lord!" *Labbayka yā rabbanā.* The phenomena of the double personality are most curious. At one moment his voice is the direct voice of God; at another, he is hampered by his laboring and disquieted human soul. The metaphor is of boiling water and high-running waves.

Now, all this is exactly paralleled in Muḥammad's early utterances. They form pictures like this, and they are as if spoken by Allāh himself. And his later utterances were cast in this form only because he had begun in it. That was the way in which prophets gave forth their message; he had begun in that way, and must keep it up to the bitter end. Probably, if Muḥammad had been in a state to realize from the first, all that was implied in the use of this form he would have done anything rather than use it. It identified him at once with the *kāhins* as a class, and, as one possessed by a Jinnī—so only could his contemporaries explain him—connected him directly with the old Arabian heathenism and polytheism from which he was striving to break loose. But the spirit came upon him in his hours of weakness and solitude, and naturally the form which it took and its manifestations were those characteristic of appearances and workings from the Unseen in the world of his time. That he was subject to fits of some kind can be open to no doubt. The narratives are too precise, and his own fears too evidently genuine. That he was possessed by a Jinnī—for him, with his beliefs, an evil spirit—was his first thought, and only gradually did he come to the conviction that this was divine inspiration, and not diabolical obsession.

But it is plain that these seizures, to which he was liable, and his general condition puzzled him to the end. When he had worked out the practical conclusion that they were the means of divine inspiration, he continued to be interested in allied phenomena. In part he was driven to this. For example, he had to explain how the *kāhins* were sometimes right in their predictions. But one very singular group of traditions shows him puzzling over the case of a Jewish boy named Ibn Ṣayyād, who exhibited exactly the same phenomena as he himself. Naturally the subject is obscure in the extreme; the traditionists have no liking for it. But on that very account these narratives may be taken as genuine. The boy had just attained to puberty, i. e., was some twelve or thirteen years old. He was liable to epileptic or cataleptic fits, and in these was wrapped up in a rough mantle[1] and lay muttering to himself. In this way he was supposed to have revelations, and appears to have been regarded by the Jews of al-Madīna as a prophet of their own. One tradition is that Muḥammad met him playing with other boys, struck him on the back with his hand, and said, "Dost thou testify that I am the messenger of God?" He looked at him and said, "I testify that thou art the messenger of the Gentiles." Then he continued, "I testify that I am the messenger of God." Muḥammad struck him to bruising,[2] and then said, "I believe in God and

[1] Cf. *Qur.* lxxiii, lxxiv.

[2] The word is uncertain; cf. Goldziher, *Muhammedanische Studien,* Vol. II, 244.

his messengers." Then to Ibn Ṣayyād, "What dost thou see?" He replied, "There comes to me a truth-teller and a liar." Muḥammad said, "The matter is confused to thee." Then he went on, "I conceal from thee something."[1] The boy said, "It is *ad-dukh*." Muḥammad was thinking of his chapter of the *Qurʾān*, *Ad-dukhān*, "The Smoke," and this answer came too close. So he replied, "Get away; thou wilt never exceed thy power." ʿUmar asked permission to strike off his head, but Muḥammad refused and said, "If it is he, then thou hast no power over him, and if it is not he, there is no good to thee in slaying him." The question was whether he was the Jewish Antichrist or not, and Muḥammad could not make up his mind. On another occasion, Muḥammad tried to catch him unawares in one of his fits. He went out to the palm grove where the boy was and hid himself behind the palm stems to listen. The boy was lying on his side, wrapt in the mantle, out of which a murmuring came. But the boy's mother caught sight of Muḥammad, and warned her son, who ceased. Apparently, he was able to shake off the fit at once. But Muḥammad was much displeased; "If she had let him alone, the thing would have been cleared up."[2]

[1] Apparently the formula for testing a soothsayer before accepting his advice; cf. pp. 4 and 9.

[2] Ṣaḥīḥ of al-Bukhārī, Vol. VIII, p. 40 (*Book of Adab*), edition of Būlāq, A. H. 1315.

There is humor enough in this picture of one prophet trying to investigate another after the method of the Society for Psychical Research, but for the boy it was not a humorous situation. Muḥammad apparently satisfied himself that he was not dangerous. He became a Muslim and was alive in the year 63 of the *Hijra.* But all his life this suspicion followed him, and though one of his sons handed down traditions which are accepted[1] he himself was ostracised. The poet al-Farazdaq took refuge once at al-Madīna, and unwittingly entered the house of Ibn Ṣayyād; he found that the people would have no dealings with him.[2] Other traditions[3] show him complaining of this, and pointing out that he was a Muslim, with children, living both in al-Madīna and Mecca—none of these things being possible in the Antichrist. But others, again, show him with a certain malicious sense of his own importance, and fond of scaring people. His diseased personality—without Muḥammad's genius—is made very distinct.

To return to Muḥammad, it is plain, as I said, that he recognized here phenomena similar to his own, but was gradually satisfied that no danger lay in them, however they were to be explained.

So, while the general vocabulary as to his revela-

[1] *Nawawī*, p. 789.

[2] *Aghānī*, Vol. XIX, p. 25.

[3] *Maṣābīḥ*, Vol. II, p. 140, edition of Cairo, A. H. 1318.

tions was borrowed from that used in describing how their knowledge came to the *kāhins*, it had to be made very clear that the influence upon him was an angel or even the Holy Spirit—for him a convertible term—of all which the Christians and Jews spoke. But, in spite of his utmost endeavors to emphasize this distinction, his opponents called him a poet—evidently thinking not of the later artistic poet who wrote verses in correct meter, of which Muḥammad by nature was absolutely incapable, but of the ecstatic poet who stood in relations with the Unseen; or they called him possessed of a Jinnī, on the same idea; or, which was striking the closest of all, a *kāhin*, soothsayer. He *was* a *kāhin*, but with an enormous difference, the difference which separated what I have called the soil of prophetism among the Hebrews, the mass of *nebhī'îm* with their ecstatic excitements without ethical content or clear religious ideas, from the great reforming and constructive figures, from Amos and Hosea, from Isaiah and Jeremiah.

But again I must guard myself: Muḥammad cannot be compared to these last, on any absolute scale. Only as both contrast with their soil will the comparison hold. What raised Muḥammad from it was two ideas: the duty of the care of the poor, of almsgiving and helpfulness; and the unity and absolute sovereignty of Allāh. Of those germinative conceptions of the relations between God and man to which the Hebrew prophets attained, he had no idea except in one point. With his hard doctrine of the unity of Allāh, intermediaries were swept away. The whole polydaemonistic scheme with a one God somewhere in the background, to which the Arabs seem to have attained, vanished. There was left no interceder with that one God; no beings from whom revelations might come. When an angel spoke with him—Gabriel or the Holy Spirit, or whatever the term might be—there was no semi-divine personality there. On the one hand there was Allāh; on the other, his creation, including angels, Jinn, devils, men. Even such a conception of a unity of nature with God as we find among the Hebrews in the Benê Elôhîm, the Sons of God, has vanished with him. The angels were created of light—that is their only distinction. Allāh is throned alone—the Creator, Ruler, Destroyer—unto him there is none like.

But having swept away at one stroke all lesser beings from whom revelations could come, having apparently closed the unseen world to man, and fixed a gulf that none could pass, with another stroke he bridged that gulf and drew man immediately into the presence of God. God, himself, the One, reveals himself to man through prophets and otherwise, and man, in prayer, can come directly to God. This is Muḥammad's great glory. The individual soul and its God are face to face. Yet in the absoluteness of this conception lay its philosophical weakness and failure. How can the One know and be known by that which is other than itself? How can unlikes ever meet? The conception of a fatherhood of God, of a genetic relationship, runs through the Hebrew prophets, and breaks down his aloofness and separateness. The conceptions again, on the one hand, of a suffering God, who has borne our flesh and knows its sorrows and, on the other hand, of a Holy Ghost, the God immanent who works in mankind, form the soul of the Christian church. But to these Islām can come, only by breaking with Muḥammad.

As we shall see abundantly hereafter, the devout life within the Muslim church led to a more complete pantheism than ever did the Christian trinity. In the struggle to bring God and his creation together, the creation had to become an aspect of the creator, and finally to vanish into him. Only in this way could the crass dualism be overcome, and that monism which is the basis or result of all mysticism be reached. There are stray expressions which suggest that Muḥammad—a devout soul, if ever there was one and a mystic in spite of his creed—was adrift himself on that sea, and was nearing that shore. But his brain, oriental to the core, contradictoriness never troubled, and Allāh could be throned apart in unapproachable grandeur and yet near to every human heart. His creed remained frankly dualistic, and to the clearly thinking mind, the ladder between earth and heaven seemed removed. How the inevitable pressure of religious inspiration restored it must be our future subject.

LECTURE II

THE MUSLIM CONCEPTION OF PROPHECY AND SOOTHSAYING

It is time now to turn to the Muslims themselves, and ask what they understand under prophecy; what for them a prophet is. In putting an answer before you, I choose a statement, not by a theologian but by a historian—a historian, it is true, of marked philosophical leanings. This is Ibn Khaldūn, who was born at Tunis, lived a restless life—part statesman, part scholar, part lawyer,—was on embassy at one time to Peter the Cruel at Seville, and at another to Tīmūr in his camp before Damascus, and died at Cairo as chief justice in A. D. 1406. His great work was a *Universal History*, which, as a history, does not merit much praise. But to it he prefixed an introduction, his justly celebrated *Muqaddima*, which was unique in its own time and for at least three centuries thereafter. For an estimate of it as a contribution to philosophical history, or rather as the foundation of that science, I refer you to Robert Flint's *Historical Philosophy in France and French Belgium and Switzerland.* Professor Flint was not an Arabist, but he was all the better able to estimate the value of a book that alone would suffice to vindicate the scientific weight of the Arabic literature. Hereafter I shall translate a good deal from it. It gives very fairly the final result of the centuries of theological development which preceded — a result which abides to this day. Ibn Khaldūn therein voices the catholic church of Islām.

You will observe that he is as absolute a supernaturalist as Muḥammad himself or any primitive Semite. Yet he tries to reduce his supernaturalism to scheme, if not entirely to rationalize it. The fact of those rifts in the shell of nature, through which the unseen world touches us, he in no way denies. But he tries to explain the method so as to bring it into accordance with the process which we see going on around us. This leads him, on the one hand, to a queer semi-evolutionary doctrine which he borrowed from the Aristotelian philosophers, and, on the other hand, to a doctrine of the human mind which seems halfway between phrenology and the more modern and fashionable hypothesis of subliminal selves. In fact, I think, when you have heard what he has to say, you will agree with me that he had some most interesting psychological ideas, and that he would probably have been in close sympathy with Mr. William James's *Varieties of Religious Experience.* His weak point is on the constructive side, and that our modern speculations would have strengthened. His different "souls" would pass easily into different selves, but it may be that he would have had to invert their order. Yet his doctrine of the use of magic mirrors, crystal balls and the like appears to be in absolute accord with our psychology.

His section on inspiration and vision he opens thus:[1]

> Know that God has chosen from mankind certain individuals whom he has graced with converse with Himself and has given such a constitution that they may know him, and has made to be means of access between Him and His creatures, that they may instruct men as to what is best for them, and may exhort them to accept their guidance, and may keep them from the Fire, and guide them in the way of salvation. In that which God gives to them, consisting of knowledge, and exhibits in agreement with what they say, consisting of invasions of the order of nature, is also narrative concerning things hidden from mankind, to the knowledge of which there is no path except from God by their intermediation; and they do not know it except through God's instructing them. The Prophet has said, "I know only what God has taught me." Know further that truthfulness is an essential and necessary element in what they tell in that way, for reasons which will become plain to you in connection with the explanation of the essential nature of prophecy.

Here, you will see, is a frankly supernatural definition and the end of prophecy is to save men from the Fire. This is one of the most puzzling paradoxes in Islām. As to recognizing, using and enjoying this world, Islām is a most practical religion, but on its doctrine of salvation it is absolutely and entirely other-worldly. Ibn Khaldūn then goes on to give

[1] Beyrout edition, p. 91; Būlāq, p. 77; de Slane's translation, Vol. I, p. 184.

five signs which characterize the prophetic division of the human race:

I. In the state of inspiration the prophet exhibits unconsciousness of his surroundings along with a snoring in the throat; [the last word is difficult;[1] it is used to describe the roaring of the male camel when it blows the faucial bag out of its mouth, or the snorting of an angry man, or loud snoring] —it is to all appearance as though he were fainting or swooning. But there is nothing of the kind; in reality he is only immersed in meeting the spiritual messenger. This takes place when they apprehend that which is cognate to them but entirely inaccessible to the physical senses. Thereafter that descends to the physical senses, either through the hearing of a humming of speech—then the prophet understands it—or there presents itself to him the form of an individual addressing him with that which he has brought from God. Thereafter that state clears away from him, and he has retained the message. The Prophet, having been asked about inspiration, said, "At times it comes to me like the ringing of a bell; that is the most grievous upon me; then it drops away from me and I have retained what it said. And at times the angel presents himself to me as a man and speaks to me; then I retain what he says." In the course of that there used to come upon him such grievousness and pressure in the throat as cannot be expressed. In a tradition stands, "There was a great grievousness in the effect of revelation upon him." ʿĀʾisha said, "Inspiration would descend upon him on a day of bitter cold; then it would drop away from him; and his brow would be running with sweat." God said[2] "Lo, we shall cast upon thee a heavy word." And because the descending of inspiration had so extreme an effect the

[1] Cf. Sprenger, *Leben Mohammeds*, Vol. I, pp. 228, 270.

[2] *Qur.* lxxiii, 5.

polytheists used to accuse the prophets of being possessed by Jinn. They would say, "He has a familiar[1] of the Jinn." But it was only by what they had observed of the outward appearance of these states that the case of the Prophet was obscured to them. "He has no guide whom God leads astray."[2]

Because of its importance I have translated this very closely. You will observe the acknowledgment of the practical identity in outward appearance between a prophet and one possessed by a Jinnī. From the traditions I could quote many other descriptions of Muḥammad's appearance under inspiration, but they would not serve any useful purpose. The individual traditions, with their details, are often suspicious, and it is practically impossible to weed them out. This holds especially of Muḥammad's earlier life at Mecca, at the time when there cannot be any question of his honesty. But that he fell into absolute trance-conditions in later life when he was consciously manipulating his revelations to suit his purpose, cannot be doubted either. It is of these later times that Ibn Khaldūn gives us here, as it were, a philosophical collective photograph. He was probably aided also by similar phenomena which he had observed among his own contemporaries. The feeling of weight and the choking in the throat seem to be characteristic for all phenomena of the subconscious life. A more

[1] Literally "an apparition or follower."

[2] *Qur.* xiii, 33.

precise interpretation of these symptoms has not yet been reached. Weil, in 1862, tried to prove that they pointed to epilepsy as opposed to catalepsy. More recently Professor Margoliouth, in his *Life of Muḥammad* (p. 46), has urged the same based on such symptoms as this unconsciousness, the sound of a bell, the belief that someone is present, a resultant headache, violent perspiration, and others, such as turning of the head to one side, foaming at the mouth, reddening or whitening of the face, all which are characteristics of epilepsy. But as Sprenger (Vol. III, p. 65) rightly points out, the traditions are too contradictory to afford a sure basis. What is certain is the existence of some pathological condition in Muḥammad, resulting in trances, and it is not at all impossible that Sprenger's judgment (Vol. I. pp. 207 f.) that it was some form of hysteria under which he suffered, may be correct. A more detailed examination in the light of the recent investigations of nervous diseases through hypnotism might reach more sure results. There are striking parallels with the descriptions of Mrs. Piper's appearance on entering and leaving trance which are scattered through the *Proceedings of the Society for Psychical Research.*

The narratives seem generally to imply that Muḥammad communicated his "revelations" only after he had come out of the trance condition. That may have been, but it must be regarded as probable also that he spoke in trance as does, for example, Mrs. Piper. And one very curious passage in the *Qurʾān* (lxxv, 16; cf. xx, 110) would suggest that he spoke automatically—like an automatic writer—out of trance. It runs, "Do not move thy tongue in it [the revelation] to hurry it." This is exactly the caution that the conscious automatic writer has to observe, namely, that he does not consciously move his hand in order to hurry the process. That the words apply to Muḥammad's action in receiving revelation is a very old traditional exegesis.[1]

The second characteristic of the prophetic class, which Ibn Khaldūn gives, need not detain us so long. Even before inspiration, prophets have a good and pure disposition; they turn away from blameworthy things and uncleanness generally. This is what is meant when they are said to be protected against sin and error; it is as though they were created with a tendency to flee these things, which are incongruous with their nature. Stories follow how Muḥammad, as a child, fell in a swoon when his person was exposed; how God cast on him, as a youth, a miraculous sleep so that he should not go to a wedding, and have part in unseemly sports; how he avoided garlic, etc., for the sake of his angel visitors.

[1] Tabarī's *Tafsīr*, Vol. XXIX, p. 101; Rāzī's *Mafātīḥ*, Vol. VIII, p. 283, edition of Cairo, A. H. 1308.

The third characteristic is that prophets summon to religion and devotion, that is prayer and the giving of the poor rate and chaste conversation. The possession of the above three characteristics alone is enough as a proof of prophecy. Ibn Khaldūn tells here one of those absurd stories of which Islām is so fond, and which seem to have shot up as did the apocryphal gospels in early Christianity; or they are like our religious novels, with the difference that they were and are fully believed. Muḥammad's letter, summoning to Islām, came to the emperor Heraclius. So he called into his presence those of the tribe of the Prophet whom he could find, and among them Abū Sufyān, the great enemy of Muḥammad, and asked them about him, especially what he commanded them. Abū Sufyān replied, "Prayer and the poor-rate and charity and chastity." Then said Heraclius, "If what thou sayest is true, he is verily a prophet, and will rule all that is under these two feet of mine." "This was enough as a proof for Heraclius," comments Ibn Khaldūn; "he had no need of an evidentiary miracle."

The fourth characteristic is that the prophet must be a person of distinction among his people. No prophet has been sent, says a tradition, save in an assured position with his people, and in wealth. This is that he may have a party and power to defend him against unbelievers, until he delivers the message of his Lord, and finish the will of God in perfecting his religion and forming a community. This characteristic is evidently deduced from the career of Muḥammad himself; it could in no way be derived either from the Old or the New Testament. And the *kāhin* of heathen Arabia, also, seldom had an assured position. But Ibn Khaldūn is perfectly right. This conception is an absolute element in the Muslim idea of the prophet. He is not a voice preaching righteousness and proclaiming God, but the militant head of a community claiming, as a right, absolute sovereignty.

The fifth characteristic of prophets is the occurrence with them of invasions of the order of nature, bearing witness to their truthfulness. These are actions whose like ordinary mankind cannot perform; they fall outside of the sphere of a creature's power. There is a dispute, however, as to how they occur and how they prove the veracity of a prophet. The scholastic theologians generally hold that they occur by the power of God, not by the action of the prophet. Even the heretical Muʿtazilites, though they say generally that the actions of a creature proceed from him himself, say of the evidentiary miracle that it is not the action of a creature—in this case, the prophet. Further, the scholastics hold that the prophet has absolutely no part in it; he only uses it as a weapon, by the permission of God; that is, before it occurs the prophet states it as a proof of his veracity in his claim; then, when it has occurred, it takes the place of a clear utterance from God that the prophet is truthful; its proof, thus, is absolute. So an evidentiary miracle proves the veracity of a prophet through (1) being an invasion of the order of nature and (2) being thus controversially used, the use is a part of it, or as the scholastics say, an essential quality. Further, this controversial use is what distinguishes the evidentiary miracle (*muᶜjiza*) of the prophet from the miracle worked by a saint (*karāma*) and from magic. In the last two there is no need of proving veracity, nor is there any controversial intention, except accidentally. If, by chance, it occurs in a saint's miracle on the part of the performer of the miracle, and has a probative force, it proves saintship only and not prophecy. Some have denied the possibility of miracles by saints, fearing this confusion, but Ibn Khaldūn thinks the distinction clear. The Muᶜtazilites, however, reject saints' miracles because invasions of the order of nature cannot be actions of a creature, since the actions of creatures are limited to custom. That the evidentiary miracle cannot be worked by a liar is proven as follows: The Ashᶜarites, orthodox scholastics, say that assertion of veracity and right guidance are both essential qualities in an evidentiary miracle. Then if it occurs without these, as it would if worked by a liar, the proof is ambiguous, the guidance into right becomes leading astray, and the assertion of veracity becomes a lie. So the essentials are changed; the essential qualities transformed. Its occurrence is thus impossible. The Muʿtazilites simply say that the occurrence of proof as ambiguity and of right guidance as leading astray is abominable and cannot have place with God.

The philosophers, on the other hand, meaning the students of Greek philosophy, Aristotelians and neo-Platonists, hold that the invasion of the order of nature in a miracle is an act of the prophet, although that invasion is strictly outside of his power. They base this on their general position as to essential necessity. The occurrence of events, one from another, depends on causes and conditions; all goes back at the last to the Necessary, the agent *per se*, not by choice. The soul of the prophet, for them, has essential peculiarities, among which are the production of these invasions of the order of nature by his own power, and the obedience of the elements to him in producing things. The prophet, for them, is endowed with control over things whenever he turns to them and has reached full age for that purpose. This is given to him by God. So the invasion of nature on the part of the prophet occurs equally, whether it is with controversial intention or not, and is a proof of his veracity by proving that he has that control over things which is peculiar to the prophetic soul. For the philosophers, therefore, the distinction by controversial intention between the evidentiary miracle and the saint's miracle and magic fails. They distinguish the prophet from the magician by the quality of his actions. The prophet's actions are good; the magician's bad. Saints, on the other hand, have a more limited sphere of wonders. The prophet ascends to heaven, and penetrates dense bodies, and restores the dead to life, and speaks with angels, and flies in the air. But the saint can only multiply things and tell something of the future, and the like. These philosophers, you will observe, were evidently working very hard to get a scientific statement for the belief of their time. We know the same phenomenon. All this, says Ibn Khaldūn, meaning apparently the entire doctrine of the miracles of prophets and saints, has been confirmed by the Ṣūfīs, the professed Muslim mystics, in the books on their discipline. For him, we will find, the mystical experience is the ultimate proof. Finally, the greatest and clearest of all evidentiary miracles is the *Qurʾān* itself. It combines both the thing to be proved, that is the inspiration, and the proof; therein is its uniqueness, the very self-evident soul of inspiration itself.

These five characteristics, then, are the outward signs of a prophet. But what is the nature of the prophet? what this prophetic soul of which we have just heard? what his part in the scheme of the universe? Here we enter on deep waters, and I must ask your very close attention and also your indulgence with the strain which I shall throw on the English language. Scholastic philosophy cannot be made very luminous; and when it must be translated from Arabic, its state is twice confounded.

You will remember, of course, that the universe, for Ibn Khaldūn, was the Ptolemaic universe, the universe of Dante and Milton, consisting of concentric spheres. Also he is ruled by a conception of the unity of nature and its processes derived from neo-Platonism; all life is in a process of emanation, tending to gradual particularization from the universal, but possessed always by a longing to return to the one, perfect unity. This joins the Aristotelian conception of the whole of nature as instinct with a vital impulse towards some higher manifestation, and of organic life as on an ascending scale of complexity with man as the final end. Only Aristotle regarded the species as fixed, but Ibn Khaldūn seems to have accepted the possibility and actuality of a true developing from one into another. That he had from the neo-Platonic admixture; as also the stretching of the process on into the spiritual world. A semi-pantheistic attitude is thus reached, which with many Muslims became absolute pantheism. With him it is only mysticism:

Know [says Ibn Khaldūn,[1]]—God guide aright us and

[1] Beyrout edition, p. 95; Būlāq, p. 80; de Slane's translation, Vol. I, p. 196.

thee!—that we observe this world, with all that is in it of created things, to be in a scheme of arrangement and ordinance, a linking of causes to results, and a joining of things to things, and a changing of some existences into others; its marvels therein unending; and its limits unbounded. I begin, then, with the physical world, perceptible to the senses.

First, the world of the elements. We can observe how it ascends upward by steps, from earth to water, then to air, then to fire; each joined to the other, and each fitted to change into that which is beyond it, upward and downward, and actually changing on certain occasions. The upper of these is always finer than that which precedes, until the world of the spheres is reached, which is finest of all and is in stages, one joining to another upon a scheme of which sense can perceive nothing but the motions only. Yet by these motions some have been guided to a knowledge of their measures and positions, and to what exists beyond them of essences to which these effects on them are due. Consider next the world of becoming—this changing world of ours—how it begins with minerals; then come plants; then animals, after a wondrous scheme of progress upward, the last of the region of the minerals joining the beginning of the region of the plants, such as grass and what has no seed; and the last of the region of the plants, such as the palm and the vine joining the beginning of the region of animals, such as the snail and shell-fish, both of which have the power of touch only. And "joining" in the case of these created things means that the last of a region of them is curiously fitted to become the beginning of the region of that which comes after it.

The world of animals is wide, and its species are numerous, and it extends in the development of this changing world up to man, the possessor of reflection and thought. The species mount up to him from this world which we perceive with our senses, which includes sense and apprehension, but which does not extend to thought and reflection actually. That is the beginning of a region which extends from man onward, and here ends what we can directly observe.

Then we find in the worlds, as they vary, differing effects; in the world of sense, effects from the movements of the spheres and from the elements; in the world of change in which we are, effects from the movement of growth and apprehension; all testify that there is a producer of effects separate from bodies. It is spiritual and is in contact with the things of this world because this world and these things in it are in contact throughout. It is, therefore, the soul which apprehends and sets in motion, and above it, without question, there must be another being which gives it its powers of apprehending and setting in motion, and is in contact with it also, and whose essence is pure apprehension and absolute rationality. It is the world of angels.

So there must needs belong to the soul a fitness to be stripped of the nature of mankind and to put on the angelic nature, so as to become actually of the genus of angels, on an occasion, for a moment. But that can happen only after the soul's spiritual essence is actually perfected, as we shall mention hereafter.

And it has contacts with the regions beyond it, like the other ordered existences, as we have said above. In these contacts there are two directions, upward and downward. The soul joins with the body downward and acquires through it sensuous apprehensions which fit it for attaining to actual operation of the reason. Upward it joins the region of the angels and through that gains apprehension of divine knowledge and of the Unseen. For the world of events [this world in which things happen] exists in the intellectual operations of angels apart from time. All this, according to what we have said above, proceeds from the ordered arrangement which we find in all existence consisting of the contact of its essences and powers, one with another.

Next, this human soul[1] cannot be seen, but its effects are plain in the body, as though the body and all its parts, joined and separate, were instruments for the soul and its powers which are either active like grasping with the hand and walking with the foot and speaking with the tongue, and like the total motion in the body through alternate efforts; or they are apprehensive.

Then, just as the powers of apprehension are arranged and ascend up to their highest and to the highest of the thinking power which is called the logical soul, so the external senses with their instruments of hearing, seeing, etc., ascend to the internal senses. The first of these is the "general sense" [the Aristotelian "common sense"][2] the power which apprehends sensuous percepts, seen, heard, touched, etc., all in a single state; thereby the general sense is distinguished from the external senses, because the percepts do not press upon them all at once. Then the "general sense" passes it along to the imagination. It is a power which presents the perceived thing in the soul as stripped of external matter. The instrument of these two powers in their rule is the first hollow of the brain, the anterior portion to the first, and the posterior portion to the second. Then the imagination ascends to the power of forming opinions and to the memory. The power of forming opinions is for the apprehension of ideas connected with individualities, like the enmity of Zayd and the friendship of ʿAmr, the love of a father and the voracity

[1] On the psychological scheme which follows compare Ibn Sīnā's little treatise edited, with German translation, by Landauer in *ZDMG.*, Vol. XXIX, and translated into English by E. A. Van Dyck, *A Compendium on the Soul*, Verona, 1906.

[2] Zeller, *Aristotle and the Earlier Peripatetics*, Vol. II, pp. 68 ff., of the English translation. See especially note 3, p. 68.

of the wolf. The memory is for the storing up of all the apprehended and imagined things and is like a treasury of them, preserving them for time of need. The instrument of these two powers in their rule is the posterior hollow of the brain; the first of it to the first, and the latter to the other.

Then they all ascend to the intellectual power whose instrument is the middle hollow of the brain. It is the power by which takes place the movement of meditation and inclining toward intellectual processes. So the soul is moved thereby constantly on account of the longing involved in it toward deliverance from the surveillance of the power which holds it back and from the equipment which belongs to human nature. So, in its rational operation, the soul comes out into action, making itself like to the Heavenly Spiritual Host[1] and it enters the lowest of the ranks of the Spiritualities when it apprehends without bodily instruments. Toward that it is constantly moving and heading. Then, sometimes, it passes over completely from human nature and its form of spirituality to the angelic nature of the upper region, not by any acquiring of a new thing, but by the constitution and primitive creation wherein God has made it.

And human souls are of three kinds. First, a kind too weak by nature to attain this degree. These souls are limited to motion in the lower direction, toward sensuous and imaginary apprehensions, and to the combining of ideas from the memory and to the power which forms opinions according to limited rules and specific arrangement. They acquire hereby the sciences, conceptual and affirmative, which belong to the intellect when in the body, and all of which belong to the imagination and are of limited range, since, on the side of its beginning, the soul extends to elements only and does not pass beyond them. If it is corrupt, then all beyond these is barred to it. This, for the most part, is the limit of human

[1] *Qur.* xxxvii, 8.

apprehension in the body; to it the apprehensions of the learned attain and in it their feet are firm.

Souls of the second kind set out through that intellectual motion toward the spiritual reason and toward the kind of apprehension which, on account of the equipment therefor which has been made in them, has no need of bodily instruments. The range of their apprehension is wider than the elements which are the range of the primary apprehension belonging to humanity, and they go on freely to internal observations. These are a kind of ecstasy as a whole; they have a limit at their beginning but not at their end. They are the apprehensions of the learned of the saints, the people of the religious sciences and of divine knowledge; they are attained after death by the saved, in the state between death and the resurrection.

The third kind are created with the power of passing over from humanity, its flesh and its spirit, to the angels of the upper region, so that, for a moment, they become angels actually, and in that moment witness the Heavenly Host in their region, and hear spiritual speech and the divine allocution. These are prophets; God has created for them the power of their momentarily passing over from humanity. And this is the state of inspiration; a constitution on which God has constituted them and a nature in which He has formed them. Through the traits of character which have been combined in them, consisting of the striving and uprightness by which they look toward God, and through the desire which is fixed in their natures for the service of God, unveiled in that looking and making easy its path, he has removed them from the hindrances and entanglements of the body so long as they remain mixed with these through their human nature. So, whenever they wish, they set out for that region by means of that power of transition and that constitution in which they are constituted, not by any acquisition or art.

Then, when they set out and pass over from their humanity, and encounter in that Heavenly Host what they encounter, they turn to the channels of physical apprehension with that as a revelation to be sent down by means of these channels, for the sake of transmitting it to creatures. So, at one time, one of them hears a humming sound, as though it were a suggestion of speech, from which he may take the sense which has been brought to him, and the humming sound does not cease until he has retained it and understood it. And, at another time, the angel who brings the revelation to him presents himself as a man, and talks to him, and he retains what the angel says. The encountering of the angel, and the return to the channels of physical apprehension, and his understanding what is brought to him, all of that is as though it were in a single flash, or less than a glance of the eye. It does not happen in time, but it happens, all of it, together. So it appears as though it were swift, and therefore it is called inspiration (*waḥy*) because *waḥy*, in Arabic, means "hastening."[1]

Know, further, that the first state—the state of hearing a humming—is the stage of the prophets who are not apostles sent with books, as the distinction is made, and the second—the state when an angel appears like a man talking—is the stage of the prophets sent with books, and on that account is more perfect than the first. This is the meaning of the tradition in which the prophet explained inspiration when he was asked about it. He said, "At times it comes to me like the ringing of a bell, and that is the most grievous upon me. Then it falls away from me and I have retained what it said. And at times the angel presents himself to me as a man and speaks to me; then I retain what he says." The first of these was more grievous, only because it was the initial step in passing from potentiality to actuality in reaching

[1] But see p. 252 below.

the spiritual world. So he was under somewhat of a strain. Therefore when he turned, in this state, to the channels of physical apprehension, these limited themselves down to hearing; every other way would have been too hard. But when the inspiration was repeated, and the encountering of the angel occurred often, reaching the spiritual world became easy. So when he turned to the channels of physical apprehension he reached them as a whole, and, especially, the clearest of them, which is apprehension by sight.

Know, too, that in the state of apprehension as a whole, is a general difficulty and grievousness, which the *Qur'ān* has pointed out. God has said, "Lo we shall cast upon thee a heavy word." And ʿĀʾisha said, "To that which he had to endure from the revelation belonged a great grievousness." And she said also, "Inspiration would descend upon him on a day of bitter cold; then it would drop away from him; and his brow would be running with sweat." On that account there used to befall him when in that state such unconsciousness, roaring and choking in the throat as is well known. The cause of that was that inspiration, as we have explained, is a separation from the physical nature for the sake of angelic apprehensions, and an encountering of the speech of the soul. So there arises a grievousness from the separation of the self from the self, and its transition from its region to that other region. This is the meaning of the choking which was spoken of as occurring at the beginning of revelation, when he [Muḥammad] said, "Then he choked me until pain reached its limit with me; thereupon he let me go, and said, 'Read!' I said, 'I cannot read;' and so a second and a third time, as stands in the tradition."

But practice sometimes brings by degrees—first one thing and then another thing—to a measure of ease, in comparison at least with what came earlier. On that account the sections of the *Qur'ān*, both chapters and verses, revealed when he was in

Mecca, were shorter than when he was in al-Madīna. Consider what is handed down as to the revealing of chapter ix, dealing with the raid of Tabūk, how the whole or the greater part of it was revealed while he was traveling upon his camel. At Mecca, on the other hand, there would be revealed to him only a part of a chapter, some very short one, at one time, and the rest would be revealed at another time. Similarly, the last of that which was revealed in al-Madīna was the "Verse of the Religion"[1] and its length is well known, while at Mecca there used to be revealed very short verses. In that there is a suggestion by which you may distinguish between Meccan and Madīnan chapters and verses.

This, then, for Ibn Khaldūn is the sum of the nature of prophecy. You will notice how careful he is to keep the conception of the unseen world vague. He felt, undoubtedly, our own shrinking from an elaborately concrete heaven of the Miltonic and Dantean type. Beyond the veil there is something from which ideas come in flashes to those whose natures are such that they can perceive them. These elements of spiritual intuition are translated into terms of the senses—sight, hearing and the like—by the perceiver, because that is the only way in which he can make intelligible what he has reached. They do not come to the prophet by the senses, but he unconsciously renders them in sensuous terms, and thus they pass out to the world. Ibn Khaldūn was compelled by the theology of the *Qur'ān* to speak of angels, but it is obvious that he much pre-

[1] *Qur.* v, 4.

fers the non-concrete terms, and would rather speak of angelic influences. The case is similar in regard to the Jinn, in whom all orthodox Islām believes, and who are frequently mentioned in the *Qur'ān.* In no part of his thesaurus does he deal with them at length, and his references by the way are always under the spur of necessity. There is a curious passage, however, found only in certain MSS in which he assigns the verses in the *Qur'ān* which make mention of revelation, angels, the Holy Spirit, and the Jinn to the technical class of "obscure verses" (*mutashābihāt*), those as to whose meaning we have no certain knowledge. In this he stands alone among presumed orthodox Muslims; with others there is no trace of uncertainty as to the nature of the Jinn, as we shall see hereafter.

He passes next to an analysis of the nature of soothsaying:[1]

That, also, [he says] belongs to the characteristics of the human soul. In all that has preceded we have seen that the human soul has an equipment for passing over from its humanity to the spiritual nature which is above it. A flash comes to mankind of the class of the prophets through the nature of their constitution, which plainly comes to them not through any acquisition, nor by seeking the aid of any of the channels of apprehension, nor through conceptions, nor through bodily actions in speech or movement, nor through anything at all. It is simply a transition from the human to the angelic nature

[1] Beyrout edition, p. 99; Būlāq, p. 84; de Slane's translation, Vol. I, p. 206.

through innate constitution, in a flash, in less than a glance of the eye. Since that is so, and since that preparedness exists in human nature in general, logical subdivision follows. There must be another class of human beings who fall short of the first class to an extent which means absolute contrariety; because the lack of seeking aid for that spiritual apprehension is the contrary of seeking aid for it, and how far apart these are! Logical division, then, gives this other class of human beings, having such a constitution that their reasoning power can be set in motion intellectually through will aroused by desire, but who through weakness of nature, fall short. They, therefore, cling for aid to particular things, perceived by the senses or imagined, such as transparent bodies and bones of animals and rhymes and words and birds and beasts as these present themselves. So they wait for that sense-perception or imagination, seeking aid of it to bring about that transition to spiritual perception which is their object; it is to them like a strengthener, and this force which is in these things as a beginning for that spiritual apprehension is the essence of soothsaying. Yet because these souls have a defective constitution and fall short of completeness, their apprehension is rather in particulars than in universals. On that account, the aiding imagination in them is so strong, because it is the instrument of particulars. It has free passage, then, in the particulars, whether waking or sleeping, and is present with these as a strong helper, presenting them and being to them like a mirror in which they are constantly seen.

But the soothsayer cannot attain completely to the apprehension of rational things because his inspiration is Satanic. The loftiest of the states of inspiration of which this class of men is capable is attained by seeking aid from rhymed prose and balanced speech, that the soothsayer may be diverted by that from the senses and strengthened in some degree for his limited attaining of the spiritual. So, on account of that mental agitation and the external things which strengthen it, there comes into his mind something which his mind then conveys to his tongue. And he sometimes speaks truth, and agrees with the fact, and sometimes lies, because he fills out what is lacking in himself with something external to his perceiving self and separate from it and unsuitable. So truth and falsehood encounter him together, and he is undecided as to the case, and often takes refuge in opinion and conjecture, out of desire to attain success in his apprehension, as he thinks, and equivocating to those who help him.[1]

The users of this rhymed prose are those who are peculiarly designated by the name of *kāhins*, because they are the best of all this kind. The Prophet has said, in speaking of such as they, "This belongs to the rhymed prose of the *kāhins*." He thus made rhymed prose theirs peculiarly. Also, he asked Ibn Ṣayyād,[2] investigating his state, "How does this thing come to thee?" Ibn Ṣayyād said, "It comes to me in truth and in falsehood." The Prophet said, "The affair is mixed for thee," meaning that the peculiarity of prophecy is truth, and lying never at all befalls it. This is because prophecy is a joining of the self of the prophet with the Heavenly Host, without any helper and without seeking aid in an external thing, but the possessor of soothsaying, since he is driven to invoke the aid of external perceptions, these enter into his apprehension and it is confused thereby, and lying comes to him on that side. Thus his apprehension cannot be prophecy. We said that the best of the degrees of soothsaying was in the state of using rhymed prose. This is only because

[1] An exact description of the impression produced by "trance-mediums" of whose honesty, in their normal state, no doubt seems possible; such, for example, as Mrs. Piper.

[2] See further, p. 66 below.

the essential nature of rhymed prose is lighter than all the other things seen and heard, used to produce that effect, and this essential lightness shows how close is the attainment and the apprehension of the spiritual things, and, therefore, how comparatively slight is the weakness in that case.

Some assert that this soothsaying has been cut off since the time of prophecy, through the pelting of devils (*shayṭāns*) with shooting-stars, which took place before the mission of Muḥammad; and that that pelting was to keep them away from knowledge of what was said in the heavens as stands in the *Qur'ān*.[1] The soothsayers informed themselves about that only by means of the devils. So soothsaying, from that day, was nullified. But that, as a proof, is not valid. The knowledge of the soothsayers, just as it came from the devils, came also from themselves, as we have explained. Also, the verse in the *Qur'ān* shows only that the devils were hindered from one kind of the things said in the heavens; that is, what was connected with the mission of Muḥammad; and they were not hindered from anything else; also, it was only before the sending of the Prophet that this cutting-off took place, and perhaps they returned thereafter to what they had been doing. This is the plain meaning, because all these sources of knowledge were obscured in the time of the Prophet's life, just as the stars and lamps are obscured in the presence of the sun; because prophecy is the mighty light before which every other light is dim or passes away.

Some of the philosophers have asserted that soothsaying existed only before the coming of the Prophet, and then was cut off, and that thus it happened with every prophet, because, they said, the existence of a prophet involves a certain situation of the spheres which requires the appearance of a prophet. If then, that situation of the spheres be complete it requires the appearance of a prophet in his complete-

[1] *Qur.* xv, 18.

ness. But if it falls short from completeness, it requires the existence of a nature of that same kind, only incomplete. But that is the essential nature of a soothsayer, as we have explained. So before that perfect situation of the spheres is completed, the imperfect situation occurs and requires the existence of the soothsayer, either one or more. Then, whenever the situation of the spheres is complete, the existence of the prophet in his perfection is complete, and the travailings[1] which indicated such a nature as that are accomplished, for nothing of them is felt afterwards. All this is based upon the idea that an incomplete spheral relation requires part of what would be its effect if complete; but that is not admitted. Perhaps, rather, the spheral relation requires such a thing only when its scheme is entire, and if any of its parts be lacking, it does not require anything; not that it requires that effect imperfectly, as they say.

Further, these soothsayers, when they are contemporary with a prophet, know his truth, worthiness, and the evidence of his miracles, since they have some of the ecstatic nature of the prophet, just as every man has in sleep. Only, the rational nature of that relationship to the unseen world exists in the soothsayer more strongly than in the sleeper. The only thing that keeps them back from admitting all that, and causes them to fall into denial, is the influence of their desire that this relationship may be prophecy on their part. So they begin to oppose, just as did Umayya ibn Abī-ṣ-Ṣalt; for he desired that he might be a prophet. So, too, it happened to Ibn Ṣayyād and to Musaylima and others. Then, when the Faith conquered and those hopes were cut off, they believed with the best kind of belief, as happened to Ṭulayḥa al-Asadī and Qārib ibn al-Aswad; both of these, in the Muslim conquests, gave evident signs of belief.

[1] Cf. Romans 8:22; but the Būlāq text and de Slane's translation read, "the situations of the spheres."

This, then, is Ibn Khaldūn's doctrine of the *kāhins* and prophets. Their nature, broadly, is the same. Only, the *kāhin* required certain mechanical inducements to distract the attention of his ordinary self, and give freedom to his subliminal self. If we make allowance for the psychological inheritance of Ibn Khaldūn from Aristotle, through the Muslim scholastics, we shall be compelled to admit the close agreement of his theories with the modern doctrine of the working of the different selves. But you will observe, also, that one point of contact between the *kāhins* and Muḥammad is not taken up by Ibn Khaldūn. He states the use of *saj*ᶜ, rhymed prose, as the "lightest" of the means used by the *kāhins* to produce the ecstatic state, apparently meaning by that that it was the simplest, the least mechanical of those devices; but he gives no hint that the whole of the *Qur*ᵓ*ān* is composed in precisely the same rhymed prose, and that in form, as well as spirit, Muḥammad belonged to the company of the *kāhins*. This, in him, is a curious bit of conservative inheritance. Earlier theologians had been exceedingly careful to obscure the likeness between Muḥammad and the *kāhins*, and had, in consequence, entered into elaborate proofs that the *Qur*ᵓ*ān* was not written in *saj*ᶜ, and that to apply the technical terms of *saj*ᶜ to it was simple unbelief. Ibn Khaldūn sees very clearly the closeness of the resemblance between Muḥammad and the *kāhins*, but he has not reached the point that the *Qurʾān*, the Uncreated Word of God, is written according to their artistic forms.

Another point, which we could hardly expect Ibn Khaldūn to notice, is the question whether Muḥammad did not, after all, have means of bringing on the ecstatic condition, somewhat similar to those of the *kāhins*. The records are so scanty that we can only frame hypotheses. Hypnotic parallels would indicate that he may have suggested to himself the state by this very use of rhymed prose. He seems to have disliked the use of it by others. It is also possible that while in the hypnotic condition—if it was hypnosis—he may have put himself under auto-suggestion of its return at a certain time. If we could trust in the slightest the stories of his Meccan period, this might explain the great break in his revelations when he feared that he had been deceived and deserted. The case may have been, simply, that he had not caught the knack of suggesting to himself a return. His doubts, too, would give him a suggestion of the opposite kind. It is peculiarly unfortunate that the fullest descriptions of his state under inspiration belong to his latest period, and cannot be free from the suspicion that he was acting up to his accepted rôle. Still, however it may have been with the revelations which in many cases were too clearly manufactured or manipulated by himself, the ecstatic or hypnotic conditions in which he professed to receive them may have remained perfectly genuine. When he had come out of the state which he had learned so easily to assume he could give anything as the revelation received therein. And it is always possible that what he vehemently desired may have seemed to come to him in that state. The self-deceptions of oriental ecstatics and mystics most be accepted as certain, though they are among the most puzzling problems of the history of religions. There will be much more of this hereafter.

LECTURE III

THE MUSLIM CONCEPTION OF INTERCOURSE WITH THE UNSEEN WORLD IN SLEEP

Ibn Khaldūn now goes on to the doctrine of intercourse with the Unseen through vision or dreaming. This had been fully admitted by Muḥammad, according to tradition, and he was here on more universally accepted ground than in his account of the *kāhins*. He develops his theory as follows:[1]

The essential nature of Vision is that the rational soul through its spiritual essence gains for a moment information as to the forms of events. Inasmuch as the soul is spiritual, the forms of events exist in it actually, as is the case with all spiritual essences, and it becomes spiritual through being stripped of all material substance and of the channels of bodily apprehension. This happens to the rational soul from time to time, for a moment, because of sleep, as we shall mention. So it acquires thereby knowledge of the future events for which it looks, and returns with that knowledge to its channels of apprehension. Then, if that acquisition is weak and lacking in clearness, through the use of metaphor and imagery in the imagination in order to state it, it has need of interpretation on account of these metaphors. And sometimes the acquisition is strong and can do without metaphors; then it has no need of interpretation to clarify it from the imagery of the imagination.

The cause of the occurrence of this flash of perception in the soul is that the soul is potentially a spiritual essence, seeking

[1] Beyrout edition, p. 102; Būlāq, p. 86; de Slane's translation, Vol. I, p. 211.

to fulfil itself through the body and the bodily channels of apprehension, until its essence may become pure rationality, and it may become perfect actually, and so be a spiritual essence apprehending without any bodily instruments. So its class, as to the spiritualities, is under the class of the angels, the People of the Upper Region, who need not seek to fulfil their essential nature through any channels of apprehension, bodily or otherwise. The equipment which leads to this perception belongs to the human soul, so long as it is in the body. There is a special kind of it which belongs to saints; and a kind that is general, belonging to mankind as a whole. The last is the basis of Vision.

As to that which belongs to the prophets, it is a capability of passing over from the human nature to the pure angelic nature, which is the loftiest of the spiritual things. This capability shows itself in them repeatedly on the occasions of inspiration. And the state of inspiration, when it enters the domain of the bodily channels of apprehension, and there occurs in these what occurs of apprehension, is most plainly like to the state of sleep, although the state of sleep is lower than it by far. On account of this likeness, Muḥammad used the expression about vision that it was one of the six and forty parts of prophecy.

Ibn Khaldūn goes on to explain how some derived this exact figure from a comparison of the total number of the years of Muḥammad's prophetic office, twenty-three in all, and that first half-year in which his inspiration came to him in vision only. In his case, dreaming had been one forty-sixth of the whole. To this, however, Ibn Khaldūn demurs. Other forms of the tradition give other numbers, one even seventy. He evidently had our own objection to any such exact reckoning of a spiritual relation, but his stated objection is that Muḥammad's twenty-three years held of him only and, therefore, could not be a basis for a general law. What is meant is that dreaming and prophetic inspiration are essentially the same, with a very wide distance between them.

When this is plain to thee, thou wilt know [he goes on] that the idea of proportion is the relationship of the primary capability, embracing all mankind, to the relative capability peculiar to the class of prophets, belonging to their constitution, since it is the less common capability. And, although this capability is general to all mankind, yet along with it are many hindrances and restraints preventing the attainment of it actually. Among the strongest of these are the external senses. But God constituted mankind with the quality that the veil of the senses might be raised in their natural sleep, and so the soul encounters, at this raising, knowledge of that for which it looks—in the World of Reality (*ʿālam al-ḥaqq*)—and apprehends, from time to time, a flash in which is attainment of the thing sought. On account of that, the Prophet called these moments of attainment "the Comforters" (*mubashshirāt*, "Givers of good tidings.") He said, "There remains of prophecy nothing but the 'Comforters.'" They said, "What are the 'Comforters,' O Apostle of God?" He said, "Sound Vision, which the sound man sees, or which is shown to him."

The cause of this lifting of the veil in sleep I will now describe to thee. The apprehensions and the actions of the rational soul are only by means of the physical, animal spirit. It is a fine vapor, whose seat is in the right hollow of the heart, as is laid down in the anatomical books of Galen and others, and it is sent forth along with the blood, in the arteries and veins, and gives sensation and motion and all the bodily actions. Its fine part ascends to the brain; then the brain is turned from its coldness, and the actions of the powers which are in its chambers are accomplished. So the rational soul apprehends and reasons only through this vapory spirit, and is joined to it only on account of the law of production which requires that the fine shall not make an impression on the coarse. Since, then, this animal spirit is the finest among the bodily substances, it becomes a *locus* for any workings of any essence different from itself in corporeality; in this case, the rational soul. So the workings of the rational soul are carried out in the body by means of the animal spirit.

We have already said that apprehension by the rational soul is of two kinds—an apprehension by means of what is external, namely the five senses, and an apprehension by means of what is internal, namely the powers of the brain, and that all this tends to hinder the rational soul from apprehending the spiritual essences above it; yet to apprehend these it is equipped by its constitution. And since the external senses are physical, they are exposed to sleep and indolence through weariness, and the soul faints by multitude of business. So God has created in it a search for rest in order that its power of apprehending may be perfectly renewed. That takes place only by the withdrawal of the animal spirit from all its external senses and its return to the internal sense. Cold in the night, which causes the body to faint, helps this. The natural heat seeks the recesses of the body, going from exterior to interior and accompanying its vehicle, the animal spirit. On account of this, sleep comes for the most part to mankind in the night.

So, when the spirit withdraws from the external senses and returns to the internal powers, and the hindrances and restraints are lightened from the soul and it returns to the forms which are stored in the memory, there present themselves from the memory, by combination and solution, imaginary forms mostly customary, because these forms are taken usually from apprehensions which are frequent. Then the "general sense," which is the union of the external senses, brings them down and apprehends them according to the different manners of the five external senses.

Often, even, the soul turns aside for a moment to its spiritual essence, in spite of the resistance of the internal power and perceives by means of its spiritual perception, because it is so created, and acquires some of the forms of things [the ideas], which then become joined with its essence. Thereafter, the imagination takes these forms, thus perceived, and presents them either as they essentially are, or by metaphor in habitual molds. The metaphors, in such cases, are what require interpretation.

On the other hand, the soul's manipulating, by combination and solution, the forms given by the memory before it has apprehended anything directly, produces the "bundles of dreams" of the *Qur'ān.*[1] Muḥammad said, "Vision is three: vision from God, vision from the angels, and vision from the devil." This division corresponds with what we have mentioned; the clear is from God; the metaphorical, which calls for interpretation, is from the angels; and the "bundles of dreams" are from the devil, because they are all vain and the devil is the source of the vain.

This is the essence of vision and of what causes it and of the sleep which accompanies it. It is the peculiar property of the human soul and exists among men in general; no one is free from it. Every one of human kind has seen in his sleep what has occurred to him in his waking hours, times more than once. And there has resulted to him the certainty that in sleep the soul apprehends the unseen world. Then, since that takes place in the world of sleep, it must needs be

[1] *Qur.* xii, 44; xxi, 5.

possible in other states. For the apprehending essence is one, and its properties are general to every state.

The most of this which occurs to mankind is apart from their intention and outside of their control. The soul is only looking for something; then the dream comes to it in that moment in sleep; it is not that the soul wills the vision, and so sees it. In the books of those who have written about ascetic and mystical exercises, certain names are given. If they are pronounced at the time of going to sleep, a vision of what is looked for will come from them. These are called *al-ḥalūmīya* [apparently derived from the Hebrew *ḥălôm*, "dream"]. The author of a book of the kind has mentioned one of these, which he calls "the *ḥalūma* of the perfect nature." It is, that at time of sleep, after the completion of religious exercises and with complete intention of mind, these foreign words should be pronounced [here follow certain unintelligible combinations of letters, which are unpronounceable as the vowels are not given. They are probably of Hebrew or Syriac origin], and that the seeker should bear in mind his need; for he will see in slumber the unveiling of that concerning which he asks. It is related that a certain man did that after a preparation of some nights as to his food and religious exercises. Then a form appeared to him saying, "I am thy perfect nature." Then the man asked his question and was told what he had been looking for. To me, myself, have come, through these names, strange appearances, and I have learned by them details of my circumstances into which I was looking.

But that does not prove that seeking a dream produces it. Only, that these names produce a preparation in the soul for the occurrence of a vision. So the more prepared the soul is, the nearer it is to that for which it is prepared. It is for the individual to make what preparation he pleases, but that will not assure him the bringing about of that for which he is prepared. Control of preparation is not control of the thing itself.

Again you will observe how modern Ibn Khaldūn's position is. It is so modern that I have hesitated as to using him as a representative of Islām and its attitudes. But exactly because he is so modern, his evidence is all the more overwhelming. In this case, for example, he has no shadow of doubt as to the reality of true dreams. His classification of dreams, in general, is that of the whole Muslim world. But he feels the necessity of rationalizing it for himself. There his psychology—a physiological psychology too—comes in. It is an innate quality of the soul which gives this power; a primary, unexplainable thing which must be taken for granted. Spells and exercises can only prepare the soul for the appearance of this power; they do not force the power out. Exactly so the hypnotic condition is induced, not caused, by mechanical means. One automatic writer, for example, begins invariably by writing the words, "Rome was not built in a day." But the sentence is never completed; the suggestion is enough. With another the first words written are, "Let me name your name," or part of that sentence. Ibn Khaldūn would recognize here at once the counterpart of his barbarous gibberish for use at bedtime. It goes to put the rational soul in the attitude which enables it to free itself from the trammels of the senses and to exercise its own power of apprehension.

This becomes still clearer in the special section[1] which he has devoted to the science, or rather art, of the interpretation of dreams. People have always dreamt dreams, he says, and there have always been interpreters of dreams. But the Muslim oneirocritic science and art are peculiar to Islām and are not derived from any preceding system. This opinion is probably due to Ibn Khaldūn's close joining of dreaming and prophecy; the interpretation of dreams must be semi-sacred and due entirely to Muslims. On general principles, however, we may be tolerably certain that their books are based on those of the Greek oneirocritic writers. And, as a matter of fact, we find in the *Fihrist*, a *catalogue raisonné* of Arabic literature of about 1000 A. D. in the section (p. 316) on the interpretation of dreams, mention of translations of the works of Artemidorus and Porphyry, the neo-Platonist.[2] The Prophet, he goes on, and his Companions all interpreted dreams. After morning prayer, for example, Muḥammad used to ask whether anyone had had a dream. Dreams, suitably interpreted, kept up the hearts of his followers. And the amount of interpretation necessary would vary with the character of the dream. The rational soul, by its nature, has an absolute power of perception in the spiritual world.

[1] Beyrout edition, p. 475; Būlāq, p. 396; de Slane's translation, Vol. III, p. 114.

[2] On Muslim dream-books see an article by N. Bland in the *Journal of the Royal Asiatic Society*, Vol. XVI, p. 153.

This it can exercise in the sleep of the body and its senses. But it is only ideas which it gets in that way. So it brings them back to the body with its apparatus of the internal senses. Then the imagination takes them and decks them out in such images from the stores of the memory as are suited to represent them. Thus in sensuous form they are brought to the "common-sense" of Aristotle and so perceived by the sleeper.

On the other hand, if the imagination brings images from the memory, uninformed with ideas from the rational soul, the sleeper sees dreams which have no meaning. Sometimes these are called Satanic dreams, as being stirred up by Satan with intention to mislead.

The problem, then, of the interpreter is to work back to the idea perceived by the rational soul in its own spiritual world, through the images in which the imagination has expressed it. This problem is sometimes very simple, as the idea may be clothed in forms so immediate to it that there can be no question of the meaning. Sometimes it is more difficult, when the clothing is in metaphors: a snake, for example, stands for enmity, or a sea for a sulṭān. The sensuous clothing will always be derived from the range of experience of the dreamer; he can never see a thing in his sleep that he has not seen awake, though new ideas may be conveyed to him under the old forms. So the interpretation will depend upon a knowledge of the range of experience of the dreamer; with different people the same thing may mean different ideas.

Further, true dreams have marks which attest their verity. One is that the sleeper at once awakes, hastening, as it were, under the shock, to re-enter the domain of sense. Another is that the impression of the true dream does not fade but imprints itself with all its details on the memory and cannot be forgotten. The reason is that true dreams are flashes of perception by the rational soul, are not imparted in time, have nothing to do with the operations of the brain, and, therefore, are not subject to the accidents of time or memory. In this, too, there is kinship between true dreams and prophecy.

But now, leaving Ibn Khaldūn for a time, I must, by an accumulation of examples, bring home to you how absolute is the Muslim trust in this minor form of revelation. It is a part of the paradox of Islām. Viewed in one way, Allāh is throned afar from his creation in unattainable glory, and between him and it there can be no contact save through miracle, and then only irrationally. But viewed in another way, Allāh and the spiritual world are very close to every human heart. There is no man but has enjoyed in his hours of sleep some measure of inspiration and some access to that world. In this way all men are prophets to some extent, and every man, unless by evil life he has given the devil power to deceive him by night as well as by day, can learn of God's truth. But the matter goes even farther. Dreams are on record, and the veracity of the narrators of them cannot be doubted, in which God himself was personally seen; the dream-books give sections to the interpretation of such appearances. This was too common to be an eccentricity; it was part of the normal possibility. Here is what al-Ghazzālī, to whom I have already referred, has to say on its manner and actuality.[1]

He who does not know the true nature of vision [or dreaming] does not know the true natures of the different kinds of vision, and he who does not know the true nature of the vision of Muḥammad and the other prophets, nay, even of the dead in general, does not know the vision of God in dream. So the ordinary man imagines that whoever sees Muḥammad in a dream has seen his actual person. But just as an idea which comes to the soul is rendered by the imagination with a word, so every impression made on the soul has a form assigned to it by the imagination. How, too, could there be a vision of the person of the Prophet in a dream, when that person has been committed to his grave at al-Madīna and has not left that to go to the place where the sleeper saw him. And even if we let that go, the Prophet is often seen by a thousand sleepers in one night in a thousand places and in different forms. And instinct supports reason in declaring that one person cannot be seen at one time in two places nor in two different forms. Whoever does not grasp that has contented himself, in the sphere of reason, with names and descriptions instead of realities and ideas. After that we need neither rebuke him nor speak to him.

[1] *Al-Maḍnūn*, p. 5, edition of Cairo, A. H. 1303.

But perhaps he will say that what he sees is the image (*mithāl*) of the Prophet, not his person (*shakhs*). Then it is either the image of his person or the image of his actual sanctified spirit which is apart from form or shape. If of his person, which is bones and flesh, what need have we of that person? His person, in itself, is an object of the imagination and the senses. Then, whoever saw it after death, apart from his spirit, would not see the Prophet but a body which used to move when the Prophet moved it. How then can he see the Prophet, when he sees the image of his person? The truth is that it is the image of the Prophet's sanctified spirit, the site of prophecy, which he sees; not his spirit or substance or person, but his image in actuality.

But it may be asked, "What then does his saying mean, 'He who has seen me in dream, has seen me; for the devil does not make himself like to me'?" It only means that what the dreamer sees is an image, acting as a link between the Prophet and himself, instructing him as to the truth. Just as the prophetic substance, that is the sanctified spirit which remains of the Prophet after death, is free from color and form and shape, and yet knowledge from it reaches his people by means of a truthful image, possessing color and form and shape, while the prophetic substance is free from that, so similarly, the essence of God is free from shape and form, but knowledge from Him reaches the creature by means of a sensuous image of light or some other beautiful form, fitted to be an image for the essential intellectual beauty which has neither form nor color. That image then is truthful and real and a link in passing on knowledge. So the sleeper says, "I saw God in dream," not meaning that he saw his essence, just as he says, "I saw the Prophet," not meaning that he saw his essence and his spirit, or the essence of his person, but that he saw his image.

But it may be said, "The Prophet has a like (*mithl*) but

God has no like." That ignores the distinction between the "like" and the "image." "Image" is not an expression for "like," for "like" is an expression for that which is equal in all its qualities, but "image" does not call for equality.[1] The reason is something to which there is nothing like, yet we can use the sun as an image [symbol] for it, because of their relationship in one point. Sensuous percepts are shown by the light of the sun, and intellectual percepts by reason. This measure of relationship suffices in an image. Nay, a sulṭān may be represented in sleep by the sun, and a wazīr by the moon. They are not equivalents in form or idea. Only a sulṭān bears universal rule and affects everything, and so far the sun is related to him. And just as a wazīr is an intermediary between the sulṭān and his people in conveying the effect of just decrees, so the moon is an intermediary between the sun and the earth in carrying the effect of light. But these are images and not equivalents.

Further, many dreams were presented to the Prophet in which milk and a cord, and the like, bore a part. He explained that milk meant Islām; as milk is the food of the external life, so Islām of the internal. And the cord was the *Qur'ān* by which we were drawn to safety. Similarly, God has no equivalent, but he has images resembling intellectual relationships to his qualities. Whenever we wish to teach an enquirer how God creates things and knows them and wills them, and how he speaks, and speech exists in its own person, we use man as an image for all that. And if man did not know the quality from himself, he would not understand the image in the case of God. An image is possible in God's case, and an equivalent is false; for an image explains but an equivalent resembles.

But it may be said, "What you have mentioned does not

[1] Al-Ghazzālī is evidently using this word *mithāl*, which I have rendered "image" in the sense of "symbol."

lead to the conclusion that God is seen, nay, to the conclusion that the Prophet even is not seen—for seeing a symbol is not seeing the thing itself—how, then, did he say, 'Whoever sees me in dream sees me'? This must be an illicit metaphor meaning 'as though he saw me.'" We reply that exactly the same thing is meant when anyone says that he saw God in dream. He does not mean that he saw him in his essence as he is. For it is generally admitted that the essence of God cannot be seen, but that an image which the sleeper believes to be the essence of God, or to be the essence of the Prophet can be seen. The existence of such dreams cannot be denied; even if one individual has not seen them unanimous tradition must compel him to believe in them. Only the image sometimes is truthful and sometimes is lying. When it is truthful, it means that God makes the vision a link between the seer and the Prophet to teach him something; it is within the power of God to create such a link between a creature and his attaining of the truth.

You will notice that al-Ghazzālī is essentially at one with Ibn Khaldūn, though he does not work out the psychology of the situation with such detail. What goes on in the brain of the dreamer is not his center of interest, rather the divine working behind the curtain. But that dreams consist of ideas conveyed to the sleeper and by him clothed in familiar forms and, so to speak, dramatized, in that he agrees with Ibn Khaldūn.

Here now are some stories of Muslim dreams. You will find them marvelously clear and coherent, more suggestive of Du Maurier's "dreaming true" than of our usual jumbles. But, just as with us, there are individuals who dream rarely but then with extraordinary clearness and connection, it may be that Orientals, simply from their belief in them, may attain frequently to that clarity. Further, I have been careful to pick, as my illustrations, cases which we have absolutely at first hand.

The following would be admitted even by the Society for Psychical Research. The dreamer himself, Ibn Khallikān, a theologian, a lawyer, a grammarian and a littérateur, who died in 1282 (A. D.) has told it in his *Biographical Dictionary*,[1] of which an autograph MS is preserved in the British Museum. He says:

> I once saw al-Mubarrad in dream and had a very strange affair with him; so I desire to tell it. I was in Alexandria in the year 636 [A. H.] and remained there for five months. I had there al-Mubarrad's book, the *Kāmil*, and the *ᶜIqd* of Ibn ᶜAbd Rabbihi, and used to read in them.

He then tells of a contradiction in the *ᶜIqd* of a statement of al-Mubarrad's in the *Rawḍa*, another of his books, which interested him, and goes on:

> A few nights after I had come upon this passage, I saw in dream as though I was in Aleppo in the college of the Qāḍī Bahā ad-Dīn, known as Ibn Shaddād, where I had been a student. And it was as though we had prayed the afternoon prayer in the place where the general custom was that prayer should take place. Then, when I had finished my prayer, I rose to go away; but I saw at the rear of the place a person

[1] Wüstenfeld's edition, No. 647; de Slane's translation, Vol. III, p. 33.

standing and praying. One of those present said to me, "That is al-Mubarrad." So I went to him and sat beside him, waiting until he finished. When he had finished, I saluted him and said, "I have just been reading your book, the *Kāmil.*" He said to me, "Have you seen my book, the *Rawḍa?*" I said, "No." I had not seen it before that time. Then he said, "Come and I will show it to you." So I went with him, and he went up with me to his house, and we went in, and I saw in it a great many books. He sat in front of them, searching for it, and I sat over against him. Then he took out a volume and handed it to me. I opened it and left it in my lap. Thereafter I said, "They have got hold of something against you here." "What have they got hold of?" he asked. I said, "You have accused Abū Nuwās of error in such and such a verse," and I quoted it to him. "Certainly," he said, "there is an error there." "No," I said, "he was right, and they say that you were wrong in blaming him." "How is that?" he said. So I told him what the author of the *ʿIqd* had said, and he bit the end of his fore-finger and kept staring at me absentmindedly as though confounded. Then I awoke from my dream while he was still in that state.

Al-Mubarrad, I may say, died in A. D., 898, almost 400 years before Ibn Khallikān.

Another dream, to which Ibn Khallikān alludes briefly,[1] was of a MS, a single gathering, containing traditions handed down orally, and traced back to a certain Surayj. In both cases he seems to have had no question that his dreams were veridical; that he had had a conversation with al-Mubarrad, and had seen and read an actual MS.

[1] Wüstenfeld's edition, No. 20; de Slane's translation, Vol. I p. 47.

Ibn Khallikān is a thoroughly representative Muslim figure. But if it should be thought that a theologian and lawyer might be touched with superstition, take the case of al-Bērūnī, who died in 1048 (A. D.), probably, almost certainly, the greatest scientist of his time. He was a man of a thoroughly critical, objective mind, an astronomer, a chronologist and a calm-headed student of custom and religion. Yet he had his dream, which he himself narrates.[1] It was in the last night of his sixty-first year, and he dreamed that he looked for the new moon in the quarter where it should appear. Then he heard a voice, "Leave the new moon alone; thou art its son, one hundred and ninety times." This he took to mean that he would live still one hundred and ninety lunar months. That his actual life fell short a month testifies, if anything, to the historicity of the story.

Frequently, to return to the religious world, a dream is given as a reason for going on a pilgrimage to Mecca, and even for giving one's self to the religious life. Even more than in Christendom, conversions in the theological sense have been worked among Muslims by dreams.

By such means, as he himself tells in his *Travel-Book*,[2] was Nāṣir ibn Khusraw turned from the

[1] *Chronologie orientalischer Völker*, p. xii.

[2] Schefer's edition, p. 3; cf. E. S. Browne, *Literary History of Persia*, Vol. II, p. 221.

world. He was a secretary in the service of the state at Merv, and devoted to wealth and the pleasures it brings. In October, 1045, (A. D.) he confesses that he took the opportunity of a favorable astrological situation to address to Allāh a special prayer for wealth. Under such circumstances, he believed it would be heard. Then he went to a neighboring town, and gave himself up for a month to wine. He was plainly in a completely unregenerate condition, and jumbled together religion, astrology, his worldly ambitions, and his pleasures. But one night he saw in dream a figure which addressed him thus: "How long wilt thou drink the wine that deprives man of reason? It were better that thou shouldst return to thyself." He answered, "The wise have found nothing better than wine to dissipate the cares of this world." "The loss of reason and of the possession of thyself," the figure replied, "do not give peace to the spirit. The wise cannot commend to any to give himself to be guided by madness; there is rather need to seek that which will increase wisdom and inheritance." "How," he replied, "can I get it for myself?" "He who seeks, finds," added the form, and indicated with a gesture the direction of Mecca.

This dream changed his life. However his own psychological condition may have been prepared, there was no question to his mind of the suddenness with which his conversion came. With the morning he determined to give up everything for which he had lived for forty years. His secretaryship he resigned; his wealth he abandoned except what was needed for the journey; and on March 6, 1046, he set out from Merv on pilgrimage to Mecca. Thereafter his life was that of a wandering religious, and he died as a hermit in the mountains of Badakhshān, in 1088. His is in many respects a perplexing personality, and legend has cast round him a nimbus of mingled miracle and heresy, but the great fact of this sudden conversion is firm.

Another sudden conversion by a similar means befell al-Ashʿarī, the founder of the Ashʿarite system of scholastic theology, now dominant for 800 years in the Muslim church. He had been brought up a Muʿtazilite, that is, in the heretical school which denied, on rationalistic principles, such doctrines of Islām as that the *Qurʾān* was the Eternal Word of God, that God would be seen by the believers in Paradise and that God created all the actions of his creatures. Generally, they applied argument to theology, and did not, like the orthodox Muslims, content themselves with statements of the faith of the fathers as derived from the *Qurʾān* and the personal words of Muḥammad.

As a Muʿtazilite, then, al-Ashʿari lived, taught, and fought for thirty or forty years. But he sprang of the blood of the desert, and with the Semitic consciousness for direct and mandatory faith he grew to be weary at heart of the dry logicalities of his fellows. Also the sequel makes it evident that he was coming to recognize—though the recognition was still below the surface of his consciousness—that a purely rationalistic theology is absurd, and that the mysteries of the universe cannot be expressed in terms of human thought. His soul was yearning within for a direct "Thus saith the Lord!"—a voice of authority and peace. He was on his way to a spiritual crisis, which came one Ramaḍān in his snatches of sleep, wearied with fasting and prayer. The story has reached us in several different forms; I give here the one[1] which seems to me to hang best together psychologically. It will be remembered that to him, as a Muᶜtazilite, dreams had little value. It is the more remarkable, then, to find his experience taking that form:

While I was sleeping on one of the first ten nights of the month of Ramaḍān, I saw the Prophet, and he said to me, "O ᶜAlī, help the tenets handed down from me, for they are true." Then when I awoke great distress fell upon me, and I ceased not to be full of thought and care on account of my dream and because of the position which I held that the proofs were clear which contradicted those tenets. At last, on one of the middle ten nights, I saw the Prophet in dream, and he said to me, "What hast thou done in the matter concerning which I commanded thee?" I said, "O Apostle, what can I do? I have extracted from the tenets handed

[1] Spitta, *Zur Geschichte Abuʾl-Hasan al-Ašᶜarī's*, p. 118; Arabic text emended.

down from thee certain positions which theological reasoning permits, and I have followed the sound proof which can be applied universally to the Creator." Then he said, "Help the tenets handed down from me; for they are true." I awoke heavy with grief and sorrow and determined to abandon theological reasoning; I gave myself also to the study of the traditions of the Prophet, and to reciting the *Qur'ān*.

Then, when the twenty-seventh night came, in which night it was our custom in al-Baṣra that the professional reciters of the *Qur'ān* and the people of science and excellence should gather and recite the whole of the *Qur'ān*, I was with them, according to that custom. But such a drowsiness seized me that I could not stand up. And when I reached my house I slept; and I was in great distress through sorrow, on account of the recitation that night which I had lost. Then I saw the Prophet, and he said to me, "What hast thou done in that which I commanded thee?" I said, "I have abandoned theological reasoning and applied myself to the Book of Allāh and to the record of thy sayings and doings." But he said to me, "Did I command thee to abandon theological reasoning? I commanded thee only to help the tenets handed down from me, for they are true." Then I said, "O Apostle of God, how can I leave the tenets whose elements I have clearly apprehended and whose proof I know this thirty years for a dream?" He said to me, "If I did not know that God will give thee a special aid from himself, I would not stand up from beside thee until I had expounded to thee those positions. And, since thou reckonest this my coming to thee a [mere] dream, was my seeing Gabriel a [mere] dream? Thou wilt not see me in this fashion hereafter; so apply thyself to these things, for God will give thee a special aid from himself." Then I awoke, and said, "After the truth there is naught but straying." And I began to defend the traditions dealing with dreaming and the intercession of the Prophet and the vision of God, etc. And there used to come to me something of which, by Allah, I had never heard a particle from my opponents, nor had I seen concerning it in any book. So I knew that it belonged to that aidance of God most High, concerning which the Apostle of God had given me good tidings.

That al-Ashᶜarī had some such dreams as these and with such consequences I make no doubt, although, unfortunately, the precise form is left uncertain to us. Out of doubt, too, is the momentous character of these dreams; they marked a turning-point in the religious history of Islām. This was what is called, "the return of al-Ashᶜarī" from the Muᶜtazilites to the orthodox, bringing back with him the weapons of scholastic disputation which had before been found among the Muᶜtazilites only. From his time on, the orthodox defended their faith with syllogisms as well as traditions; this fell in 300 of the Hijra, A. D. 913.

Let me leap now, suddenly, to quite modern times and to an experience of Burton's at Mecca. There he met a company of pilgrims which attracted his especial attention:

They were Panjabis, [he tells us[1]] and the bachelor's history was instructive. He was gaining an honest livelihood in his own country, when suddenly, one night, Hazrat Ali, dressed in green, and mounted upon his charger, Duldul—at least so said the narrator—appeared, crying in a terrible voice, "How long wilt thou toil for this world, and be idle

[1] *Pilgrimage*, Vol. II, p. 184, edition of London, 1898.

about the world to come?" From that moment, like an English murderer, he knew no peace; conscience and Hazrat Ali haunted him. Finding life unendurable at home, he sold everything; raised the sum of twenty pounds and started for the Holy Land. He reached Jeddah with a few rupees in his pocket; and came to Mecca, where, everything being exorbitantly dear and charity all but unknown, he might have starved, had he not been received by his old friend.

But the truth is that there is hardly a Muslim of eminence but stories are told of dreams seen by him or affecting him. Here are two about al-Ghazzālī. The first has much psychological truth, and is given thus in his own words:[1]

I used at first to deny the ecstatic states of the saints and the grades of advancement of the initiated, until I companied with my Shaykh Yūsuf an-Nassāj at Ṭūs, and he kept polishing at me, until I was graced with revelations, and I saw God in a dream and he said to me, "O Abū Ḥāmid!" I said, "Is Satan speaking to me?" He said, "Nay, but I am God that encompasseth all thy ways; *Am I not* [*thy Lord*]?"[2] Then he said, "O Abū Ḥāmid, abandon thy formal rules, and company with the people whom I have made the resting-place of my regard in my earth; they are they who have sold the Two Abodes for my love." Then I said, "By thy might, I adjure thee to give me again to taste good thought of them!" Then he said, "I do so; that which separated between thee and them was thy being occupied by the love of this world, so come out from it by free will before thou comest out from it abjectly [at death]. I pour forth upon thee lights from the

[1] "Life" in *Journal of the American Oriental Society*, Vol. XX, p. 89.

[2] *Qur*. vii, 171.

protection of my holiness, so seize them and apply thyself." Then I awoke in great joy and went to my Shaykh Yūsuf an-Nassāj and related to him the dream. And he smiled and said, "O Abū Ḥāmid, these changing states and grades we obliterate with our feet; yea, if thou companiest with me, the glance of thy insight will be anointed with the ointment of succor until thou seest the empyreal throne and those around it. Thou wilt not be satisfied with that until thou witnessest that to which glances cannot attain, and thou wilt be purified from the uncleanness of thy nature and ascend beyond the limits of thy reason and hear discourse from God most High, like Moses, Verily, I am God, the lord of the worlds."[1]

In this, without question, there is genuine autobiographical value. The following,[2] however, is only of value as showing us what passed current with the people; yet it is told by an Abū Bakr ash-Shāshī who died only two years after al-Ghazzālī himself:

In our time there was a man who disliked al-Ghazzālī and abused him and slandered him. And he saw the Prophet (God bless him and give him peace!) in a dream; Abū Bakr and ʿUmar (may God be well pleased with both of them!) were at his side, and al-Ghazzālī was sitting before him, saying, "O Apostle of God, this man speaks against me!" Thereupon the Prophet said, "Bring the whips!" So the man was beaten on account of al-Ghazzālī. Then the man arose from sleep, and the marks of the whips remained on his back; and he was wont to weep and tell the story.

It would be easy to go on almost interminably with such tales as these, but I imagine that my point is

[1] *Qur.* xxviii, 30.
[2] "Life," *loc. cit.*, p. 109.

now sufficiently made. The means of access to the unseen world open to all, the universal crack in the shell of which I spoke, is the faculty of dreaming. All members of the Muslim world, orthodox, heretical, unbelieving, theologians, philosophers, and the man in the street, believed and believe in dreams. There is a book, not nearly so well known as it should be and might be for its varied interest and its vivid picture of its author, his adventures and the world in which he lived. It is the account of his life and travels, dictated in 1355 (A. D.) at Fez by Ibn Baṭūṭa, after his return from twenty-eight years and more than 75,000 miles of wandering. He is a much more garrulous, free-spoken and wider traveled Marco Polo, and is almost as trustworthy an observer and describer. In certain ways he has marked kinship to Pepys. I shall have to use his book hereafter, but, in the meantime, you will find in its pages—there is a good edition of the Arabic text, with a fairly adequate French translation by Défrémery and Sanguinetti—numerous cases of dreams very much to our present point. For him, the crack in the shell was even wider than usual.

LECTURE IV

OTHER MEANS OF INTERCOURSE: WIZARDS, MAGIC, TALISMANS; UTILITARIANISM IN ISLĀM

We can now return to Ibn Khaldūn's philosophizings. In the following terms[1] he makes a fresh attempt to grapple with our connections with the Unseen.

We find among men certain individuals who give information about events before these take place, by a nature in them by which their kind is distinguished from other men. In that, they do not have recourse to an art; nor do they draw inferences from an influence exercised by the stars and the like; we simply find that they have channels of apprehension dealing therewith which are necessarily involved in the constitution with which they have been endowed. Such are wizards and gazers into transparent bodies, like mirrors and cups of water, and gazers on the hearts and livers and bones of animals, and those who augur by birds and wild beasts, or who cast pebbles and grains of wheat and date stones. All these exist in the world of man; denial of them is not possible for anyone. Similarly, the mad have cast upon their tongues words from the Unseen, and they tell them. Similarly, a sleeper, when he has just fallen asleep, and a dead man, when he has just died, speak concerning the Unseen. So, too, it is with ascetics, i. e., the Ṣūfīs. They have well-known channels of information as to the Unseen, by way of grace from God (*karāma*). We will now speak about all these

[1] Beyrout edition, p. 105; Būlāq, p. 89; de Slane's translation, Vol. I, p. 218.

modes of apprehension, beginning with soothsaying, and taking up the rest, one by one.

But first, an introduction on the way in which the human soul is equipped to apprehend the Unseen after all these fashions. The soul is the essence of a spirituality potentially existent and so distinguished from the other spiritualities as we have mentioned above; it passes into actuality only in the body and its states. That everyone perceives. And everything that is potential has a substance and a form. The form of the soul, by which its existence is complete, is apprehension itself and rational thought. It exists, in the first instance, in potentiality, equipped to apprehend and receive forms universal and particular. Then, its growth and existence become complete in actuality, through being joined with the body and through the arrival of its sensuously perceived apprehensions to which the body accustoms it, and through the universal ideas which are drawn from these apprehensions. So it rationally considers the forms, again and again, until it acquires in actuality a form consisting of apprehension and rational thought, and so its essence is completed. The soul, then, is like matter, and forms alternate upon it, through apprehension, one after the other.

On that account, we find that a child, in the beginning of its growth, is not able to apprehend that which belongs to the soul essentially, neither in sleep, nor by revelation, nor otherwise. That is because its form, which is its very essence, namely apprehension and rational thought, is not complete; nay, not even the extraction of universals can be completely carried out.

Then, whenever its essence is actually complete, it comes to have, so long as it is together with the body, two kinds of apprehension. One kind, through the instruments of the body, which the bodily channels of apprehension bring to it, and one kind through its essence, without any intermediary.

It is screened off from the second kind by being immersed in the body and in the senses, and by their preoccupations. The senses are always drawing it to that which is without through the physical apprehension which is their primary nature. But often it plunges from the external into the internal; and the veil of the body is raised for a moment, either through a property which belongs to man in general, like sleep, or through a property which exists in some men, like soothsaying and divining with pebbles, or through a discipline, as that which gives Ṣūfīs their revelations. So the soul turns, then, to the essences which are above it, of the heavenly host, on account of the connection which exists between its region and their region, as we have shown above. These essences are spiritual, and are absolute apprehension and actual intelligence; in them are the forms and essentials of existence, as has preceded. Then, something of these forms shines out in them, and the soul acquires knowledge from them. Often, those apprehended forms are carried back to the imagination, which casts them in accustomed molds. Then, these apprehensions are brought to the senses, either simple or in the molds of the imagination, and so are reported. This is an explanation of the equipment of the soul for the apprehension of the Unseen.

Let us return to the exposition which we promised of the kinds of this apprehension. The gazers in transparent bodies,[1] such as mirrors and cups of water and hearts and livers and bones of animals, and those who divine with pebbles and grains, all are of the kind of the *kāhins*. Only, they are weaker as to their fundamental nature, because the *kāhin*, for the lifting of the veil of sense, does not need much assistance, but these seek assistance by limiting all the channels of sense-apprehension down to one only. The noblest

[1] *Scryers* in English; cf. N. W. Thomas, *Crystal-gazing;* also Andrew Lang, *Making of Religion.*

of these channels is vision, so vision is concentrated upon an object with a uniform surface (*marʾī basīṭ*), until it gains an apprehension, by vision, of that of which it must give information. And often it is thought that those who observe see what they see in the surface of the mirror, but that is not so. They simply continue gazing at the surface of the mirror until it vanishes from their sight, and then there appears, between them and the surface of the mirror, a curtain, as though it were a cloud, on which forms show themselves. These are the things which they apprehend, and thus they can indicate what is desired to be known, either negatively or affirmatively. So they report about it, just as they have apprehended it; but as for the mirror and the forms which were (supposedly) apprehended in it, they did not really apprehend these in that way. There only grew for them, through it, this other kind of apprehension, which belongs to the soul and is not really apprehension by vision. The spiritual apprehender forms his apprehension only as though it were according to sense.

The case is the same with gazers on the hearts and livers of animals and water in cups and so on. Some of these, we have observed, distract the senses by means of vapors only, or by spells by way of preparation. Then they tell what they have apprehended. They maintain that they see forms shaped in the air, telling them by symbols and indications the things a knowledge of which is desired. The absence of these last from the influence of sense is less than in the case of the first. The world is full of marvels!

There follows a section on those who draw omens from the flight of birds, etc.; and then another, of more interest, on divination through the insane:

The logical souls of these have a weak connection with the body, because their constitution is, for the most part, disordered, and the animal spirit is weaker in them. So the soul of one of these, on account of the pain of what is lacking in him and of his disease which distracts his senses, is not plunged and submerged in the senses. And often another satanic spirituality importunes the soul to join him, clinging to it; and that soul is too weak to drive it off, so it is convulsed thereby. Then, when this convulsion has taken place, either through an essential disorder in the constitution, or by importunity from satanic spirits which join it, the madman loses contact with his senses completely, and apprehends a flash of the world of his soul; and sense forms are impressed upon it. The imagination then transforms these; and often he speaks from his tongue only, in that state, without willing to speak.[1] Apprehension, on the part of all these, has mixed in it truth and falsehood, because their contact with the spiritual world comes to them, even although they have lost contact with their senses, only after aid has been sought in externalities, as we have explained. Thence comes the false element in these appearances.

There follows his opinion of those whom he calls wizards (*ᶜarrāf*). These profess to have connection with the Unseen, but are really guided by their intelligence and by free conjecture. They use, as a basis, the opinion which they have gained from the first stages of this connection with the spiritual world and their apprehension thereof, and claim by that a knowledge of the Unseen. He further refers by name to some of the most celebrated *kāhins* of the heathen Arabs and to their wizards; then he goes on to speak of the approach to the Unseen at the beginning of sleep, and at the first moments of death;

[1] These phenomena would now be called technically "possession" and "automatic speech."

how the tongue then speaks without intention—again automatic speech—when the veil of sense has been raised. So, some tyrannous rulers used to take men and kill them, that they might know from their speech, at the point of death, what the future would bring. He gives, further, a gruesome receipt how to dissolve away a living man in a barrel of oil, until nothing was left of him but the veins and sutures of his head. The head would then answer questions about the future. This he blames as belonging to the actions of the magicians, but accepts it as proving the wonders of the human structure. This story of the head that answers questions, I may say, is very widely spread in Islām, but mostly as a tale of ancient magic. It was localized, apparently, among the heathen of Ḥarrān in North Syria, and connected with their star worship. In Islām itself it was probably never practiced.

Others sought to attain the same results by bringing about an artificial death—the phrase is Ibn Khaldūn's. By ascetic exercises and discipline, they sought to destroy all the physical powers; then to obliterate their effects upon the soul; then to foster the soul by religious exercises and increase its power in itself. When this death descended upon the body, then sense and its veil were removed, and the soul could attain to the Unseen. Others strove to attain the same end by magical disciplines; these were especially in the remoter regions of the earth and in India. Ibn Khaldūn had heard of the yogis and of the elaborate Indian literature on this subject. Ibn ᶜArabī, a great mystical writer who died in 1240, revised with the help of a yogi a translation of one of these Indian texts.[1]

The traveler, Ibn Baṭūṭa, of whom I have already spoken, also had strange experiences in India and China with yogis. He observed them closely, and seems to have had no doubt as to the reality of their feats, but he shows a disposition to regard them as secret Muslims. Only a Muslim saint could work such wonders. Some of their miracles affected him with a palpitation of the heart, so that he fainted; but the performance was suspended until he recovered and could see it through. He names them as yogis (*jūkīya*) and is evidently a trustworthy witness.

Ibn Khaldūn comes next to the Ṣūfīs or Muslim mystics. He treats them twice in his book. Once here, when he considers especially their intercourse with the Unseen, and later, in a longer and more general article on their origin, history and tenets. In this place, he begins by saying, that their system of discipline is religious and free from the blameworthy ends mentioned above. Their sole object is to approach closely to God, so that they may attain those pleasures which belong to the people who truly know God and enter into union with him.

[1] Brockelmann, *Arabische Litteratur*, Vol. I, p. 446.

The essence of their discipline is starving the body and feeding the soul with meditation upon God; for when the soul grows up thus, it grows ever nearer to the knowledge of God; and when it is deprived of this meditation, it becomes satanic. Whatever comes to the Ṣūfīs by way of knowledge and of control of the Unseen, is only accidental; it is not an object in the first instance. If it were an object, then their aim would be something besides God, and that would be equivalent to polytheism. One of them has said, "He who prefers (mystical) knowledge for the sake of (mystical) knowledge professes the second:" i. e., mystical knowledge and not God himself.

Their aim, then, is God and nothing else; when anything else comes in, it is by accident only; and many of them avoid that when it presents itself and do not heed it. Still, that such things come to them is well known and is disapproved by a few theologians only, lest the miracles of the saints might be confused with the evidentiary miracles of the prophets.

The fact, however, that the saints have such miracles Ibn Khaldūn proves by narratives from the Companions of the Prophet. Thus the story runs, that ʿUmar, the second Khalīfa, was preaching one day, at al-Madīna, when he suddenly stopped in his sermon, and cried out, "O Sāriya, the hill! the hill!" Sāriya was a Muslim general, at that time, in al-ᶜIrāq. He was hard pressed in battle at that moment by unbelievers, but the voice of ᶜUmar came to him from al-Madīna and warned him of the hill that he must seize. "Many other such things happened," says Ibn Khaldūn, "in the time of the Companions, and, after them, among the pious. In the lifetime and especially in the presence of the Prophet, such things were few, and even now, when the student of Ṣūfīsm comes to al-Madīna, his ecstatic states cease, so long as he remains there." Apparently, saints are a substitute for a prophet, and therefore in the lifetime and environment of a prophet, the specific character of sainthood is not exhibited. Further, according to many theologians, Muḥammad is not absolutely dead, but lives, in a sense, in his tomb at al-Madīna. Immediately around it, therefore, the miracles and ecstatic states of saints do not appear.

What Ibn Khaldūn has to say in general upon the Ṣūfīs we may leave until later; only one class of them calls for notice now. These are idiots, who are mentally deranged like the insane, but who show along with that clear proofs of sainthood. Ibn Khaldūn opines that whoever with sound understanding knows their manner of life will recognize this, although they do not fulfil the external duties of the law. There occur in them wonderful things by way of stories of the Unseen, for they are not limited by anything, and they give their speech full course therein. The canon lawyers sometimes deny that they are saints at all on account of that dropping of the external ritual of the law which is seen in them, and because it is held that sainthood comes only through devotional exercises. But that is an error, for the grace of God comes to whomsoever God wills, and the attainment of sainthood does not stand in devotional exercises only. Since the human soul is imperishable, God endows it with what of his gifts he wills. In idiots the logical soul is not lacking; nor is it corrupt as in the case of the insane. It is only their reason which fails; and it is to it that is attached the duty of the external observance of the law. Ibn Khaldūn adds some scholastic reasoning upon this point which we need not notice; his meaning is sufficiently clear. He warns, however, that these idiot-saints are to be carefully distinguished from the insane, whose logical souls have become corrupt, and who are, therefore, like the lower animals.

To distinguish them, however, there are certain signs. First, that you will find in these idiots a distinct turn for religious meditation and devotion, although not according to legal conditions, because they are not under the law; the case is different with the insane. Secondly, that they were created in idiocy, while insanity befalls the insane after a portion of their life, on account of bodily, physical accidents. When this has befallen them, their logical soul is corrupted, and they act without reason or sequence. And, thirdly, their much busying themselves with men, for good and for evil; for they do not wait for permission, there being no obligation to the law in their case; but the insane have no such concern regarding others.

Ibn Khaldūn, then, takes up some means of reaching the Unseen, without this throwing off of the veil of the senses. The claim of astrologers he shortly rejects, with a reference to his more elaborate examination elsewhere. The art of geomancy, that is, divining the future by arrangements of dots in sand or on paper, he describes more fully. It claimed, like all the arts, prophetic origin, and in proof of its lawfulness a tradition from Muḥammad was alleged which seems to be a far-away echo of the pericope of the adulteress in John's Gospel. We need not take it up here, and I will only refer you to a note in Mr. John Payne's translation of *Alaeddin* (pp. 199 ff.), where is the only description of this art which I know in English.[1] After it all, Ibn Khaldūn concludes shortly that such arts cannot possibly reach the Unseen, and that these dots, for example, can only assist toward it when they blur the sense perception of the worker of them. The only basis for reaching the Unseen lies in the nature of the human soul itself. And here he adds a remark which shows that many claimed falsely to possess

[1] See, too, de Slane's translation, Vol. I, pp. 232 ff.

this power, and that he himself had a keen feeling of the need of some rational criterion:

> The sign [he says] of the constitution, which those have who can apprehend the Unseen, is that there comes upon them, when they turn to those things, a passing out from their natural state, such as yawning and stretching, and the beginnings of a lack of sense-perception. This differs in strength and weakness, as this constitution differs in them. Any one however, in whom this sign is not found, has no perception of the Unseen, and is only trying to make money out of lies.

Finally, Ibn Khaldūn mentions a class of efforts to reach the Unseen, based, neither on the, for him undoubted, properties in the spiritual soul, nor on the hypothesis of the influence of the stars, nor on the conjectures and fancies of wizards, but on supposed powers residing in combinations of numbers and letters. These Ibn Khaldūn rejects absolutely, but he has found it necessary to state and expose them at considerable length. I need not follow him here. In part, they exhibit the curious lack of simple arithmetical power in the Muslim peoples, which has made them fall back on Copts and Armenians as calculating machines. An arithmetical problem which involves nothing more than a simple proportion, or, at the most, requires for its statement a simple equation, appears to suggest to them the mysteries of the universe. This undoubtedly arises, apart from their lack of arithmetical ability, from their feeling, which I have already mentioned, that a very thin shell divides them from the Unseen. Proportions of numbers lead them almost immediately to suppose proportions existing mysteriously in the very nature of things. On another side this affected our own Middle Ages as the doctrine of signatures.

It was undoubtedly fostered, further, by the fact that the letters of the Arabic alphabet had numerical values, and that those values did not fit, in any way, the order of the letters in that alphabet. The values were derived from the quite different order of the Hebrew alphabet; but comparatively few Muslims knew that, and in consequence there is the feeling that the number inheres, in some mysterious way, in the personality of the letter. It is as though we should always think of the number ten when we saw the letter *x*, and also have a vague feeling that whenever *x* occurred in a word, there must, in the scheme of things, be some working of the value ten.

Somewhat similar things are used in games and guesses by us. To a Muslim, that game, for example, of telling a person to take a number and perform on it divers operations and from the result of them telling him his age, would seem to involve direct contact with the spiritual world. Ibn Khaldūn, naturally, has no patience with all this. He had Berber blood in him and could count and reckon; but the detail which he feels compelled to give to it and the elaborate simplicity of his explanation and example of proportion in arithmetic show how absolutely unarithmetical were the minds for which he was writing.

It might now be in place to take up his doctrine of the saints and their miracles. But as has been suggested already, it seems better to leave his fuller discussion of that subject until we come to deal with the actual path and experience of the religious soul on its way to God.

I take up next, therefore, his doctrine of magic and talismans:[1]

The sciences of magic and of talismans concern the nature of the equipments by which human souls are able to produce effects in the world of the elements, either with or without a helper of the heavenly things. If without a helper, it is magic; if with a helper, it is the science of talismans. Since these sciences are forbidden in different law-codes, both on account of their hurtfulness, and because there is involved in them a looking towards someone else than God, whether a star or not, books concerning them are almost entirely lacking, except as to what is found in the books of the ancient peoples before the time of Moses, such as the Nabataeans and the Chaldeans.

None of the prophets who preceded Moses laid down laws or brought commands. Their books contained only exhortations, the doctrine of the unity of God and admonitions as to heaven and hell. So these sciences existed among the people of Babel, Syrians and Chaldeans, and among the people of Egypt, the Copts and others. These peoples had on them writings and traditions; but only a little has been translated for us from their books on this subject, like the *Nabataean Agriculture*, one of the books of the people of Babel.

[1] Beyrout edition, p. 496; Būlāq, p. 414; de Slane's translation, Vol. III, p. 171.

Then men took this science over from them, and became well versed in it; and, thereafter, books were composed like the *Scrolls of the Seven Stars*, and the *Book of Ṭimṭim, the Indian*, on the forms [or figures] of the Scale and the Stars, etc. Then Geber appeared in the East, the greatest of the magicians in this community, and examined the books of the experts and extracted the art, testing thoroughly and extracting its cream. He composed, also, other works, and wrote much upon this art and on the art of natural magic, because that art is one of the branches of magic. For the changing of specific bodies from one form to another can take place only by a force of the soul, not by mechanical art, and that is part of the nature of magic, as we shall mention in its place. Then came Maslama ibn Aḥmad of Madrid, the leader of the Spanish people in mathematics and magical things. He expounded all these books and corrected them, and gathered their divergent views in his own book. No one has written on this science since him.

I have translated this passage at length, because of its historical suggestiveness. It was the fate of the whole science of history among Muslims, and Ibn Khaldūn himself does not rise above it, to seek to know too much; to abhor all vacuum, and not to be too critical toward books which professed, on very slender evidence, to be authorities on the remotest times. All divisions of Muslim literature have suffered from the pseudograph; and here Ibn Khaldūn makes mention of one of the most celebrated and fatal of these books, which, after misleading all Muslim writers, misled even a European scholar in the nineteenth century. The *Nabataean Agriculture* was written at the beginning of the tenth century by a certain Ibn al-Waḥshīya, a scion of an Aramaic family. His book is no translation, but a frank forgery, in which he invents a complete ancient literature and exalts the old Babylonians over the conquering Arabs. It is upon his book and upon their own conception of the history of revelation through a series of prophets, that Muslims base their ideas of the ancient civilizations.

With Geber we touch honester and more solid ground. He seems to have lived in the latter part of the eighth century, and to have written much upon chemistry. He is the greatest name, of course, in the history of alchemy, but whether all the books ascribed to him, and, if so, which, are really his, we are absolutely in the dark. The difficulty is that they, in their European translations at least, show a scientific knowledge, which chemists find almost unbelievable of his time. Maslama of Madrid, on the other hand, is a perfectly historical character, who died 1007 A. D. Ibn Khaldūn often refers to him.[1]

But though Ibn Khaldūn's ancient history was led astray by these forgeries, and his criticism vitiated by these assumptions, yet, when he comes to philosophize the whole question, he shows the same grasp of the possibilities of the mind. We must

[1] See, on him, de Slane's long note, Vol. III, p. 172, and on the whole subject the article on Muḥammadan alchemy in Hastings' *Encyclopaedia of Religions and Ethics*, Vol. I, pp. 289 ff.

remember here, as everywhere, that he takes a great deal for granted which, not many years ago, we would have declined to think about at all, and only within the last few years have accepted as worthy of any consideration. The limits of what science is willing to discuss, which are so apt to hamper us, did not exist for him. The occult phenomena, to which we are now turning again, because they have simply been forced upon our notice, had met him in still richer abundance. Only he felt no need of turning away from them. He accepted them and set to work to rationalize them.

This is how he did it:

Although human souls are one as a species, yet they divide up into a great many kinds, each with different properties. These properties are inborn constitutions; so, the souls of the prophets have a property which prepares them for the divine and for intercourse with angels, and for the influence on the things of this world which necessarily follows. In magicians, on the other hand, there is a peculiar psychic power by which they influence these things and draw down and apply the spiritual force of the stars, and thus exercise an influence which is either psychic or satanic. The influence, then, of the prophets is by the help of God and by a divine peculiarity, while the souls of the diviners have a peculiar ability to learn about hidden things through satanic forces. Similarly, each kind of human beings is distinguished by a peculiarity which is not found in any other.

The souls of magicians, further, are of three kinds. The first of these exerts its influence through an effort of the will only, without using an instrument or a helper. This is what the philosophers call magic. The second uses as a helper the intervention of the spheres, or of the elements, or of the peculiarities of numbers. This they call talismanic art, and this kind is weaker than the first. The third kind has an influence on the imaginative powers. The user of this influence can control the imagination to a certain extent, and impress upon it different kinds of appearances and resemblances and forms, according to his purpose; he affects the senses of those who see those things by the force of his soul influencing them. Then it is to him who sees as though he saw those things externally; and yet there is nothing of the kind there. So it is related that some have been caused to see gardens and rivers and castles that had no external reality. This the philosophers call conjuring. Those, then, are the three divisions.

Ibn Khaldūn then goes on to discuss the theological and ethical implications in this. He points out that this peculiar power exists in the magician potentially, just as do all human powers. It can be brought to actuality only by practice. Practice, in the case of magic, consists in turning the attention toward the celestial spheres and the stars and the upper worlds and the evil spirits, and magnifying, worshiping and submitting one's self to them. But this is turning toward other than God, which is unbelief. Magic, then, must be largely reckoned as a form of unbelief. On the ethical side, there can be no question of its corrupting influence.

Again, it is necessary to distinguish between these three kinds of magic, when we consider whether there is in magic any external reality. In the third kind, it is plain that there is none. But as to the first two kinds, their reality is certain. On that point, Ibn Khaldūn has no doubt; all reasonable men admit it, and the *Qur'ān* speaks of it with perfect clearness. There we have the case of the two angels at Babel, Hārūt and Mārūt, who taught mankind magic. The Prophet, too, had spells cast upon him. A chapter of the *Qur'ān* speaks of "the evil of those who blow upon knots," and ʿĀʾisha tells how those magic knots unloosed themselves, when this chapter was recited over them. The people of Babel, Chaldeans, Nabataeans, Syrians—this is Ibn Khaldūn's ethnography—stood in repute as magicians, and the *Qur'ān* tells us how the magicians of Egypt competed with Moses. In the temples of upper Egypt traces are still left of them. This reference by Ibn Khaldūn is rather obscurely expressed, but it seems to point to the paintings and sculptures in Egyptian tombs, and to the mummies and figures found there.

Egypt, for all Muslims, has been a land of mystery, of ancient stories, hidden treasure, and enchanters. The Egyptians themselves, of Ibn Khaldūn's own day, were believed to be peculiarly expert magicians. He gives a very obscure account of one whom he had seen at work. I must admit that I cannot translate this passage with any certainty, and de Slane, in his French rendering,[1] makes the same confession. But the general drift seems to be as follows: The

[1] Vol. III, p. 177.

magician built up out of different materials suited to his purpose, a figure of the individual whom he wished to enchant; these bore an actual relationship, either real or symbolic, to the person and character of his victim. Then he uttered sounds over that figure, and after gathering some saliva in his mouth, blew it repeatedly at the figure, apparently mixing in with this, at the same time, words of enchantment. He held over the figure, too, a cord which he had prepared and made a knot upon it by way of drawing to his assistance one of the Jinn and strengthening the spell. The idea was that an evil spirit went out from him when he blew, attached to his saliva, and fell upon his victim.

This is not very lucid, I confess, yet one can easily recognize in it a number of the permanent elements in magical operations such as appear in all countries and times.

But Ibn Khaldūn had other experiences which are more intelligible. He had met professors of magic who could point to a garment or to a skin, pronounce words secretly at it, and it was cut or torn. They could point, also, with a slicing gesture at sheep pasturing, and their entrails would fall out of them to the ground. He had heard, too, that in India there were some who would point at a man, and he would fall dead. It would then be found that his heart had vanished. They would point, too, at pomegranites, and all the seeds would be found to have vanished. Ibn Khaldūn does not tell us here what Ibn Baṭūṭa of his own personal knowledge does, that the Indian magician was supposed to have devoured what was thus spirited away.

To pass to talismans, Ibn Khaldūn had observed wonders worked by the use of what we call "amicable numbers." For example, if you take the numbers, 284 and 220, each of them is equal to the sum of the aliquot parts of the other. This peculiarity seems to have struck the oriental imagination, and given rise to a belief that this relationship could be used to promote love and friendship. Upon two symbolic images, constructed according to astrological rules, these numbers were placed, one on the one and the other on the other. Their possessors, then, would become friends. Ibn Khaldūn seems actually to say that experience had borne this out. He tells of other kinds of talismans, consisting partly of figures, as of a lion or a snake or a scorpion imprinted under certain conditions upon certain kinds of steel, partly of what we call "magic squares."

He then comes back to the very remarkable "slitting" magic, which is of the greater interest to us that he had had personal experience of it. It flourished peculiarly in western North Africa; and the people who professed it terrorized their neighbors by the threat of using it against their cattle and sheep. Naturally, both parties concealed the matter out of fear of the authorities, but Ibn Khaldūn had met a company of these "slitters," had witnessed their operations, and they had told him that they had a peculiar art and practice, through heathen prayers and by drawing in the assistance of the Jinn and the stars. This was laid down for them in a book which they had and which they studied. They could exercise this art upon anything except a free man, that is upon goods and cattle and slaves. As they put it, "We can only work upon that in which money walks."

This, [says Ibn Khaldūn] is what they assert: I asked one of them and he told me about it. As for what they do, that is plain and evident. I have been present at much of it, and have seen it without any doubt.

The philosophers distinguished between magic and talismans, but they lay it down that both together are due to an influence belonging to the human soul. They give as a proof of this influence how the soul affects the body apart from the ordinary operations of nature or physical causes. Nay, there are effects which arise from spiritual conditions, such as heat caused by joy, or from ideas, such as those which result from fear. One who is walking upon the edge of a wall, or upon a tight-rope, when fear of falling comes strongly upon him, will most certainly fall. Only by long practice can the fear of falling be removed, and then such walk safely. If, then, the soul has this influence upon its own body, without physical natural causes, it is possible that it can have a similar influence upon another body, since its relationship to bodies in this kind of influence is one; for it is not enfolded in the body or shut up in it. So it follows that it can exert an influence upon all material objects.

This, you will notice, is precisely the theory which

lies behind the "mental science" and "Christian science" of our own day. It is also practically involved in the infinitely more scientific "meta-psychical," to use Dr. Maxwell's word, investigations which are now going on. There lies in it an indubitable element of truth. But the philosophers further distinguish between magic and talismans:

> In magic the magician has no need of a helper, but the user of a talisman seeks help from the spiritualities of the stars, and the secrets of numbers, and the peculiarities of things, and the situations of the spheres, these working upon the world of the elements, as astrologers say. Magic, they say, is the union of a spirit with a spirit. But in the use of a talisman there is the union of a spirit with a material object; in idea, a joining of the upper, heavenly natures with the lower natures. The upper natures are the spiritualities of the stars, and on that account the holder of a talisman mostly seeks aid in astrology. The magician, again, according to the philosophers, cannot acquire the art of magic, but must have it constitutionally. He has the peculiar ability to exercise this kind of influence.
>
> Their distinction between magic and miracle, then, is that miracle is a divine ability, giving the soul this power of influence; the prophet is aided by the Spirit of God. But the magician does it of himself, by his own psychical power, or by satanic aid, under some conditions.

The distinction of the philosophers, then, went down to the very nature of the thing. But Ibn Khaldūn himself is inclined to follow the external signs of the difference:

> A miracle is what is worked by a good man, for good

objects and for purified souls, and by way of proof of the prophetic office. Magic is worked only by an evil man, for evil purposes and with evil results. This, according to philosophical theologians, is the distinction between the two.

I do not understand that Ibn Khaldūn would entirely reject the view of the philosophers, as given above, but only that he regards his own distinction —he here evidently reckons himself with the philosophical theologians—as more simple, and as giving also the essentials in the case. That a distinction between miracles and magic was felt to be necessary will explain why I give so much time to magic now. Just as in the case of an Oriental, it is impossible to separate between his philosophy and his theology, so it is impossible to separate between his religion and what we have, in a somewhat narrow spirit, got into the habit of calling "superstition," or, more liberally, "folk-lore."

But not prophets only and magicians can thus bend the order of the world. The Ṣūfīs, too, or saints, have their miracles, and exercise a similar influence. This is really a far more important distinction. Muḥammad was the last prophet, and a consideration of the nature of the prophetic miracles is thus largely a subject for the schools. But the miracles of the saints are happening every day, as we shall see, and a knowledge of them is a most practical matter. They take place only by the power of God and in proportion to the faith of the saint and the closeness of his intercourse with God. Thus, by the very nature of the case, it is impossible that he can give himself to evil, but is held closely by the command and the permission of God. Him, too, magic cannot oppose; it collapses and vanishes at his touch. So the enchanted flag of Persia, signed with magic numbers in planetary hour, ensuring victory, fell before the Companions of the Prophet at al-Qādisīya, where the empire of the Chosroes went down for ever.

Last among the influences exerted by the soul, Ibn Khaldūn mentions the evil eye, the Eye as it is called simply in the East. He who has it, sees a thing, admires it, envies the owner, and smites him with his eye. There is no doubt of this; but it differs from all other magic, in that it needs not the will of him who has it. It works automatically and he cannot control it. So, if anyone kills by magic or talisman, he is to be put to death; but not if he kills with the Eye.

Finally, as to all this, Ibn Khaldūn makes a very curious and illuminating statement. It is perfectly evident throughout his book that he is discussing these matters in a spirit of the keenest intellectual curiosity and interest. Such subjects interested him, as they are interesting so many of us now. But that is the paradox of which he seems himself to have been unconscious. According to Muslim law, he says, actions are allowable if they are important for us (*a*) religiously, that is for our final salvation, or (*b*) temporally, for our living in this world. If a thing does not concern us from either of these points of view, and if there is in it any hurtfulness, either actual as in the case of magic, or imagined as in the case of astrology, it is legally forbidden. But, further, if it is not of importance to us, nor is hurtful, it is still to be avoided; letting such things alone is a drawing near to God, for part of the beauty of a man's *islām*, resignation to God, is leaving alone what does not concern him.

This, you will see, throws an astonishing flood of light upon Muslim ideals. Contrary to his own plain, but evidently unconscious practice, Ibn Khaldūn teaches that the true Muslim must give up and avoid anything that is not directly of moment for his life in this world or the next. All that we would reckon as the "interesting" is swept away; the useful alone is in point. And this is not Ibn Khaldūn's view only. With him the theologians of Islām agree. If they have a section on the excellence of science (*fī faḍli-l-ʿilm*) there is certain to follow it another on the praiseworthy and the blameworthy sciences (*al-ʿulūm al-maḥmūda wal-madhmūma*). Knowledge for its own sake has no place; it must be of use for this world or the next. And this is not simply theological; it is in the very texture of the Muslim mind. We can say, "This is an interesting book;" in Arabic you cannot express that idea. I turn to Badger's *English-Arabic Lexicon* and find a large quarto page on "Interest" and its derivations. But it only helps you to say that the book gives pleasure or amuses or is desirable or useful or touching or surprising or important or sways you or captivates you, never that it arouses that disinterested intellectual curiosity which we so strangely call "interest." Even curiosity, in the highest and finest sense, we cannot render. It is either deep, devoted study and research, or intrusive spying.

Here, beyond question, we have one of the keys to the fatal defect in the Muslim mind. Exceptions, of course, there have been, conscious and unconscious, but the whole trend of usage and weight of influence have gone to limit and destroy free intellectual workings; the object must be plain from the first, and be one of certain classified kinds. Investigation which does not know where it is going to come out, and what it may produce, and does not care, is under the Muslim ban. Amusement, even, must justify its existence by its usefulness; recreation must seek protection behind wise saws about making Jack a dull boy and tales about the surprising humors and unbendings of saints. The free, self-determining, self-developing soul may not walk its own path, however innocently, but must fit itself to the scheme and pattern of schools.

And this does not hold of the Arabic world only.

Here is what one of the keenest observers of Islām in recent years has to say on the matter:

Few things throw a more instructive light on the character of a nation than an examination of the ideas which cannot be expressed in their language. Now the Turkish language, copious as it is, contains no equivalent for "interesting." You can say, this is a useful book, or a funny book, or a learned book, or a book which attracts attention, but you cannot precisely translate our expression, "This is an interesting book." Similarly you cannot render in Turkish the precise shade of meaning conveyed by the phrase, "I take an interest in the Eastern question, or the Mohammedan religion." The various approximate equivalents imply either a more active and less intellectual participation than that denoted by interest, or else suggest that these serious subjects are something queer and funny which it is amusing to hear about. This lacuna in the language has its counterpart in the brain. The ordinary Turk does not take an interest in anything, and his intelligence seems incapable of grappling with any problem more complex than his immediate daily needs. A natural want of curiosity, and a conviction that their own religion contains all that man knows or needs to know, keep the provincial population in a state of ignorance which seems incredible and fantastic.[1]

This certainly is too strongly expressed to apply to the much keener-witted Syrian, Arabian, or Egyptian. But the lack of the idea of free, untrammeled interest, and the rejection of everything that may in some remote development loosen the sense of dependence on God characterize all; which, to come round to our starting-point, makes only more sur-

[1] *Turkey in Europe*, by "Odysseus," p. 98.

prising Ibn Khaldūn's fresh, open-eyed attention to the phenomena of life.

I have spent so much time on this because it is not alien, nay, is very pertinent to our present subject. One of the most astonishing things in Muslim religious feeling is that even its mystical attitudes are utilitarian. Normally, among all peoples, the mystic is so plunged in the experiences of the moment that the future fades out of reality. When he is struggling to find peace he is not concerned with his salvation from hell-fire, but only that the choking burden of the present may be lifted from him. When he has reached peace, the vision and the light of God are on his daily path, and in them he walks. God is in the world and he is with God. I should be loth to say that this mystical disinterestedness is not also found in Islām, but far more frequent and always possible is the coarser, harder fear of the Fire; the sense of God as the relentless Watcher in whose presence no soul can stand.

We have seen already, how the conversion even of such a saint as al-Ghazzālī was such simple fear; fear as of an earthly sovereign who might doom to death if unrecognized; such fear as our revivals too often have known. Certainly there mingled in it the baffled struggles of his intellect, snared in the net of this most unintelligible world, overborne by the burden of its travail and mystery. But once he had reached the sense of a God behind the veil—the

Allāh of the theologies of his day—the fear of that Allāh overwhelmed him. Thereafter he might have moments of reconciliation and communion, but always watching was the dread of a quickly offended possibly implacable deity. "Only by the mercy of Allāh," said the Prophet, "can I hope to enter the Garden; and so all Muslims have said. The love of God is an afterthought.

So, too, Ibn Khaldūn[1] warns against plunging into speculation on the mysteries of the divine Unity. It is sufficient for eternal salvation simply to confess that Unity in the broad. To go farther will lead to nothing but disappointment and, it may be, unbelief. The Prophet said, "Whoever dies testifying that there is no God but Allāh, will enter the Garden."

Still more curious is the position of Averroes. He led a double existence with two sharply distinguished sets of views. Openly he was a broad-school Muslim, who, while he admitted that the mass of the people should be taught the simple statements of the *Qur'ān* without explanation or discussion, claimed for himself and all educated men the right to speculate and explain these statements so as to meet the requirements of philosophy. But this was simply for protection. On the other side, he was a neo-Platonic-Aristotelian philosopher, separated by

[1] Beyrout edition, p. 459; Būlāq, p. 383; de Slane's translation, Vol. III, p. 42.

three great heresies from the Islām of his time. He held the eternity of the material world; he held that God cannot know individuals, cannot exercise providence in any usual sense, can only produce and embrace the Whole; he held that the race alone was eternal, but all individuals must pass away. Naturally, then, he was driven to two positions on the matter of salvation. In his books intended for the reading of ordinary, educated men, he followed the regular Muslim doctrine and taught that true knowledge is the knowledge of God, and especially of the religious law, and of happiness and unhappiness in the world to come.[1] In his philosophical writings, on the other hand, intended for students of Aristotle, he denounces all popular myths about the future life. Among dangerous fictions, he says, we must count those which tend to present virtue as simply a means of arriving at happiness. If virtue is nothing more, no one will abstain from pleasure except in the hope of being recompensed with usury; a brave man will not seek death, except to avoid a greater evil; a just man will not respect the goods of another, except to acquire double.[2] Nothing could show the normal Muslim position and its results more clearly.

Before leaving the subject of magic and talismans,

[1] *Philosophie u. Theologie von Averroes . . . . übers. von M. J. Müller*, p. 18.

[2] Renan, *Averroes et l'Averroisme*, p. 156.

one or two general considerations will be in place. First, you must not think that such things belong to a past age of Islām and have now lost their hold except upon the most ignorant. That is not so. From the one end of the Muslim world to the other, an unquestioning faith in the magician still reigns. Scattered among the educated classes, it is true, you will meet a good deal of absolute Voltairean unbelief, but even these individuals are liable to set back at any time. The shell that separates the Oriental from the Unseen is still very thin, and the charm or amulet of the magician may easily break it. The world of the *Arabian Nights* is still his world, and these stories for him are not tales from wonderland, but are, rather, to be compared to our stories of the wonders and possibilities of science, such as M. Jules Verne used to write and which we now owe to Mr. H. G. Wells. So Lane, in his time, found the magic mirror in Cairo, and he and others had some most interesting experiences. You will find these brought together in Mr. N. W. Thomas' book on *Crystal Gazing*. Only I would add that when Mr. Thomas says, (p. 94) that Lane was eventually inclined to ascribe the magician's success to a certain renegade Scotsman, he goes too far. Scots have been responsible for a good deal, but not, in Lane's final opinion, for this. A note by his nephew to a later edition of his *Arabian Nights* (Vol. I, p. 60) says that there were cases which remained to him inexplicable. The magic mirror, I may add, is still in popular use in Cairo. Only now no professional magician is needed. Books have been printed describing the mode of using it and all classes experiment for themselves. Very few doubt the truth of its revelations.

More recent evidence is given in Professor E. G. Browne's *Year Among the Persians*. There he met a magician who produced in his presence some most interesting telekinetic phenomena similar to those which Dr. Maxwell has described in his *Metapsychical Phenomena* (pp. 318 ff.) as performed by a medium whom he calls Meurice. They included moving a comb and a watch lying about three feet from the magician. Unfortunately, Professor Browne did not follow the matter up, being disgusted apparently by some lies which he found the magician was telling about him. He had also heard stories of the magic mirror, but had had no experiences himself. A tale told to him of experiences in learning to control the Jinn I shall take up later.

But, secondly, while belief in the power of magic is spread generally throughout Islām, and few doubt that the magician by his spells can break the thin shell of custom and law, and work what the results only can distinguish from God-given miracle, this does not affect the Muslim religious attitude so much as might be thought. The overwhelming fact of the personality, the will and power of God is over all, and under that shadow men feel secure. At the opposite extreme from Islām, in this respect, are those lowest religions, in which the gods, as innocuous, are ignored, and demons—practically magic and witchcraft—are feared and propitiated. But in Islām the puzzle is, rather, how any forms of black magic can survive and any magician dare to set himself against Allāh. That the art was and is cultivated is certain; but probably the student soothes his conscience and allays his fears by doubts as to the precise nature of the spirits he invokes, much as he of mediaeval Europe felt sure that in the end he could cheat the devil, who was notoriously stupid.

Finally, if you would appreciate the tremendous difference of atmosphere which this distinction involves, compare with the *Arabian Nights* the *Golden Ass* of Apuleius. Both books are instinct with piety of a kind; in each case, in a setting, for us, most certainly queer. It has been said, that the *Golden Ass* is the first book in European literature showing piety in the modern sense, and the most disreputable adventures of Lucius lead, it is true, in the end, to a religious climax. The *Arabian Nights*, on the other hand, is, in spite of everything, so pious that the sense of the all-seeing eye and the need of submission to the all-guiding hand become oppressive. But how different in each is the feeling toward the Unseen! Few books, in spite of fantastic gleams of color and light, move under such leaden-weighted skies as the *Golden Ass*. Theré is no real God in that world; all things are in the hands of enchanters; man is without hope for here and hereafter; full of yearnings, he struggles and takes refuge in strange cults. But the world of the *Arabian Nights* is God's world. There is sun and air and the sense of an ultimate justice. Joy comes with the morning there. And so, for all his belief in magic and his sense of the power of enchanters, the Muslim is a man. He stands on God's earth, beneath his sky, and at any time can enter that presence and carry his wrong to the highest court. Between him and Allāh there stands nothing, and he is absolutely sure of Allāh.

LECTURE V

INTERCOURSE THROUGH THE JINN; SPIRITS, DEMONS, GHOSTS IN ISLĀM.

The next point of contact with the Unseen to which I turn has much more immediate connection with religion, as we understand that word. Though Ibn Khaldūn has, from time to time, been compelled to make mention of the Jinn, he has no section dealing explicitly with them; on them he never relieves his mind. The simple reason is that he could not; that his views on them were too far from those of the Muslim world to be stated in such a book as he was writing. He accepted the great fact of the institution of prophecy; he accepted the personal mission of Muḥammad and the authority of the book revealed through him, because he also felt compelled to accept man's absolute dependence on God, and to admit that the researches, the reasonings, and the systems of the philosophers had been a failure. Viewing life from the side of reason he was an agnostic; by that path the ultimate realities could not be reached. But the reason is not the only pathway to reality, and is only one side of man's nature. On another side, that of the life of the soul, man came forth from God and can still have contact with God. This has already been made plain, again and again. Nor is it peculiar in the slightest to Ibn

Khaldūn. He derived it from al-Ghazzālī; he was a convinced Ghazzālian.

And so, too, were the rest of Islām. This, which some might compare with the pragmatic or humanistic position to which many of us have drifted in these last years, is the standard attitude of Islām toward the problem of religion and metaphysics. All metaphysical systems have failed and must fail. The thinkers of Islām had been through them all, and had come out with empty hands. Reason, however subtle, could find no means of passing from "me" to "thee," from the effect to the cause. But the soul of man could go out from the body in many ways; could meet the outstretched help of God and therein find peace and rest. It is true that the soul, when it returned, must translate its message in terms of human experience; the veil of the senses, in which the body clothed it, required that. But the message was delivered, however its garb might vary; so much man could know with absolute certainty.

Starting from this position, then, Ibn Khaldūn looked out on the world with all its varied, changing phenomena, and tried to interpret and realize it in terms of these ideas. It seemed to him that the pieces of the puzzle fell together of themselves. All through the world he found this reaching and groaning of the soul after its source. As the Christian church speaks of the fullness of time, so he felt that all these yearnings led up to the final revelation in Muḥammad. That revelation, then, in the *Qur'ān* he had to interpret again to himself in terms of the phenomena around him.

And he succeeded in great part. He found in life corresponding phenomena for everything in the *Qur'ān* except the individual personal spirits, the angels and the Jinn. Of such things he had had no experience and, therefore, to these words he could attach no ideas. The spiritual world, in the broad, he knew, but not personalities therein. In all this to which we have now come, you will remember, that Ibn Khaldūn stands by himself. No other Muslim ever looked with such clear, untroubled vision at the facts of life, reckoned with them all, and tried to rationalize them all, as did he. So he had never known angels and, it is plain, had had no personal experience of the Jinn. Soothsayers and magicians he had known, tested, and accepted; he had had dreams and found them valid; of the miracles of the saints he was firmly convinced; but he had never seen any of the Jinn, and so he blocked them out from his reckoning.

Only in one passage in his book, and that, too, as we have seen already, occurring only in a few MSS and apparently added as an afterthought, does he speak of them. There,[1] he puts the verses of

[1] De Slane's translation, Vol. III, p. 68; the passage is not in the Būlāq or Beyrout texts.

the *Qur'ān* which mention them in the "obscure" (*mutashābih*) class. All *Qur'ān* verses are divided into "clear" (*muḥkam*) and "obscure;" a division which delivers Muslims from the difficulties of the doctrine of inspiration, much as do our human and divine elements in the Scriptures. Naturally, theologians are little agreed as to what the true "obscure" verses are, and reckon in that class those which their systems find hard to digest.

But Ibn Khaldūn, in thus, out of his respect for facts, disregarding the Jinn entirely, was really ignoring one of the most primitive sources of old Arabian religion. The Jinn were the nymphs and satyrs of the desert; all wild, solitary nature was full of them; in a sense they typified that side of the life of nature which was still unsubdued and still hostile to man. They were in constant connection with wild animals and often appeared in animal forms. Whether they were originally animal fetiches and what their relation was to totemism we need not here consider. Our subject does not reach so far back. But the difference between them and the primitive Semitic gods, as Robertson Smith well puts it,[1] is simply that the gods have worshipers, and they have not. That means that the gods have entered into fixed, personal relations with men, are no longer hostile, and dwell in sanctuaries that are no longer dangerous, though, it may be, awful.

[1] *Religion of the Semites*[2], p. 121.

Robertson Smith thus goes on, in what is a *locus classicus* for our subject:

In fact the earth may be said to be parceled out between demons and wild beasts on the one hand, and gods and men on the other. To the former belong the untrodden wilderness with all its unknown perils, the wastes and jungles that lie outside the familiar tracks and pasture grounds of the tribe, and which only the boldest men venture upon without terror; to the latter belong the regions that man knows and habitually frequents, and within which he has established relations, not only with his human neighbors, but with the supernatural beings that have their haunts side by side with him. And as man gradually encroaches on the wilderness and drives back the wild beasts before him, so the gods in like manner drive out the demons, and spots that were once feared, as the habitation of mysterious and presumably malignant powers, lose their terrors and either become common ground or are transformed into the seats of friendly deities. From this point of view, the recognition of certain spots as haunts of the gods is the religious expression of the gradual subjugation of nature by man.

But when we reach Muḥammad's time, the situation has greatly cleared and simplified. No essential connection remained between the Jinn and wild beasts. They had become spirits with some curious animal associations. For example, they appeared riding upon animals, as, in another connection, they were accompanied by manifestations of light. The heathen Meccans associated them with Allāh as his sons and daughters, or they were made partners with Allāh.[1] They also, as we have seen, inspired

[1] *Qur.* vi, 100.

the *kāhins* and poets, and Muḥammad was said to be possessed by one. In a word, they furnished for the Arabs their general background of the supernatural, out of which rose pre-eminently Allāh, and less eminently but more intimately to the hearts of the worshipers, the various tribal gods. Allāh, Muḥammad accepted and made the one, only God. The Jinn remained for him real, rational beings, but the creation of Allāh and under his rule. How he conceived their relations to the angels, the messengers of Allāh, on the one hand, and to the devils, especially to Iblīs, ὁ διάβολος—an effect from Judaism and Christianity—on the other, is obscure because of his own uncertainty and lack of decision. Certain it is that for him the two salvable races on earth were the Jinn and mankind, these two before Allāh were on exactly the same footing.

To the Jinn, then, he must proclaim Islām as he did to mankind. And that was done. In chap. lxxii of the *Qur'ān* we read the words of Allāh to Muḥammad, revealing that this had taken place, and telling him to inform the people of it:

> Say [O Muḥammad], "It has been revealed to me that a small company of the Jinn listened, then said, 'We have heard a wondrous *Qur'ān* [or recitation], guiding to right; so we believe in it and we certainly will not join any as a companion to our Lord.' "

The revelation goes on to give the confession of faith made then by these Jinn, and introduces incidentally some points which interest us as showing how the heathen Arabs regarded the Jinn. Men, under certain conditions, "sought refuge" with the Jinn. That is, invoked their help and protection. The Jinn used to ascend to heaven and listen there in order to learn what was decreed by God. "Now," they said, "whoever listens finds there for him a shooting-star waiting." The angels hurled these at them to drive them off.

In chap. xlvi, 28 ff., mention is again made how a small company of the Jinn gathered to hear the Prophet and then dispersed to carry the message to their brethren. There are many other references in the *Qur'ān* to the Jinn, all accepting quite simply their existence as a race on earth beside that of the Sons of Adam; the phrase, "the Jinn and mankind," occurs again and again. With them, as I have already said, Iblīs, ὁ διάβολος, is curiously confused; sometimes being reckoned a fallen angel, and sometimes one of them. Several times we are told that he refused to prostrate himself to Adam when the other angels did so. In one of these passages (xxxviii) he is explicitly said to be one of the Jinn, and mankind is asked, "Do ye then take him and his seed as patrons (*awliyā*) instead of me?" This is an allusion to the semi-worship of the Jinn by the heathen Arabs.

So far, then, the *Qur'ān*. But these references, though plain, do not carry us very far. Muḥammad is either artistically or really modest in his claims. The great controversy among Muslim theologians, as to whether Muḥammad ever really saw the Jinn, must be decided in the negative. The *Qurʾān* is explicit that all this was a revelation to him from Allāh. But tradition has not been content with that, and the fixed belief of the enormous majority of the Muslim church is that he had divers direct interviews, face to face, with these spirits. Some are most picturesquely told, with details suggesting western magic.

I choose one, not because of its superior historicity —for all are equally unhistorical—but because of its detail, which commended it to the later Muslim imagination and makes it more representative for us. It is put in the mouth of az-Zubayr ibn al-ʿAwwām, one of the earliest of the believers, and one also of the ten who were personally promised by the Prophet that they would enter the Garden:

One day the Prophet prayed the morning prayer with us in the mosque of al-Madīna. Then, when he had finished, he said, "Which of you will follow me to a deputation of the Jinn tonight?" But the people kept silence and none said anything. He said it three times; then he walked past me and took me by the hand, and I walked with him until all the mountains of al-Madīna were distant from us and we had reached the open country. And there were men, tall as lances, wrapped completely in their mantles from their feet up. When I saw them a great quivering seized upon me, until my feet would hardly support me from fear. When we came near to them the Prophet drew with his great toe a line for me on the ground and said, "Sit in the middle of that." Then when I had sat down, all fear which I had felt departed from me. And the Prophet passed between me and them and recited the *Qur'ān* in a loud voice until the dawn broke. Then he came past me and said, "Take hold of me." So I walked with him, and we went a little distance. Then he said to me, "Turn and look; dost thou see any one where these were?" I turned and said, "O Apostle of God, I see much blackness!" He bent his head to the ground and looked at a bone and a piece of dung, and cast them to them. Thereafter he said, "These are a deputation of the Jinn of Naṣībīn; they asked of me traveling provender; so I appointed for them all bones and pieces of dung."

This end is rather puzzling but it seems to occur in all the stories of this kind. I take it that it is an attempt to explain a part of the ritual law dealing with purification.[1] In one form it runs:

The Prophet said to them [the Jinn], "Yours is every bone over which the name of God has been spoken; ye shall take it and it shall be in your hands the richest possible in flesh; and dung shall be provender for your beasts." Then he said [to his followers], "So do not use these two things for purifying; they are the food of your brethren."

Of these legends there are curious later echoes. Stories came down of Muslims who saw Jinn or heard their voices, and learned from them that they had taken part in these famous deputations to Muḥammad. There is a long tale, too, of one aged Jinnī who met Muḥammad and professed Islām.

[1] Cf. al-Bājūrī on Ibn Qāsim, Vol. I, p. 63, *fi-l-istinjā;* edition of Cairo, A. H. 1307.

He had lived in the days when Cain slew Abel, and had known all the prophets from that time on. Jesus had commissioned him to greet Muḥammad if he lived into his time.

But this whole matter is far too vast for me to enter into it in detail. I will here attempt only some bits of personal experience, and the like, which may make living for you the conception in the broad.[1]

That the Muslim law in its entirety is binding on the believing Jinn is accepted as certain. Whether they have had prophets of their own kind is uncertain, but not that Muḥammad was a prophet to them. That they will enter the Garden and be rewarded therein is almost unanimously accepted. Iblīs himself, of course, is an unbeliever but differing grounds are given for his being so reckoned. He is also the supreme tempter of men and is conceived of as setting his wits against Allāh to seduce from him his creation. He brought about the Fall, but it, in Islām, is an historical event only, without theological consequences. Still, traces remain of a doctrine of original sin. The following story is strikingly to that

[1] Cf., on the whole subject, Lane, *Arabian Nights*, Vol. I, note 21 to the Introduction, and the *Arabian Nights* themselves *passim;* Lane, *Modern Egyptians*, chap. x; also Ad-Damīrī's *Ḥayât al-Ḥayawân*, ... translated from the Arabic by A. S. G. Jayakar, London, 1906, Vol. I, pp. 448 ff.; for heathen Arabia see Robertson Smith, *Religion of the Semites;* Wellhausen, *Reste;* Goldziher, *Arabische Philologie*, and articles by Van Vloten in the *Wiener Zeitschrift für die Kunde des Morgenlandes*, 1893–94.

purpose, but I have been unable to find it in Arabic. I give it in E. J. W. Gibb's translation from the Turkish:

From that time when Satan was cursed and driven from Paradise by reason of Adam (peace on him!) he pursued him with hatred and sought to take vengeance. He had a son named Khannās; and he made him assume the form of a kid, and took him before our mother Eve, and said, "Let this kid remain by thee; I shall come now and fetch it." Eve said, "By reason of thee have we come forth from Paradise; art thou come now again?" Satan replied, "If they drove you from Paradise, they have driven me thence, too; one must pass from the past." And he left the kid and went off. Saint Adam came and saw the kid, and he said, "Whose kid is this?" Eve answered, "Satan has left it, and has gone off." He said, "I will come now and fetch it." Saint Adam (peace on him!) was wroth, and he killed the kid, and threw it into the desert and went away. Satan came and said, "Where is the kid?" Eve said, "Adam came and killed the kid, and threw it into the desert." Satan cried out, "Khannās!" The kid said, "Here I am, father." And it became alive and went up to him. Again Satan left it, and went off; for though Eve entreated him, saying, "Take it, and go," he would not take it. Saint Adam came and saw the kid, and asked about it, and Eve told him what had happened. Adam said, "Why didst thou keep that accursed one's kid?" And he was angry with Eve; and he cut the kid into many pieces, and threw each piece in a different direction, and went away. Again Satan came and asked, and Eve told him what had happened. Again Satan cried, "O Khannās!" And it answered, "Here I am, father." And it became alive and went up to him. Again Satan left it and went off; and though Eve said many times, "Leave it not," it was of no avail, for Satan vanished. Again Adam came and saw the kid, and this time he smote Eve; and people have beaten their wives since that time. Adam seized the kid, and cut its throat, and cooked it, and he and Eve ate it; then he went away. Again Satan came and asked, "Where is the kid?" Eve said, "This time was Adam wroth, and he cut its throat, and cooked it, and we both of us ate it." Satan again cried, "O Khannās!" This time it answered from Eve's belly, "Here I am, father." Satan said, "My son, thou hast found thy best place; let us tempt the sons of Adam, thou from within, and I from without, till the resurrection, and urge them to many sins, and make them deserving of hell."[1]

But in one respect the Muslim Iblīs differed markedly from the Devil of mediaeval Europe. He was lost hopelessly—that was accepted—but then he was also the father of all the Jinn, believing and unbelieving. There was, therefore, with all his stratagems to mislead men, a kindly side to his nature. He was not simply stupid as in European devil-lore; he was also humorous. Often in the *Arabian Nights* he plays this double part; showing himself most interested, friendly, and amusing, while the other characters in the tale scrupulously refer to him as "Iblīs the Accursed." Outstanding examples are in the *Story of Sul and Shumūl*, recently published and translated by Seybold,[2] and in the "Story of Hārūn ar-Rashīd and Tūḥfat al-Qulūb.[3]

1 *History of the Forty Vezirs*, p. 348.

2 Leipzig, 1902.

3 Payne, *Tales from the Arabic*, Vol. II, p. 203; Burton, Vol. IX, p. 291, of 12 vol. edit.

From many of these, as for example, "The Story of Abdullah and his Brothers,"[1] it is plain that the popular imagination had brought Hārūn ar-Rashīd into close relationships with the Jinn. By his strict piety and exact observance of his religious duties—this sounds very curious, but Hārūn *was* pious in his way—joined to his position as successor of Muḥammad, commander of the faithful and representative of Allāh on earth, he had complete control, supernatural and natural, of both Jinn and mankind. The Jinn added to his wealth, taught songs and airs to his court poets and musicians, and took the oath of fidelity to his proclaimed successor. For the last point, we have better authority than the *Arabian Nights*. Ibn Khallikān tells us of it in connection with a certain poet, who was the intermediary.[2] To this poet Hārūn is reported to have said, "If thou hast seen what thou tellest, thou hast seen marvels; if not, thou hast composed a wonder." This must not be taken as implying doubt of the existence of the Jinn; that were heresy of the worst. The doubt was only of his having had intercourse with them; for it was a much contested point whether any men except prophets could see them. Some few lawyers laid it down flatly that any man who claimed to have seen them was not fit to be a legal witness; he had showed himself

[1] Payne, *Arabian Nights*, Vol. IX; Burton, Vol. VII, p. 364.

[2] De Slane's translation, Vol. III, p. 373; *Wüstenfeld*, No. 735.

impious in claiming what the law did not admit. More curious still is a Berber story in which Hārūn actually marries a female Jinnī. I know it only by reference.[1]

Around the possibility of marriage between mankind and the Jinn an immense literature has gathered. The general position is that such marriages have frequently taken place and are lawful; some few canon lawyers, however, deny their legality on qur'ānic grounds.[2] According to the present code of Ottoman law, following the school of Abū Ḥanīfa, such marriages are illegal;[3] one reason alleged is because a Jinnī may appear in either sex. But these legal doubts the broad belief of the Muslim people laughs to scorn. Probably every Muslim has heard of or been in some relation to some man or other, who was known to have married a female Jinnī. So Lane, during his residence at Cairo, had a Persian acquaintance who told him of a friend of his own, who had had such an experience.[4] The idea has also often served to cover an intrigue. A good example of this, in Alexandria, in the middle of the last century, is to be found in Bayle St. John's *Two Years in a Levantine Family* (chap. xxiv). But from the earliest Muslim times such stories were

[1] Chauvin, *Bibliographie arabe*, Vol. VI, p. 48.

[2] *Qur*. xvi, 74; xl, 9.

[3] Young, *Corps de droit Ottoman*, Vol. II, pp. 210, 215.

[4] *Arabian Nights*, Vol. I, chap. i, note 25.

current, and had become a *lieu commune* in romance. The book called *Al-Fihrist*, a *catalogue raisonné* of Arabic literature of about 1000 A. D., gives a separate section to "Names of Those of Mankind Who Loved the Jinn and Vice-versa." It is really sixteen titles of books of their love stories. Similarly, in the numerous collections of love stories there are chapters given to "Lovers of the Jinn."

Another fertile aspect of this subject is the relation between saints and the Jinn. As Muslim saints live more or less in contact with the unseen world all the time, that relation of necessity is close. Of course, we must distinguish between necessarily apocryphal stories and those which have *vraisemblance*, at least; although both, for our purpose, are of value. A story with every appearance of truth is that which al-Ghazzālī tells of his own attempt at spirit-seeing. I may say of him that one of his characteristics is extreme modesty in his claims to contact with the Unseen. He had visions of insight into spiritual truth, but he never felt that he had reached the same degree of closeness to the divine as some of his contemporaries, and he always declared that he had never been able to work miracles. This story, then, bears these characteristic marks of modesty. He applied to a celebrated evoker of the Jinn, Muḥammad ibn Aḥmad aṭ-Ṭabasī—an older contemporary of his own, who died in A. H. 482, when al-Ghazzālī was thirty-two years of age—requesting that he would bring about a meeting between himself and some of the Jinn. To that he consented, and al-Ghazzālī says, "I saw them like a shadow on a wall. Then I said to him that I would like to talk with them and hear their speech, but he said, 'You are not able to see more of them than this.'"[1] Not a very satisfactory case, except as showing al-Ghazzālī's truthfulness. The magician, apparently, had made only so much preparation.

Another very different story, a legend with large elements of folk-lore in it, is told of ᶜAbd al-Qādir al-Jīlānī who died in 1166, A. D., the founder of the Qādirite fraternity of darwīshes. Around him an immense accumulation of myth has collected, and to that the following evidently belongs. I do not mean to suggest that all the marvels of ᶜAbd al-Qādir's life are necessarily mythical. The levitations, for example, told of him have far too many analogues elsewhere to be ruled so easily out of court. The story runs thus:

One of the people of Baghdād came to him and told him that a maiden daughter of his had been snatched away from the roof of the house. "Go," said the shaykh, "this night to the ruined part of al-Karkh [a district of Baghdād] and sit beside the fifth mound and draw a circle on the ground and say, as thou drawest it, 'In the name of Allāh; according to the intention of ᶜAbd al-Qādir.'" [I presume he meant, as though ᶜAbd al-Qādir had drawn this line.] "Then, when the black of the night has come, there will pass by thee troops

[1] Al-Qazwīnī, Vol. II, p. 272, (Wüstenfeld's edition).

of the Jinn in different forms, but let not their appearance terrify thee. And when the dawn comes, there will pass by thee their king in an army of them. He will ask thee of thy need; so say, 'Abd al-Qādir hath sent me to thee,' and tell him the case of thy daughter." The man did so. "It was" he told thereafter, "as the shaykh had said. Not one of the Jinn was able to pass the circle in which I was. They kept going by in bands, until their king came, riding on a horse, and before him [whole] nations of them. He stopped over against the circle and said, 'O human being, what is thy need?' I said, 'The shaykh, ᶜAbd al-Qādir, hath sent me to thee.' Then he alighted from his horse and kissed the ground and sat just outside of the circle; and those sat who were with him. Then he said, 'What is thy affair?' and I told him the story of my daughter. He said to those around him, 'Bring me him who hath done this!' and they brought an evil Jinnī and my daughter with him. He was told, 'This is one of the evil Jinn of China.' Then he said, 'What led thee to snatch one away from under the stirrups of the Quṭb [the chief of all the saints of Allāh]?' 'She pleased me,' said the evil Jinnī. So he gave orders, and the head of the evil Jinnī was struck off, and he gave me back my daughter."[1]

This, you will observe, is exactly the same as the nocturnal procession of the demons with Pluto, their king, which we meet in European folk-lore. The part of the magician is taken by the head, for the time, of all the saints of Allāh. *Ex officio*, he has absolute control over the Jinn.

Around Ibn ᶜArabī, another great saint and mystic of later times, who died in 1240 A. D., similar tales have gathered. He wrote an account of all who had

[1] Damīrī, Vol. I, p. 185, edition of Cairo, A. H. 1313.

been his teachers, of the Jinn and mankind and angels and beasts. In that account he tells the following story as a rebuke of his pride; it is evidently told in earnest, though it may seem rather humorous to us. One time he was in a ship on the great sea. The wind blew, and a storm arose. But he cried out to the sea, "Be still, for a sea of learning is upon thee!" Then a sea monster raised its head and said to him, "We have heard thy saying. What do you say to this case of law? If the husband of a wife be ensorcelled and transformed, must she wait, before remarrying, the period of a widow, or of a divorced woman [literally the waiting period of the dead or of the living]?" But Ibn ᶜArabī, for all that he was a sea of learning, could not tell. So the sea-monster said, "Make me one of thy teachers, and I will tell thee." Ibn ᶜArabī accepted, and the sea-monster said, "If he is transformed into a beast, then she must wait the period of a divorced woman; and if into a stone, that of a widow."[1]

But an evident jest is the following. A certain shaykh had been asked about Ibn ᶜArabī. He replied with emphasis, "An evil shaykh, a liar!" "A liar, too?" someone said to him. "Yes, indeed," he said. "We were discussing, once, marriage with the Jinn, and he said, 'The Jinn are fine spirits and mankind are coarse bodies; how can they come

[1] Shaᶜrānī, *Lawāqiḥ*, p. 284, edition of Cairo, A. H. 1308.

together?' Then he was away from us for a time, and came back with a bruise on his head. We asked him whence it was. He said, 'I married a woman of the Jinn, and we had some trouble, and she hit me this bruise!'" The original teller of the story adds, "I don't think this was a deliberate lie on Ibn ᶜArabī's part; it was simply one of the jesting stories current among those of the spiritual life."[1]

Another saint who had large dealings with the Jinn was ash-Shaᶜrānī, a Cairene mystic, who died in 1565. He was a very remarkable man, and a union of the most opposite characteristics. He was a canon lawyer of originality and keenness; one of the very few creative minds in law after the first three centuries. He was a moralist, touched with high ethical indignation. Unlike most of the learned of Islām, he sought and found his own among the oppressed common people. He was a mystic who lived from day to day in constant touch with the Unseen; the spirit world was as near and real to him as the walls of the classroom in which he taught, or of the mosque in which he worshiped. In the night time, there came dreams to him, or else, when he waked, a voice would sound in his ears; a *hātif*, as they called such wandering utterances, would warn or admonish him. Of these the records of Islām are full, but in no case so full as in his. Naturally, intercourse with the Jinn was not lacking. They

[1] Damīrī, Vol. I, p. 185.

used to seek his judgment, as a jurisconsult of standing. Once a Jinnī in the form of a dog ran in at his house door with a piece of European paper in his mouth, on which certain theological questions were written. Ash-Shaʿrānī replied by writing a book, still extant, on them.

It should be understood, then, that just as among men there are ascetics and devotees, so, too, among the Jinn. In deserts and solitary places, men have often heard their voices in pious exclamation or prayer; of such the records of the saints are full. And just as they taught men, so men taught them. The great shaykhs had disciples of the Jinn as of mankind. Here is something upon that, from a most valuable and interesting book, consisting of translations of passages from the lives of the great saints of Morocco:[1]

"I once happened upon the shaikh Abooʾl Hasan," he [shaikh Muḥammad the Andalusee] said, "and he was sitting in the midst of a plantation, of which he was the owner, and around him sat a company of the Jinn who believed, to whom he was teaching the beautiful names of God.

"On seeing me, he looked up and asked: 'Has the matter concerning these been revealed to thee?'

"I replied that it had been revealed. 'These,' he went on, 'are in search of that which thou art in search of'—meaning that they, too, were seekers after the Truth."

Andalusee used also to say: "There was not in all Morocco, nor in any part of it, neither in any land, the like of the shaikh

[1] T. H. Weir, *The Shaikhs of Morocco*, p. 121. Mr. Weir's method of representing Arabic words in English is preserved here.

Aboo'l Hasan, the son of Aboo'l Kasim in his time. He had as followers upward of seventy thousand of the jinn; and when he died, they were scattered into all quarters of the earth, but none of them ever found again a teacher like him." "I had made friends with four of these jinn," he continued, "and once I asked one of the four, who was the best-read of all, which of the plants, in their opinion, afforded the most useful drugs for the purposes of medicine, so as to cure all maladies. 'There is not one among all plants,' replied the jinnee, 'more generally useful than the caper; for it unites in itself qualities which are found only separate in other plants; and if the men-folk but knew all that is in it, they would not wish for any other.' "[1]

But to all, this matter was not so simple. The Jinn might be spoken of in the *Qur'ān*, and many might have seen them and had speech with them, but others had no such good fortunes. Al-Ghazzālī, as we have seen, had but indifferent success in his attempt to reach them, and Ibn Khaldūn seems to have had none at all. These, however, were believing men, and either accepted the traditions and the testimony of others, or held their place. But there were some who were no great believers, and who had to settle the existence of the Jinn on other than religious grounds. Many of the Mu'tazilites seem in general to have rejected them; how these dealt with the qur'ānic passages I do not know. They must have explained them away in some fashion, as

[1] Compare the folk-lore stories of fairy changelings and the like who would say, "If men but knew the value of this or that" (some despised thing).

they were only heretics and not unbelievers. It is certain that they were of varying opinions on the matter.

But the philosophers were in different case. Al-Fārābī, who died in 950, was a Plotinian and an Aristotelian, but managed, being also a mystic, to remain a devout Muslim. His only trouble, then, was to discover a philosophical definition, and so get them into his system. The ordinary definition was, "Airy bodies capable of assuming different forms, possessed of reason and understanding, and able to perform hard labors."[1] But there was a doubt on the point of reason (*ʿaql*). For example, in the "Story of the Fisherman and the Jinnī," in the *Arabian Nights*, the fisherman says to himself in some texts,[2] "This is a Jinnī, and I am a human being, and Allāh has given to me reason and made me more excellent than him, and lo! I contrive against him with my reason, and he contrives against me with his Jinn-mind (*bi-jinnihi ?*)."

This distinction al-Fārābī laid hold of, and he constructed the following definitions: Man is a living being, rational, mortal; the angels are the same, rational, immortal; brute beasts the same, irrational, mortal; the Jinn, then, to fill out the analogy, are living beings, irrational, immortal. But the *Qurʾān* speaks of them as hearing and speaking; must they

[1] Damīrī, Vol. I, p. 177.

[2] Galland; Breslau; I Calcutta.

not, then, be rational? Al-Fārābī denies that. Speech and verbal utterance may be found in any living being, *qua* living being; they are different from that power of distinguishing, which is reason. The speech of man is natural to him, *qua* living being; but his speech is different from that of other kinds of living beings; each kind has its own speech. He might further have defended himself with the popular belief that the speech of the Jinn is a kind of whistling; that is why it is unlucky to whistle in the Muḥammadan East. But the truth evidently is that he was simply hard pressed.[1] His argument from classification is of a type common in Arabic and is based essentially on a realistic philosophy.

Avicenna (died 1037) avoided such subjects as far as he could, but his system had certainly no place for the Jinn. Yet once, in giving a series of definitions of things, he defined "Jinn," "Airy animals capable of changing themselves into different forms," but added, "This is an explanation of the name (or noun)," meaning evidently that the thing had no real existence; he, in this, was a nominalist.[2]

Farther with the philosophers we need not go; they practically had no effect on the views of the vast body of Muslims. Islām believes to this day in the Jinn not only among the vulgar but as an essential part of the faith. In the Azhar University at Cairo,

[1] Dieterici, *Alfarabi's philos. Abhandl. herausg.*, p. 84.

[2] Rāzī, *Mafātīh al-ghayb*, Sūra lxxii, beginning.

the legal textbooks still consider the vexed question of the marriage of men and Jinn; e. g., al-Bājūrī's great commentary on Ibn Qāsim's commentary on Abu Shujā's handbook of Shāfiᶜite law, Vol. II, pp. 113, 186, 187. We have already seen the same in the Ottoman code. So, too, is Lane's testimony for modern Cairo. Professor E. G. Browne, in his *Year among the Persians*, has a curious narrative of a friend of his, a certain unbelieving philosopher of Ispahan, who had twice gone through the training incumbent upon those who wish to gain control over the Jinn:

The seeker after this power [said he] chooses some solitary and dismal spot, such as the Hazár-Déré at Isfahán (the place selected by me). There he must remain for forty days, which period of retirement we call *chillé*. He spends the greater part of this time in incantations in the Arabic language, which he recites within the area of the *mandal*, or geometric figure, which he must describe in a certain way on the ground. Besides this, he must eat very little food, and diminish the amount daily. If he has faithfully observed all these details, on the twenty-first day a lion will appear, and will enter the magic circle. The operator must not allow himself to be terrified by this apparition, and, above all, must on no account quit the *mandal*, else he will lose the result of all his pains. If he resists the lion, other terrible forms will come to him on subsequent days—tigers, dragons, and the like—which he must similarly withstand. If he holds his ground till the fortieth day, he has attained his object, and the *jinnīs*, having been unable to get the mastery over him, will have to become his servants and obey all his behests. Well, I faithfully observed all the necessary conditions, and on the twenty-first day, sure enough, a lion appeared and entered the circle. I was horribly frightened, but all the same I stood my ground, although I came near to fainting with terror. Next day, a tiger came, and still I succeeded in resisting the impulse which urged me to flee. But when, on the following day, a most hideous and frightful dragon appeared, I could no longer control my terror, and rushed from the circle, renouncing all further attempts at obtaining the mastery over the *jinnīs*. When some time had elapsed after this, and I had pursued my studies in philosophy further, I came to the conclusion that I had been the victim of hallucinations, excited by expectation, solitude, hunger, and long vigils, and, with a view to testing this hypothesis, I again repeated the same process which I had before practiced, this time in a spirit of philosophical incredulity. My expectations were justified; I saw absolutely nothing. And there is another fact which proves to my mind that the phantoms I saw on the first occasion had no existence outside of my own brain. I had never seen a real lion then, and my ideas about the appearance of that animal were entirely derived from the pictures which, may be seen over the doors of baths in this country. Now the lion which I saw in the magic circle was exactly like the latter in form and coloring, and, therefore, as I need hardly say, differed considerably in aspect from a real lion.

So far this philosopher of Isfahán, as reported by Professor Browne. But you already know, from Ibn Khaldūn and al-Ghazzālī, that the spectres which appear to the would-be magician must be forms that he already knows. They are ideas—true ideas—which his memory and imagination clothe in corresponding appearances. Thus the idea "lion" would necessarily assume the form of a bath-house picture lion.

The most remarkable narrative of all, however, is given by Bayle St. John in his *Two Years in a Levantine Family* (chap. xx). The house in which he lived with his "family" was haunted by a ghost, an *ᶜifrīt*; ghosts now are called *ᶜifrīts*, which means strictly an evil kind of Jinnī. This ghost was the spirit of a deceased previous owner, who was supposed to have buried his money in the house, and in consequence had to guard it. The Levantine family had seen him, from time to time for thirteen years, and now took no notice of him. He never meddled with them, and they had become accustomed to his prowling about, and appearing and disappearing. Also, he had always the same appearance, and this had often been described to St. John. Then suddenly, one day, in broad daylight, he, himself, saw this shaykh, as he was called, with perfect clearness. Twice, thereafter, he saw him again, but the third appearance, the most circumstantial, is invalidated as evidence by occurring during an attack of fever. It is curious that the first two experiences agree precisely in type with the cases of "haunting ghosts" collected by the Society for Psychical Research and are utterly different from the loquacious, meddlesome ghosts of literature, eastern and western. For these two St. John could find no explanation. Nor do I think will you be able to, if you read his careful narrative. I can make only one suggestion. It is incredible to me that there should be absolutely no foundation for the unbroken belief of the East in these spirits. There must be some phenomena behind it. Is it possible to explain it as a result of auto-hypnosis—that the whole people are more or less under this hypnotic suggestion? It is conceivable, then, that St. John, living for long in such an environment, would come at last under the same suggestion.[1] It is certain that Europeans who have long lived in the East, and adapted themselves to eastern ways, come in time to be orientalized in their attitudes and ideas. Sometimes, this reaches a, for us, disgusting point; at others, it is only the possibilities of the unseen world which are marvelously widened.

[1] Cf. the case of the haunting of the old house in St. Swithin's Lane, London (*Proceedings of Society for Psychical Research*, Vol. III, pp. 126 ff.), and the gradual extension of the hallucination (veridical or otherwise) to Mr. Votas-Simpson himself.

LECTURE VI

SAINTS AND THE ASCETIC-ECSTATIC LIFE IN ISLĀM

It may be well for us now to look back to our starting-point, see how far we have come, and what journey lies still before us. You will remember that in our subject — the religious attitude and life, as developed in Islām—I found three essential elements; (1) the reality of the Unseen, as a background to life unattainable to our physical senses; (2) man's relation to this Unseen, as to faith and insight therein: the whole emotional religious life; (3) the discipline of the traveler on his way to such direct knowledge of the divine and during his life in it.

The first of these, the tremendous reality and nearness for the Muslim of the unseen world must now be tolerably clear to you. You will have observed, also, the different processes by which the Muslim endeavors to construct connections between his own life and that Unseen, his metaphysical scheme in the exact sense. Of necessity that will appear to you very unmetaphysical in the ordinary sense, full of bizarre concretenesses and materialisms. But that hangs from the nature of the case. I should like to put before you an ontology full of the most beautiful abstractions, leaving you gasping in an over-rarified atmosphere, but my sources will not permit it. Even the Aristotelian philosophers of Islām had their system of spheres, with therein dominating intelligences; it was left for Occam to lay down the final law, "We must not multiply beings without reason."

But among these pathways to the Unseen, I have not yet put formally before you that trodden by the saints, by those men who, in the beauty of holiness, have gained immediate vision of divine things and whose lives, in consequence, are permeated with the divine light and energy. Allusion has been made to them, again and again, and the Muslim conception of them as a class is already, in general terms, before you. In all strictness I should now consider the phenomena of sainthood as one of the avenues of approach to the Unseen, one of the cracks in the shell, before passing on to our second element, the emotional religious life in general. I venture, however, to combine the two, and will now take up the psychological-religious element of man's relation to the Unseen as to faith and insight therein.

Practically, we come now to an investigation of sainthood as practiced in Islām. This does not limit our subject as the word saint might suggest. There are saints of all degrees in Islām, and saintship is not the rare phenomenon of our associations. Externally, through an elaborate hierarchy rising to a single spiritual head, and internally, through a multitude of brethren of varying spiritual illumination and powers, every pious Muslim looks up a path to God and knows his place in it. This institution, externally and internally, as an organization and as a life, is of the highest interest as a force in Islām; but I can notice it now only most inadequately. Our subject, in strictness, is the emotional life of the individual.

So much, at least, must be said. From the earliest times there was an element in the Muslim church which was repelled equally by traditional teaching and by intellectual reasoning. It felt that the essence of religion lay elsewhere; that the seat and organ of religion was in the heart. In process of time, all Islām became permeated with this conception, in different degrees and various forms. More widely than ever with Christianity, Islām became and is a mystical faith. All—the simple believers, the theologians of the schools, the philosophers—came in one form or another to the essential mystical positions.

The varying, of course, was wide; it stretched from absolute Plotinian pantheism—the emission of the individuals from the One, and their vanishing again into the One—through various phases of more or less disguised pantheism to simple acceptance of life in God and of God's immanence in the world. After the strangest fashion, the absolute contrast of Allāh and his world—Allāh and not-Allāh—of the *Qurʾān* almost entirely vanished.

Then, from this soil, developed the conception of saints in the precise sense, favorites of God, gifted by him with illumination and wondrous powers, accepted and heard by him, and therefore to be honored, petitioned, practically worshiped by other men. These began as ascetics, fleeing from the wrath to come; developed into ecstatics, reveling in the conception of the love for and of God which they pictured in various sensuous ways; and often ended as antinomians in a spiritual life above the moral law and ritual duty. The worship of these, living and dead, by the populace has gone so far as to bring Islām, with certain classes, back to a polytheistic or, at least, polydaemonistic position. Into the exceedingly interesting details of this I cannot here enter. You will find them at length in Dr. Goldziher's *Muhammedanische Studien.*[1]

But, further, there was a tendency for schools of disciples to gather round such outstanding figures, exactly as did the schools of the prophets in the Old Testament. They were students around their teacher, and unfettered by any vows save those of their love and devotion. He instructed them in theology, initiated them into the specific religious life, and guided them on that pathway. They did not necessarily remain always with him. They might go back into the world and live their life there. And he on his side was not necessarily a cloistered monk

[1] Vol. II, pp. 277–378.

or a solitary; he might hold what we would call a university position as professor of theology or canon law.

This went on for centuries. Such teaching saints came and went, and with their deaths their circles of disciples broke up. The unit of organization was still the individual teacher, and for his life only. There were early, it is true, communities of begging friars who wandered in the summer, and settled in their monasteries in the winter, and were tolerably continuous of organization; but these had not yet come to call themselves by any name. The general words describing them are suggestive. The saints are *walīs* (*walī*, pl. *awliyā*, "a relative," "friend," "associate," "favorite," here "of God"); the ascetics were *sāʾiḥs*, "wanderers;" *rāhibs*, "fearers;" and *zāhids*, "ascetics." Broadly, they were all called *Ṣūfīs*, from their habit of wearing wool, *ṣūf*. Their exercises are called *dhikrs*, "rememberings," from the qurʾānic injunction, "Remember Allāh much, and praise him morning and evening,"[1]

The "remembering" consists in the repetition of names of God and certain formulas.[2]

[1] *Qur.* xxxiii, 41.

[2] For these see Hughes, *Dictionary of Islām*, p. 703, and Lane, *Modern Egyptians*, chap. xxiv. For the whole early development see Goldziher, "Materialien zur Entwickelungsgeschichte des Sûfismus," *Wiener Zeitschrift für die Kunde des Morgenlandes*, Vol. XIII, p. 35; in short, also, in Macdonald, *Development of Muslim Theology*, pp. 172–85.

But in the course of the twelfth century, these associations of personal followers and pupils began to pass into self-perpetuating corporations. What are now known as fraternities of darwīshes were fairly started. Darwīsh is derived from a Persian word meaning a mendicant "seeking doors," but it has come to be applied to all members of these fraternities or orders, whether they are begging friars or not. The strict begging friar is called *faqīr*, in Arabic, "a poor man."

Among the earliest of these orders appears to be that of the Qādirites, founded either by the ᶜAbd al-Qādir al-Jīlānī, of whom I have already given some legends, or by his immediate followers. But the number soon grew, and now there are very many of these brotherhoods scattered over the Muslim world. Some of them are of very wide spread. The Qādirites, for example, have traveled from the region of Baghdād as far as northern Africa, and are dominant even in the Fulani Emirates of northern Nigeria.[1] One of the youngest orders, and by far the most fanatical, the Sanūsites, is scattered from the Atlantic to the Philippines.

These orders are independent of one another in government; they have each their own ritual and mode of life; they differ as to the wonders which they perform in ecstasy; their theological attitudes,

[1] Major Alder Burdon, in the *Geographical Journal*, December, 1904, p. 650.

even, are different, varying as to the strictness of their adherence to the ritual law and the exactness of their acceptance of the traditional faith. They constitute, in fact, the only ecclesiastical organization that Islām has ever had; but a multiform organization, absolutely un-unified, either internally or externally. Further, each of the orders has a large number of adhering lay members, who are in exactly the position of the tertiaries of Christian monasticism. Thus, in all ranks of life throughout Islām, the influence of the orders is active. They are the nearest approach to the different churches of Protestantism, just as there are striking parallels between their meetings and the early class-meetings of the Methodists.

But, besides these great separate and visible organizations, there is one, greater, single, and invisible. This is the Ṣūfī hierarchy. At its head is a great saint, presumably the greatest of the time, chosen by God for the office, and given miraculous power above all others. He is called the *Quṭb*, or Axis, and wanders, often invisible and always unknown to the world, through the lands, performing the duties of his office. From him the hierarchy descends, in gradually widening numbers, and the whole system forms a saintly board of administration, by which the invisible government of the world is carried on.[1]

[1] Lane, *Modern Egyptians*, chap x; Lane, *Arabian Nights*, note 63 to chap. iii; von Kremer, *Herrschende Ideen* D. 172; Vollers, in *ZDMG.*, Vol. XLIII, p. 115.

It may, perhaps, make the above clearer to contrast these orders and this hierarchy with the monastic orders and the organization of the Roman church. At every point, the advantage in universality and freedom is on the side of Islām. As for the hierarchy—I assume its existence and reality since our subject is the beliefs and attitudes of Muslims—its head is spiritual, invisible, and in immediate connection with Allāh; the organization as a whole is free from the bonds of locality, the things of the world, and the entanglements which these bring. The whole, one may say, is a beautiful dream. The orders, again, are independent and self-developing. There is rivalry between them; but no one rules over the other. In faith and practice each goes its own way, limited only by the universal conscience of Islām. Thus strange doctrines and grave moral defects easily develop unheeded; but freedom is saved. As to universality, the whole Muslim people is reached and may be gathered in. The system of tertiaries, adherents, living in the world but bound to certain religious usages, which the Franciscans first introduced into Christendom and the Dominicans adopted, is of the widest and earliest extension in Islām. On this side the Muslim fraternities might be said to resemble the lodges of freemasons or other friendly societies. Further, all that is said here of men holds of women as well, down to the present day, even, as regards lay membership. There always have been, and still are, women saints in Islām. The distinction of Roman christendom, that a woman cannot be a priest does not exist for Islām, as there is neither priest nor layman there. All the Arabic terms, then, which I gave above for ascetics, mendicants, etc., can be put in the feminine, and the mode of life and exercises of the man can be predicated of women as well. Finally, for all these fraternities, a standard book of reference is Depont and Cappolani's *Confrêries religieuses Musulmanes*, Algiers, 1897.

But how did this movement and this development present itself to the Muslims themselves? That is the point of nearer interest to us. Again I take Ibn Khaldūn as representing very fairly the resultant attitude of Islām in the broad toward the Ṣūfīs. He has not treated the fraternities so far as I can find; in his time they, apparently, were not of outstanding importance. The following, then, is an abstract of his section[1] on the Ṣūfīs. Their science is one of the religious sciences which arose in the Muslim community. From the very beginning the method of the Ṣūfīs was followed by the most eminent of the Companions and their immediate successors, as a means of reaching truth and guidance. So, I may throw in, dictionaries of Ṣūfī biography begin with the ten to whom Muḥammad personally

[1] Beyrout edition, p. 467; Būlāq, p. 390; de Slane's translation, Vol. III, p. 85; there are large additions in de Slane.

promised Paradise, among them being the first four khalīfas, the "rightly guided." The original form of the method consisted in (1) persistence in acts of worship; (2) living uniquely for God; (3) turning away from the adornments of the world; (4) abstinence from the objects of the masses, such as pleasure, wealth, ambition; (5) separation from mankind in solitude for worship. All that, says Ibn Khal dūn, following the pious historical fiction which had grown up, was general among the Companions and the early believers.

But in the second century, and thereafter, people turned to the world, and stooped to be mixed with it. Then, those who turned, rather, to worship, came to stand by themselves and were called, in distinction, Ṣūfīs. The derivation of this name he gives, as I have already done, as from *ṣūf*, wool; they wore woolen garments, in contrast to the splendid array of the non-Ṣūfīs.[1] But their turning to the devotional life and separating themselves from the mass of the people had spiritual consequences. Man has perceptions, either external or internal; the latter are of his own states of joy, sorrow, hope, fear, etc. The intelligent spirit which rules the body grows through [reflective] perceptions, acts of will and states, so consciousness is traditionally divided into knowing, feeling, and willing; by these man is distinguished from the other animals. They pro-

[1] Cf. Nöldeke, in *ZDMG.*, Vol. XLVIII, p. 45.

ceed, one from the other; knowledge from proofs, and joy or sorrow from the painful or the pleasant perception. So, when the Sūfī neophyte applies himself to his religious exercises, states[1] (feelings) result in him, of one kind or another, and of greater or less fixity. He goes up then, as on a ladder, trading his dead selves under him, until he arrives at that immediate knowledge of the divine unity which is his object. He must needs mount up through these degrees, whose beginning is obedience and purity, and which faith introduces and accompanies. He may be sure that if there are any breaks in his progress, it is because he has fallen short in some way before that. He must, therefore, cautiously take account with himself as to what he does and does not, and be on his guard against heedlessness. The method, then, is this examination of the soul, and a discussion of the tastes of bliss and the ecstasies which result from its effects. Further, there are certain usages and technical terms peculiar to the Ṣūfīs, and not used by the mass of the people.

When, then, the time came that the different religious sciences were reduced to writing, and were no longer simply carried in the memories, on this science also books were written. Thus, from being a practice only, it became, in the exact sense, a science.

But, again, by means of these exercises and ecstasies, the veil of sense is often rent and the upper

[1] For the meaning of "states" cf. p. 188.

spiritual regions are directly perceived. The soul belongs to these worlds, and is thus enabled to reach a state where it beholds them, and does not simply know about them. This is absolute perception, and in this state the soul receives various divine gifts and favors from God directly, So Ṣūfīs come to know the real nature of things, and future events are unsealed to them, and, through their zeal and the forces of their souls, they can affect the things of this lower world. Yet the more they advance, the less attention they pay to such matters, and they finally reckon them as temptations and lower manifestations.

In later times there arose a party which turned more and more attention to this rending of the veil of sense. They had different methods of bringing it about, but they so disciplined the body and nourished the soul that it could exercise freely and fully its essential faculty of perception. They maintained, then, that all existence in its real essence could be perceived by it, from the highest to the lowest. But the soul must be directed by uprightness, otherwise its perceptions would be distorted, as in a convex or concave mirror, like those of magicians, Christians, etc.[1] Apparently the meaning is that by fasting and solitude anyone's soul could be enabled to see the spiritual world, but only the upright soul would see it perfectly.

[1] The Christian editors of the Beyrout edition omit "Christians" here.

Then these Ṣūfīs passed from regarding their method as a discipline of the soul, to treating it as a means of reaching a knowledge of the true nature of things. That is, from being psychological and ethical, it becomes metaphysical. In a later edition of his book[1] Ibn Khaldūn inserted at this point a long passage upon this, and especially upon the relation of God to his creatures. It is much more theological than psychological, so I shall give little of it here. The traditional attitude, that of the fathers, was that God and his creation were absolutely separate. That, of course, introduced logical difficulties, and the scholastic theologians came in time to teach that God was neither separate from nor joined to his creation. The philosophers held that he was neither outside the world, nor within it; and the later Ṣūfīs that he was identified (*muttaḥid*) with created beings, either by fusion (*ḥulūl*) in them, or because these beings were he himself, and did not contain, either in whole or in part, anything except him. "Separation" he then goes on to discuss in its two aspects of separation in place and separateness as to essence, individuality, existence, attributes. The opposite of the latter is unification (*ittiḥād*). This last, in different phases, was the view of many Ṣūfīs.

Some of these explain—but their explanation, according to Ibn Khaldūn, is obscure to a degree,

[1] De Slane's translation, Vol. III, p. 93.

and the matter evidently cannot be expressed in ordinary language—that all things are appearances, which emanate in a certain order from God. They go back to a saying of Allāh's which they allege, "I was a concealed treasure, and I desired that I might be known; so I created the creatures that they might know me." The scheme is evidently one of Plotinian emanation, beginning with the realities in the world of ideas, and these gradually realizing themselves as the spheres, and so down to the elemental world when they become individuals and appearances. This is called the "self-revealing" (*tajallà*) of Allāh, and is only really intelligible through the mystical contemplation, which sees all things in God, as it sees God in all things.[1]

But another school of Ṣūfīs laid weight on the idea of absolute unity. The multiplicity which we see around us springs from man's multiple senses. Just as there would be no color if there were no light, so the existence of all perceptible things depends on the existence of senses perceiving them, that is of percipient beings. This, you will observe, is exactly Berkeley's position, that the *esse* of a thing is its *percipi*. Eliminate, then, all perceptions and all beings return to one unity. That is God, who is spread through all beings and unites them without direction or appearance or form or substance. To

[1] Cf. the article on ʿAbd al-Razzāḳ in the *Encyclopaedia of Islām*, Vol. I, pp. 61 ff.

this theory, Ibn Khaldūn makes some "common-sense" objections, but finally urges that according to the Ṣūfīs themselves the mystical perception of the unity is only a stage. The neophyte must pass through this; and to go beyond it is hard; but when he does, he comes to a farther stage where he can again distinguish between beings, and finds them no longer swallowed in oneness.

But these conceptions have undoubtedly had great influence. So, too, has the Ismāᶜīlite and Shīᶜite belief that there is at all times in this world some representative of God, whose right it is to rule, teach, and guide his people. To this Ibn Khaldūn traces the development of the doctrine of the hierarchy of saints, from the Axis down, which I have already described; but as a good Sunnite, he, of course, rejects the Shīᶜite view. All of it is comparatively recent; he cannot find that it was professed by the older Ṣūfīs.

Ibn Khaldūn finally divides the general Ṣūfī position under four heads: (1) the discipline of the soul; the keeping it to strict account for actions; the tastes of bliss and the ecstasies which come upon it; its ascent from one spiritual stage to another; (2) the unveiling of the unseen world and the perception therein of spiritual things, of the real natures of things, and how they proceed thence; (3) control of material things by the grace of God; (4) those wild, fanciful expressions which many of them utter in ecstasy, the literal meaning of which gives no clue to the real meaning.

To the first, the discipline of the soul, no one can take the slightest objection. That way lies the very essence of eternal salvation. Nor to the third, the miracles of the saints, can any objection be taken, provided they are carefully distinguished, which is easy, from the miracles of the prophets. The existence of these wonders is absolutely certain, and was approved by the Companions. As to the second, the unveiling of the unseen world, the case is more complicated. The most of what they say is like the "obscure" verses in the *Qur'ān*. It is uttered in ecstasy, and he who is not in ecstasy cannot understand it. The words used give no clue to what they mean, for words are conventional signs for known things, and these things are not known. You will remember here Occam's form of Nominalism. It is better, therefore, to let these sayings alone, as we let alone the "obscure" passages in the *Qur'ān*. He to whom God has given knowledge of the meaning of any of these sayings, in a way which agrees with the plain sense of the faith, may say, "How noble they are for eternal salvation!" In this, you will not fail to observe precisely the phenomena of "speaking with tongues," yet with one curious difference. Here there were no "tongues;" they spoke their own language, and hence the frequent scandal. It is very probable, however, that they used qur'ānic expressions, and these, especially if they were non-Arabic speakers by race, would have a haze of vagueness and possibility over them.

But the matter went even farther. In the fourth place, the Ṣūfīs themselves recognized a class of utterances which they called *shaṭaḥāt*, "overflowings in ecstasy as of drunkenness"—all that is in the etymology and usage of the root—which were metaphorical expressions used by them when self-control had been lost. For these they were held to account and blamed by the canonists. Ibn Khaldūn thinks that in justice we should consider the following points. First, if they are people of known goodness and an evermastering ecstasy has fallen upon them to express which there is no fixed language, then they should not be blamed for using language unsuitable for other people and conditions. We may take for granted that such people do not think of it in the blasphemous sense. But, secondly, if they are not people of known goodness, a doubt may enter. And, thirdly, if they use such language when not in a state of ecstasy but in control of themselves and aware of what they say, they are plainly to be held accountable. Finally, Ibn Khaldūn agreed with the older Ṣūfīs in holding that all such attempts to get behind the veil and to comprehend the whole nature of things and all talkings about such perceptions should be repressed. The knowledge of God is too wide, and his creation too great to be so comprehended; and to cling to the guidance of God's law is best.

I now turn to some concrete examples of this religious life; and I take up first the case for which we have the fullest and most reliable data. It is that of al-Ghazzālī, who went through a well-marked and permanent conversion in 1095 A. D., spent the rest of his life, partly as a Ṣūfī wanderer, partly as a teacher of Ṣūfī theology, and died in 1111, leaving us an autobiography which is unique in Arabic for the keenness and fulness of its self-revelation. Unfortunately, he was beset by the utilitarianism of Islām, and so could not be content to let his book stand for itself as a human document, nor even as an *apologia pro vita sua.* He must needs make out of it a manual of apologetics suited to his time, and thus, undoubtedly, has dulled the personal touch. In so doing he has furnished perhaps the most striking example of the fatal Muslim didacticism which does not permit an artist, conscious or unconscious, to set a living figure before the reader and leave it to do its work, but must systematize and explain everything. In this the Muslim writers differ markedly from the poets of heathen Arabia who had a frank delight in the simple expression of themselves without thought of their audience.

But, for all this, al-Ghazzālī's book is unique, and

I must now put before you considerable extracts from it. It has been used already, you may remember, as the standard Muslim example of conversion by Mr. William James, in his *Varieties of Religious Experience.* He wrote it late in life, when he was more than fifty (lunar) years old, and only a few years before his early death. But from his first youth searching to know reality had been a passion with him, and he recognized that this passion belonged to a nature planted in him by God. It was not any choice of his own which made him keep on seeking. He means, I think, that there is nothing sinful or unnatural in such an attitude. From his early youth, then, he could no longer believe simply because he was taught so. He looked round and saw that other children were taught differently—Jews or Christians—and they grew up Jews or Christians. But there is a tradition that the Prophet said, "Every child is born a Muslim by nature, then his parents make him a Jew or a Christian or a Magian." So he was moved to ask what was the essence of this fundamental nature, and what the essence of the opposing traditional creeds taught by parents and teachers, and how he could distinguish between these traditional, accepted views, seeing that their beginnings were simple dictations and there was much contradiction in distinguishing between the true of them and the false:

So I said to myself [he goes on[1]], what I want is knowledge of the real natures only of things. I must ask, therefore, what is the essence of knowledge. It seemed to me, then, that certain knowledge is that which uncovers the thing known in such a way that there does not remain with it any doubt, nor accompany it the possibility of error or illusion, nor can the mind conceive such. Security from error must accompany the certain to such a degree that if the claim of ability to show its falsity is made by someone, for example, who can turn a stone into gold or a staff into a serpent, that would not produce any doubt or denial. For when I know that ten is more than three, if someone says to me, "No, but three is more than ten, and I will prove it by changing this staff into a serpent," and he does change it, and I see him do it, I do not doubt what I know because of that; and the only result for me is wonder as to how he can do such a thing, but never any doubt as to what I know.

Then I knew that everything which I did not know in this fashion, and of the certainty of which I was not assured in this way, was a kind of knowledge in which there could be neither trust nor surety, and knowledge with which no trust goes is no certain knowledge. So I examined all the things which I knew, and found that I had no knowledge which could be described in this way, except sense-perceptions and necessary intuitive knowledge. Then, after despairing, I said, "There is no hope of getting to the dubious except through the clear, that is through sense-perceptions and necessary intuitive knowledge. So I must test these first, that it may be clear to me whether my trust in objects of perception and my security from error in necessary knowledge is of the same kind as my trust which I had formerly in traditional knowledge and the trust which the most of men have in reasoned knowledge; or is a certified trust without treachery or limit."

[1] *Al-Munqidh min aḍ-ḍalāl,* edition of Cairo, A. H. 1303, p. 4.

So I turned zealously to consider the objects of sense and necessary knowledge, and to try whether I could bring myself to doubt them. And doubt reached the point with me, that I could not permit myself to extend trust even to objects of the senses. Doubt as to them kept spreading, and I said, "How can you be sure of objects of sense, while the strongest of the senses is vision, and it looks at a shadow and sees the shadow standing unmoved and judges that there is no motion. Then, by test and observation after a time, it knows that the shadow does move, and not suddenly but gradually, bit by bit, never standing still. And it looks at a star and sees that star small as a gold piece, but geometry proves that it is greater than the earth. In such cases, then, the senses decide in one way but reason in another; it gives the lie and accuses of deceit in a way which cannot be answered."

So I said, "My trust in the objects of the senses, too, is gone; perhaps there can be no trust save in those intellectual results which are axiomatic, as our saying that ten is more than three, or that negation and affirmation cannot exist together in one thing, and that a thing cannot be both created and eternal *a parte ante*, existent and non-existent, necessary and impossible." But the objects of the senses said, "What assurance have you that your trust in conclusions of reason is not like your trust in the objects of the senses? You used to trust in me; then came the test of the reason and gave me the lie, and if it had not been for the test of reason you would have gone on believing me. Then, perhaps, behind the perceptions of the reason there is another test; whenever it appears reason will be given the lie by it, just as reason appeared and gave sense the lie. That such a perception has not appeared does not prove its impossibility."[1]

At an answer to this my soul somewhat paused and justified

[1] The confusion here between singular and plural, sense and its results, is in the original also.

her confusion by alleging the phenomena of dreaming. She said, "Do not you see that in sleep you believe in certain things, and you imagine conditions and believe that they have reality and fixity, and in that state you do not doubt them? Then you wake up, and you know that to all your imaginations and beliefs there was neither foundation nor use. Then, how are you sure that all which in your waking-time you believe in, because of either sense or reason, is not fact simply in relationship to your then condition? But it is possible that a condition may surprise you, the relationship of which to your waking-state is like the relationship of your waking-state to your dreams; and your waking-state is a sleep in relation to it. Then, whenever that condition comes upon you, you will be assured that all which you have vainly imagined by your reason consists of baseless phantoms only. Or, perhaps, that condition is what the Ṣūfīs claim to be their condition; since they assert that they have open soul-perception in their states, which come when they plunge into their souls and are apart from their physical senses, of certain states which do not agree with those results of reason. Or, perhaps that condition is death, since the Prophet said, 'Mankind are asleep, and when they die, they are aroused.' So, perhaps, the life of this world is a sleep, in relation to the other world; and when a man dies, things appear to him which are opposed to what he observes now. Then it will be said to him, 'We have uncovered from thee thy veil, and thy sight, today, is piercing.' "[1]

When these thoughts came to me, a deep impression was made upon me, and I desired some treatment against them, but it was not easy. They could be refuted only by means of proof; and no proof can be set up, except by combining primary facts of knowledge; but when these are not granted, a proof cannot be put together. This disease troubled me and

[1] *Qur.* l, 21.

remained with me almost two months. During that time, I was an absolute sceptic in mind, if not in statement.

At length God healed me of that disease, and my soul returned to health and balance, and the necessary intellectual truths came back, accepted and certain. That was not by means of a proof or by any form of words; but by a light which God cast into my breast. That light is the key of the most of knowledge; and whoever believes that the mystical unveiling is based upon abstract proofs narrows the wide mercy of God. When the apostle was asked what was the meaning of "opening," in the saying of God, "Whom God wills to guide, he opens his breast to Islām,"[1] he said, "It is light which God throws into the heart." And when he was asked, "And what is its sign?" he said, "Removing from the abode of deceit and return to the abode of eternity." About this same thing the Prophet said, "God Most High created his creatures in darkness; then he sprinkled upon them some of his light." It is from that light that the unveiling ought to be sought, and that light is cast forth suddenly out of the divine bounty on certain occasions, and should be watched for; as the Prophet said, "Lo, in the days of your earthly life, thy Lord hath outbreathings; be ready to meet them." And the point of all these narratives is to show that all diligence should be used in seeking, until that is reached which was not sought. Fundamental conceptions cannot be sought, for they are with us. And if that which is with us is sought, it cannot be found, and vanishes. He who seeks what is not sought cannot be suspected of falling short in seeking what is sought.

When, then, God healed me of this disease, by his grace and wide bounty, I observed that the different kinds of seekers around me divided into four classes. There were the scholastic theologians who claimed to be guided by judgment and

[1] *Qur.* vi, 125.

discussion. There were the allegorists [holders of an inner meaning] who asserted that they possessed a doctrine of their own, and that they were distinguished from others in that they learned from an infallible Head. There were the philosophers, who asserted that they followed logic and absolute proof. And there were the Ṣūfīs, who claimed that they were distinguished by being in the presence of God, and that they possessed immediate soul-perception and unveiling.

Then I said to myself, "The truth must needs lie with one of these four, for these are they who walk the paths of the seeking of the truth. If, then, the truth is hidden from them, there remains no hope of success in gaining it. For there is no hope in returning to a traditional faith, after it has once been abandoned, since the essential condition in the holder of a traditional faith is that he should not know that he is a traditionalist. Whenever he knows that, the glass of his traditional faith is broken. That is a breaking that cannot be mended and a separating that cannot be united by any sewing or putting together, except it be melted in the fire and given another new form."

Al-Ghazzālī now turns to a discussion of these different pathways to truth, one after the other. It is here that his desire to write a manual of apologetics interferes most with the value of his book as an autobiographical revelation of himself. We can hardly believe that he worked through these different schools in the calm and orderly fashion which he now sets down. But in the putting together of this systematized search for truth, it is perfectly clear that he is simply arranging, in what he thinks is logical form, the experiences which had come to him, broken and irregularly, in the life of his soul.

There can be no question, for example, that his strange drop into absolute skepticism and his recovery, not by argument but through the wideness of God's mercy, are narrated as they actually took place. Similarly, as we now turn to his account of his experiences on the path of the Ṣūfīs, we shall not, I think, have any doubt that here, too, there is a genuine page from his inner life.

That this was his first acquaintance with Ṣūfī methods, I do not think. Nor that he had not, himself, in earlier life, experimented in their practices. As a young man, he had evidently experimented in everything, and later had found everything vain. You will remember, for example, the story of his dream, which I have already given,[1] and of the advice of his shaykh to him. I find it hard to put that dream in his life, after his conversion, and, therefore, feel compelled to believe that he is now returning to ground already trodden.

His second trial of Ṣūfīism he describes as follows:[2]

Then I gave my attention to the path of the Ṣūfīs. I knew that their path could be complete only by means of both theory and practice. On the side of theory, its result is climbing the steep ascent of the soul and removing from the soul its blameworthy characteristics and qualities, until one may attain by it to being alone in the mind with God, and to the adornment of the mind with the constant thought of God.

[1] *Supra*, p. 92.

[2] P. 28 of text cited above.

Now the theory of it was easier to me than its practice. So I began to acquire it by the study of their books [al-Ghazzālī here gives a list of several] until I had reached the summit of their theoretical objects and had learned as much of their path as could be gained by studying and hearing about it.

It was plain to me that it was impossible to attain the most characteristic elements by study; these called for experience [*dhawq*] and state [*ḥāl*] and change in one's qualities. How great a difference there is between one who knows the definition of health and the definition of satiety and the causes and conditions of both, and one who is in health and is satisfied! Or between one who knows the definition of drunkenness, that it is an expression for a condition which results from vapors which ascend from the stomach to the abodes of thought, gaining control of them, and one who is actually drunk! He who is drunk does not know the definition and science of drunkenness; he is drunk and has no knowledge at all. The sober man knows the definition of drunkenness and its elements, and yet nothing of drunkenness is with him. A physician, again, when he is ill, knows the definition of health and its causes and its remedies, although he is lacking in health. Similar is the distinction between knowing the nature, the conditions, and the causes of self-restraint, and having, as your condition, self-restraint, and the keeping of the soul from the world.

So I knew, of a certainty, that to the Ṣūfīs, states and not definitions were of importance; and that I had got all that could be got by way of learning; that what was left could not be reached by hearing and studying, but only by experience and the following of a certain course of action.

From the sciences which I had studied and the ways which I had gone in searching out the kinds of sciences, both religious and intellectual, I had attained to an assured belief in God and in prophecy and in the Last Day. These three fundamentals of faith were fixed in my soul, not by an abstract, definite proof, but by connections and associations and experiences, all the elements of which cannot be put in short. It had become plain to me that I had no hope of attaining to the salvation of the world to come except by piety and the restraint of the soul from lust; and that the beginning of all that must be the cutting of the ties of the heart to this world, the abode of deceit, and the return to the abode of eternity; and by striving toward God with absoluteness of purpose.

That, too, I knew, could not be completely carried out, except by turning away from ambition and wealth and by flight from entanglements and restraint. I looked at my conditions, and lo, I was plunged in restraints which sur-sounded me on all sides. I looked at my works; the best of them were studying and teaching; and lo, in them, I was striving after knowledge that was unimportant and useless with regard to the world to come. Then I considered my purpose in studying; and lo, it was not purely for the sake of seeing the face of God, but its inciter and mover was the search for repute and for the spread of renown.

I became assured that I was upon the extremity of a crumbling edge, and was looking down into the Fire, if I did not turn and amend my state. So I continued meditating upon that for a time, and, having still freedom of choice, one day, I would fix my resolve upon going away from Baghdād and separating myself from those conditions, and another day I would relax that resolution. I would put forward one foot and draw back the other. I could not have a pure desire of seeking the world to come in the morning, without the army of lust making an attack and breaking it in the evening. The lusts of the world kept dragging me by their chains to abiding; and the crier of faith kept proclaiming, "Journeying! journeying! there remaineth not of life, save a little.

The long journey is before thee; and all that thou are doing, of labor and of knowledge, is a vain phantom. If thou dost not prepare thyself now for the world to come, when wilt thou prepare thyself? And if thou wilt not cut thy ties now, when wilt thou cut them?" Thereupon my desire would be aroused and my purpose fixed. But the devil would return and say, "This is an accidental condition; beware lest thou heed it, for it will pass swiftly; and if thou obeyest it, and abandonest this ample honor and settled position, free from perturbation and embitterment and this conceded authority, clear of hostile strife, perhaps thy soul would have adjusted itself to it and return will not be easy to thee."

So I continued swaying between the attractions of the lusts of this world and the summons of the other world almost six months, the first of which was Rajab, A. H. 488. In that month, the matter passed the bound of choice to compulsion, in that God locked my tongue till it was bound so that I could not teach. I would put pressure upon myself to teach a single day, in order to satisfy certain persons, but could not bring my tongue to utter a word. Then, this laming of my tongue brought upon me a sorrow in my mind; my digestion and desire for food and drink were destroyed; I could not swallow a drop nor digest a mouthful. My strength began to fail, and the physicians despaired of my cure. "This is a mental trouble," they said, "which has come to affect the physical organization, and it can be healed only by rest of the mind from the care which has befallen it." Then, feeling my weakness and giving up entirely my own will, I took refuge with God, as one under necessity and with no resource left. And he, "Who answers the driven when he calls,"[1] answered me and made easy to me my turning away from ambition and wealth and family and companions.

Al-Ghazzālī goes on to tell how he managed to

[1] *Qur.* xxvii, 63.

extricate himself from his impossible position at Baghdād at the court of the Khalīfa. He used as a pretext that he wished to go on a pilgrimage to Mecca, although his real intention was to go to Syria and stay there, immersing himself in the ascetic and contemplative life of the Ṣūfīs. Apparently, his departure caused as great a commotion as if some distinguished professor with us, or a bishop, perhaps, were to announce that he had at last been converted and had determined to abandon the world. In the church of Rome such a man would enter a monastic order; in Protestantism I fear that there would be no place for him. Al-Ghazzālī became a wandering Ṣūfī monk. He went to Syria, and spent there almost two years in retirement and solitude. He passed through the Ṣūfī religious exercises, purifying his mind and heart, laboring with his failings in character, and giving himself entirely to the thought of God. After a time, the desire that he might really make the pilgrimage to Mecca rose in him; the clouds had passed from him and his religious life was again normal. It was as though a man with us had withdrawn from the communion of the Lord's Supper, and had again found his way back. So he went to Mecca and performed his religious duties there, and was drawn gradually again into the current of events. For ten years his life was divided between the cultivation of his own soul and caring for others in the world. The cares and ties of the world, the necessities of life, and the prayers of his children, now drew him back; his yearning for the communion and peace of the mystic now drove him into the solitudes. So the years passed:

And [he said[1]] there were revealed to me in the course of these periods of solitude things which cannot be numbered nor exhausted. The amount which I mention now, for the benefit of others, is that I know of a certainty that the Ṣūfīs only follow the path to God; that their mode of life is the best of modes, and their path the most sure of paths, and their characteristics the purest of characteristics. If the intellectual with their intellect and the learned with their wisdom and students of the mysteries of the divine law with their knowledge were to join to alter anything of the Ṣūfī mode of life or its characteristics, or to exchange these for something better, they would find no way of doing that.

All actions of the Ṣūfīs, whether of movement or of rest, whether internal or external, are derived from the light of the lamp of prophecy. And other than the light of prophecy there is none on the face of the earth from which illumination can be sought. In a word, whatever is said as to their pure path is so. Its first condition is a cleansing of the mind entirely from all that is not God. Its key of entrance—just like the first cry of prayer, which means that all else is now unlawful—is the plunging of the mind totally in God. But that is its end only as to what comes under free will and acquisition from its beginnings; it is really only the beginning of the path, and what comes before it is like a vestibule. From the beginning of the path, unveilings and clear soul-perceptions begin; and the traveler therein, while awake, sees angels and the souls of prophets, and hears their voices,

[1] P. 32 of text cited above.

and learns from them. Then his spiritual condition advances from witnessing of forms and similitudes to stages where the limit of language is too narrow, and no rendering in words is possible, for such expression would contain manifest errors, against which there could be no guarding. A point of nearness to God is reached which some have thought to render as *ḥulūl*, "fusion of being;" some as *ittiḥād*, "identification;" and some as *wuṣūl*, "union." But all these expressions contain error, and he who is in that condition ought not to say more than the poet:

And there happened what happened of that which I mention not;
So think of a good thing, and ask not concerning the Good.[1]

He who has not been granted actual experience of anything of this, can know of the essence of prophecy only the name. The miracles (*karāmāt*) of the saints are in reality the beginnings of prophets. That was, too, the first condition of the Prophet when he went to Mount Ḥirā, and was alone there with his Lord, engaged in religious exercises, until the Arabs said, "Muḥammad is passionately in love with his Lord." Whoever follows the Ṣūfīs in their course can verify this condition by experience, [*dhawq*] and whoever is not granted actual experience can be assured of it by the test of listening. If he consorts much with them, he will understand that as a certainty through their circumstances. He who companies with them will gain from them their faith; for they are not such that their companion can be lost. But he who cannot company with them, let him know assuredly the possibility of that of which we have been speaking by certain proofs, such as we have laid down in the *Book of the Marvels of the Heart.*[2] Verification, then, by proof is knowledge; having intimate contact with the essence of that condition is

[1] Or, perhaps, "So think a report, and ask not concerning the report."

[2] Translated below, pp. 220 ff.

experience; receiving on the test of listening, with approval, is faith; these are three stages.

On this basis, then, al-Ghazzālī would put the proof of the fact of prophecy. The soul witnesses to it, either by absolute experience of strictly similar phenomena, or by first-hand observation of the existence of such similar phenomena, or by certain proofs which I hope to take up later. The basis of it all is, therefore, what the Ṣūfīs call "states." The word is a puzzling one to translate, and must be rendered differently in different contexts. Primarily, it means only a psychological condition, arising without effort or apparent cause, as opposed to results of reasoning. It is feeling, as opposed to reason; an immediate consciousness, as opposed to derivative knowledge.[1]

The data of such phenomena of the inner life were for al-Ghazzālī and his school, that is practically for al-Islām after him, the only certain basis for religious faith and knowledge. He never really abandoned

[1] Ibn ᶜArabī, the great western mystic, thus distinguishes: "Knowledge is of three grades: (*a*) rational, any knowledge axiomatic or as a consequence of consideration of a proof under the condition of stumbling on what that proof means; (*b*) knowledge of 'states;' these are reached only by 'tasting' and the merely intellectual man cannot know this or get to it by a proof; such is knowledge of the sweetness of honey, the bitterness of aloes, of emotion and longing; he only who has experienced these can know them; (*c*) knowledge of the secrets; it is above the sphere of reason and is a knowledge breathed into the mind by the Holy Spirit; it is peculiar to prophets and saints; by it they take mysteriously all knowledge to themselves" (Comm. on *Iḥyā*, Vol. VII, p. 245).

his skeptical position as to the results of reason; and, in fact, he tended to ascribe all human knowledge more or less directly to revelation either through prophets or saints. For him, as for Ibn Khaldūn, philosophy was bankrupt, and he retained only so much trust in reason as to enable him dialectically to destroy the possibility of a metaphysical system, on the one hand, and to establish the authority of psychological states, on the other. In the revelation of man's emotional nature, not in the results of his reason, lie fact and certainty; for, on that side, there is a spark in man of the divine nature; but reason is a mere utilitarian drudge, limited to a narrow round, and beyond that to be distrusted. Further, the Ṣūfīs used the word "states" to indicate also those conditions of joy or sorrow, elation or depression, which descend upon the heart of the devotee in constant change. And as a last development, a "state," in the highest sense, is a state of ecstasy when the devotee has passed out of himself, is unconscious of the world, and conscious only of God. But none of these could be controlled by the will; the spirit came and went. As with the Scholar Gypsy, "it took heaven-sent moments for that skill." Yet this "skill" was man's only guide. That it was unto this last that the church of Islām came, in spite of the crass and, one might almost say, materialistic monotheism of Muḥammad, is one of the strangest developments in all the history of religion. The wheel came full circle and seems now nailed in its place.

Another word worthy of notice is that which I have rendered above "experience." Literally, it means "taste," and is either the act of tasting, or the taste itself. Then it has various derived applications; tasting in any way; taste in language and literature; tasting the savor of the divine truth or essence in the soul; all such soul-experiences.

In accordance with the above al-Ghazzālī gives in the following words his final results as to the nature of man and the character of man's intercourse with the unseen world:[1]

Then, after I had persevered in withdrawal from the world, and in the solitary life for almost ten years, there became plain to me and certain, in the course of that, by innumerable causes—at one time by spiritual experience, at another time by demonstrative knowledge, and at another time by acceptance on faith—that man is created with a body and with a heart. I mean by "heart" his spiritual essence which is the *locus* of the knowledge of God, as opposed to the flesh-and-blood organ in which dead bodies and the lower animals share. Further, it became plain to me that as the body has a health in which is its happiness and a sickness in which is its destruction, so the heart, similarly, has a health and a soundness (none is saved "except he who cometh to God with a sound heart"[2]) and a sickness, in which is its eternal destruction for the world to come, as God hath said, "In their hearts is a sickness."[3] That ignorance with regard

[1] P. 38 of the *Munqidh*.

[2] *Qur.* xxvi, 89.

[3] *Ibid.*, ii, 9.

to God is a destroying poison; and that disobedience of God, through following the lusts, is the heart's grievous ailment; that knowledge of God is its reviving remedy, and obedience to God in opposition to the lusts is its healing medicine; that there is no way of treating it, to do away with its disease and to gain for it health, except by medicines; just as there is no way of treating the body, except by the same.

And just as the medicines for the body produce an effect in gaining health through a property in them, to which the intellect cannot attain, but with regard to which physicians must be believed who have learned that property from the prophets who, in turn, came to know the properties of things, through the prophetic property, so it became plain to me that the intellect could not attain to the mode of the working of the medicines of the heart, which are exercises of devotion, in their definitions and amounts, defined and prescribed by the prophets, but that, with regard to this, the prophets must be followed who attained unto these properties by the light of prophecy and not by means of reason. And just as medicines are made up of kind and amount, and some are double of others in weight and amount; and as in the difference of these amounts there lies a secret belonging to their properties; so acts of devotion which are the medicine of the disease of the heart are compounded of actions, differing in kind or amount, as "prostration" is double of "bowing," and the prayer of the dawn is half the prayer of the afternoon in amount; and in this there is a certain secret belonging to the properties, which cannot be learned except by the light of prophecy.

Those, therefore, have been most foolish who have desired by means of reason to discover for those things a law, or have imagined that they were so given by accident—not on account of a secret in them which required them, by way of this property. And just as in medicines there are bases which are fundamental and additions which are supplemental, every one of which has peculiar effects on the working of the bases, so supererogatory acts of devotion and usage are complements completing the effects of the basal acts of devotion.

In a word, the prophets are the physicians of the diseases of hearts; and the only use and authority for reason is that it should teach us this, and should bear witness to the truth of prophecy and to its own inability to attain to what the eye of prophecy can reach, and that it should take us by our hands and commit us to prophecy, as the blind are committed to their guides and the sick to their physicians. This is the work and the bound of reason, and beyond this it may not go, except to make known what the physician has taught it. These things I learned with the assurance of absolute perception in the course of my solitude and my retirement from the world.

Thus does al-Ghazzālī build an ingenious defense of the mechanical details of the Muslim ritual law upon his agnostic theory of knowledge. I shall come back, later, to his *Science of the Heart*, but, in the mean time, must leave him with one remark. The exercises by which, in his case, the ecstatic state was induced, seem to have been of a simply devotional and personal character. We have no details of his pursuing them at this time under the special guidance of a shaykh, although, during his earlier life, we have already seen him working under such influence. Thus, with him, if there was any hypnotism in the case, it must have been exercised by himself. It is significant that the course of preparation through which he went as a young man, under the personality of a teacher, came to nothing and left him capable of absolute unbelief. His real conversion, as we have seen it, sprang from within himself, and was induced or fostered by no foreign influence.

Of the reality of the change in him there can be no question. His own modesty as to the rank in saintḥood which he had reached is significant. So the following story has great psychological probability, as it evidently describes his effort to free his mind from the burden of all his legal and theological studies, and to present it as a *tabula rasa* to the new impressions. A later mystic tells it:

Al-Ghazzālī was wont to say, "When I wished to plunge into following the people [the Ṣūfīs] and to drink of their drink, I looked at my soul, and I saw how much it was curtained in"—at this time he had no shaykh—"so I retired into solitude and busied myself with religious exercises for forty days and there was doled to me of knowledge what I had not had, purer and finer than I had known. Then I looked upon it, and lo, in it was a legal element. So I returned to solitude and busied myself with religious exercises for forty days, and there was doled to me other knowledge, purer and finer than what had befallen me at first, and I rejoiced in it. Then I looked upon it, and lo, in it was a speculative element. So I returned to solitude a third time for forty days, and there was doled to me other knowledge; it was finer and purer. Then I looked on it, and lo, in it was an element mixed with a knowledge that is known [i. e., not simply perceived, felt], and I did not attain to the people of the inward sciences. So I knew that writing on a surface from which something has been erased is not like writing on a surface in its first purity and cleanness, and I never separated myself from speculation except in a few things." On this there is the remark, "May God have mercy on Abū- Ḥāmid al-Ghazzālī; how great was his justice and his guarding himself from any claim!"[1]

And here, finally, is a remark by an intimate friend which shows how much he was changed from the supercilious, self-confident scholar of his earlier life:

However much he met of contradiction and attack and slander, it made no impression on him, and he did not trouble himself to answer his assailants. I visited him many times, and it was no bare conjecture of mine that he, in spite of what I saw in him in time past of maliciousness and roughness toward people, and how he looked upon them contemptuously, through his being led astray by what God had granted him of ease, in word and thought and expression, and through the seeking of rank and position, had come to be the very opposite and was purified from these stains. And I used to think that he was wrapping himself in the garment of pretense, but I realized after investigation that the thing was the opposite of what I had thought, and that the man had recovered after being mad."[2]

[1] "Life" in *Journal of American Oriental Society*, Vol. XX, p. 90.

[2] *Op. cit.* p. 105.

LECTURE VII

SAINTS AND THE ASCETIC-ECSTATIC LIFE IN ISLĀM.—*Continued*

Our next example of the mystical life takes us to India under the Mogul emperors, during the reigns of Akbar, Jahāngīr, Shāh-Jahān, and Aurangzīb. Stretching through these reigns, there lived at Balkh, Cashmere, and Lahore, a saint of national celebrity, whose life, sayings and doings have been made public by von Kremer[1] on the absolutely first-hand evidence of a book written by an immediate disciple, who lived a curiously mixed life, in part as a Ṣūfī student, and in part as an official of rank at the Mogul court. The saint was Mollā-Shāh, who was born in Badakhshān in A. D. 1584; educated at Balkh and Lahore, received into the Qādirite order of darwīshes; became a pantheistic Ṣūfī, but went through the external rites of Islām in order not to offend the people; developed great personal magnetism by which he surrounded himself with many devoted disciples; lived through several attacks for heresy, and managed to conciliate even the puritan Aurangzīb; and died in the odor of sanctity at Lahore, in 1661. His disciple and biographer was Tawakkul Beg, whom as a young man he initiated into the mystical life and led to the

[1] *Journal asiatique*, February, 1869, p. 105.

point where he clearly perceived the inner light, the unity of all things, and himself vanishing, as an individual, in the One.

The interest in the account lies in the plain hypnotism employed and in the comparatively minor importance of devotional and ascetic exercises. It is true that Mollā-Shāh, himself, according to this account, had reached his own unveiling by such exercises, and without the hypnotic help of a teacher. But for his own pupils, he had discovered a simpler and shorter course, in which he used his will and personality to open, as the phrase is, the knot of their hearts. That method is described by Tawakkul Beg as applied to himself and some others. His absolute faith in his master and evident devotion to his memory make his narrative a very trustworthy document.

For a long time he found it difficult to prevail upon Mollā-Shāh to operate upon him. The master said that he recognized that the young man had a true vocation and that he was naturally saddened by seeing so many of his fellows admitted to the spiritual life. But if he were initiated, he would certainly abandon the public life, for which his father, who had no idea of mysticism, intended him. What answer could Mollā-Shāh give, if he made this old soldier's son a darwīsh? Finally, Tawakkul Beg cut the knot when his father left Kashmīr and sought to take his son with him. He ran away, returned to

Cashmere, and was at last received by Mollā-Shāh. He thus describes his initiation, which I translate from von Kremer's French rendering:

I passed all that night without being able to close an eye, and set myself to recite the one hundred and twelfth chapter of the *Qur'ān* one hundred thousand times, which I accomplished in some days. It is well known that the Great Name of God is contained in that chapter, and that by the power of that name, whoever reads it one hundred thousand times is able to attain accomplishment of all his desires. So I formed a wish that the master would grant me his affection, and, as a matter of fact, I convinced myself of the efficiency of this means. For scarcely had I finished reciting that chapter for the one hundred thousandth time, when the heart of the master was filled with sympathy with me, and he gave orders to Senghin Muḥammad, his representative [*vicaire*, in von Kremer's French], to conduct me, the following night, into his presence. During that entire night he concentrated his mind upon me, while I directed my thought toward my own heart; but the knot of my heart did not open.

So three nights passed, during which he made me the object of his spiritual attention, without any effect being felt. On the fourth night, Mollā-Shāh said, "This night, Mollā-Senghin and Ṣāliḥ Beg, who are both very open to ecstatic emotion, will direct all their mind on the neophyte." They obeyed this order, while I remained sitting, the whole night, with my face turned toward Mecca, concentrating, at the same time, all my mental faculties upon my own heart. Toward the dawn, some little light and clearness showed themselves in my heart; but I was not able to distinguish either color or form.

After the morning prayers, I went with the two persons whom I have just named, to the master who saluted me and asked them what they had made of me. They replied, "Ask himself." He then turned to me and asked me to tell him my experiences. I said to him that I had perceived a clearness in my heart; whereupon the shaykh brightened and said to me, "Thy heart contains an infinity of colors; but it has become so dark that the gaze of these two crocodiles of the infinite ocean [of mystical knowledge] have not been able to give it either brightness or transparency. The moment is come when I myself must show how it is clarified."

Thereupon, he made me sit before him, my senses being as though intoxicated, and ordered me to reproduce his own image within myself; and, after having bandaged my eyes, he asked me to concentrate all my mental faculties on my heart. I obeyed, and in an instant, by the divine favor and by the spiritual assistance of the shaykh, my heart opened. I saw, then, that there was something like an overturned cup within me. This having been set upright, a sensation of unbounded happiness filled my being. I said to the master, "This cell, where I am seated before you—I see a faithful reproduction of it within me and it appears to me as though another Tawakkul Beg were seated before another Mollā-Shāh." He replied, "Very good! The first apparition which appears to thee is the image of the master. Thy companions [the other novices] have been prevented by other mystical exercises; but, as far as regards myself, this is not the first time that I have met such a case." He then ordered me to uncover my eyes; and I saw him, then, with the physical organ of vision, seated before me. He then made me bind my eyes again, and I perceived him with my spiritual sight, seated similarly before me. Full of astonishment, I cried out, "O Master! whether I look with my physical organs or with my spiritual sight, always it is you that I see."

After these things, I saw advancing toward me a dazzling figure, and when I had told the master of it, he directed me to ask the apparition its name. I addressed to it that question, in my mind, and the figure replied in the voice of the heart, "My name is ᶜAbd al-Qādir al-Jīlānī." I heard this answer with my spiritual ear. The master then counseled me to pray the saint to accord to me his spiritual assistance and succor. When I had asked this, the apparition said to me, "I have already granted to thee my spiritual assistance; it is by it that the knots of thy heart have been opened." Filled with profound gratitude, I undertook the duty of reciting every Friday night the whole *Qur'ān* in honor of this great saint, and during two entire years, I never neglected that usage. Mollā-Shāh then said to me, "The spiritual world has been shown to thee in all its beauty. Remain, then, seated, effacing thyself entirely in the marvels of that unknown world."

I conformed strictly to the directions of my master; and from day to day the spiritual world was opened further before me. The day following, I saw the figures of the Prophet and of his principal Companions, and of legions of angels and of saints pass before my inner sight. Three months went by in this manner, after which the sphere where all color is effaced opened before me, and then all these images disappeared. During all this time the master did not cease to explain to me the doctrine of union with God and of mystical insight; but he was not willing to show me the absolute reality. It was not until after a year that the science of the absolute reality with regard to the conception of my own proper existence reached me. The following verses were revealed, in that moment, to my heart, whence they passed to my lips unconsciously:

I knew not that this perishable carcass was naught but water and clay.
I did not recognize either the faculties of the heart or of the soul, or of the body:

Unhappy am I that without Thee, so much of my life has passed.
Thou wast I, and I knew it not.

When I submitted to Mollā-Shāh this poetic inspiration, he rejoiced that the idea of union with God had at last been manifested to my heart; and, addressing his friends, he said, "Tawakkul Beg has heard from my mouth the words of the doctrine of the union with God, and he will never belie its secret. His inner sight has been opened; the sphere of colors and of images has been shown to him; and thereafter the sphere where all color is effaced has been revealed to him. Whoever, after having passed through all these phases of the union with God, has obtained the absolute reality, does not permit himself to be led again astray either by his own doubts or by those which skeptics can suggest."

How different this is from al-Ghazzālī's experience needs no saying. Here there is no ethical element; there is nothing but the stimulation of emotional religiosity with, so far as this narrative goes, no suggestion for conduct. The object is to reach a certain assurance of the existence of the Unseen and a direct knowledge as to the relation of the individual to that Unseen. If it were not that the operation is in terms of emotion and intuition purely, we might say that what is given here is a metaphysical basis for life. Perhaps Dr. Maxwell's "metapsychical" would again be the better term.

But, further, this is reached by most evident "suggestion" in the hypnotic sense. We can see, too, that the path along which the neophyte is led is a well-known one, with well-marked stages, as definite as in the development of an old-fashioned conversion.

The references to stages showing color and form and to a later one, where color vanishes, are interesting. In this case, their arrangement and sequence is not complicated, nor does it seem to be of a mechanical fixedness. But that also was found, and some Ṣūfī teachers held that the neophyte passed through seven stages of purification, each marked by the appearance of a different colored light. Others rejected this entirely. Such lights might be met, they said, but it was a dangerous thing for the neophyte to pay too great attention to them. They belonged to the body, and did not come from the spiritual world. The elaborate classification of them, they argued, and the expectation of each of them at a definite stage was to universalize and to turn into a dogma the purely subjective and personal. You will find more on this matter in Fleischer's *Kleinere Schriften.*[1] His hope expressed then (in 1862) that others would take up the subject and study it further, has not, as regards Islām, so far as I know, been fulfilled. In the discussions, however, of late years, of the emotional religious life, such phenomena have occasionally been touched.[2]

[1] Vol. III, p. 440.

[2] See, for example, William James, *Varieties of Religious Experience*, p. 251, and *Proceedings of the Society for Psychical Research*, Part LI, p. 97 (the recent Welsh revival).

To return to Tawakkul Beg. He had now been initiated as a darwīsh into the Qādirite order, and might have passed the rest of his life in a cloister, or as a wandering ascetic. But no such vows hold the darwīsh back from return to the world as are binding in the monastic orders of the Roman church. And so, on his father's petition, addressed to Mollā-Shāh, Tawakkul Beg went back into the world, and passed ten years in the service of the state; yet not, as one might imagine, in any peaceful capacity, but as a soldier. Again he returned to his master, and spent more than a year with him, who, thereafter, again dismissed him, telling him that his profession was that of arms, and giving him a letter of introduction to Prince Dārā Shukōh, son of Shāh Jahān. With him he must have passed through the troublous days of the contest for the empire in the last years of Shāh Jahān's life, when Aurangzīb swung himself to power and Dārā Shukōh went down to absolute ruin and death.

But these changes have left no reflection in the story of Mollā-Shāh's influence as retold by von Kremer. The only danger for him seems to have lain in the incautious utterances, from time to time, of his disciples. These sometimes proclaimed too openly the doctrine of the absolute unity, and were naturally accused of heresy, or they carried out too logically its consequences, and neglected their ritual and even their moral duties. Islām has generally shown itself strangely tolerant toward both of these deviations; and, indeed, will permit anyone to say and do almost anything he pleases, if he only shows signs of clear religious frenzy. That we have already seen formally laid down by Ibn Khaldūn.[1] But occasionally the Muslim conscience becomes excited, or there is a scrupulous ruler who takes his position seriously, and then there is danger for free-thinkers and free-livers. Once, at least, Mollā-Shāh was saved from imminent danger by the friendship of Prince Dārā Shukōh, and on another occasion he had to temporize with Aurangzīb.

Descriptions are given by Tawakkul Beg of two other such hypnotic initiations, but they add little to Tawakkul's own narrative. One was that of Dārā Shukōh himself, who had the greatest difficulty in prevailing on Mollā-Shāh to operate on him. Another was that of Fāṭima, a sister of Dārā Shukōh, who had a long correspondence with the master; was initiated by her brother acting for him; passed through all the normal visions; and attained to pure union with God and intuitive perception. Mollā-Shāh said of her, "She has attained to so extraordinary a development of the mystical knowledge that she is worthy of being my representative."

She thus describes some of her experiences:

I seated myself, then, in a corner with my face turned toward Mecca, and concentrated all my mind on the image

[1] Cf. p. 173.

of the master, calling up, at the same time, in my imagination, the personal description of our most holy Prophet. Occupied with this contemplation, I arrived at a state of soul in which I neither slept nor waked, and then I saw the holy company of the Prophet and of his first adherents, with the other saints. The Prophet and his four friends [Abū Bakr, ᶜUmar, ᶜUthmān, and ᶜAlī] were seated together, and a certain number of the principal Companions surrounded him. I perceived also Mollā-Shāh; he was seated near the Prophet, upon whose foot his head lay, while the Prophet said to him, "O Mollā-Shāh, for what reason did you illumine that Tīmūrid?"

When my senses had returned to me, my heart, under the impression of this distinguished sign of the divine favor, bloomed like a bed of roses, and I prostrated myself, full of boundless gratitude, before the throne of the absolute Being. Filled with unutterable happiness, I did not know what to do to express all the joy of my heart. I vowed a blind obedience to the master, and I chose him, once for all, as my spiritual guide, saying, "O how signal a happiness! What an unheard of felicity has been given to me—to me, a feeble and unworthy woman! I render thanks and praises for it without end, to the All-powerful, to the incomprehensible God, who, when it seemed that my life must pass uselessly, permitted me to give myself to the search for him, and accorded to me, thereafter, to attain the desired end of union with him, giving me thus to drink of the ocean of truth and the fountain of mystical knowledge. I nourish the hope that God will permit me to walk with a firm step and unshakable courage on this path which is comparable to the *Ṣirāṭ* [here the narrow bridge to Paradise] and that my soul will always taste the supreme happiness of being able to think of him. God be praised, who, through the particular attention of the holy master, has accorded to me, a poor woman, the gift of conceiving, in the most complete manner, of the absolute Being, as I have always ardently desired. Whoever does not possess the knowledge of the absolute Being is not a man—he belongs to those of whom it is said, 'They are as the brutes, and more ignorant still.'[1] Every man who has attained this supreme felicity becomes, through this fact itself, the most accomplished and the most noble of beings, and his individual existence is lost in the absolute existence; he becomes like a drop in the ocean, a mote in the sunshine, an atom over against totality. Arrived in this state, he is above death, future punishment, the Garden, and the Fire. Whether he is man or woman, he is always the most perfect human being. This is a favor of God who dispenses it to whomsoever it seems to him good. The poet ᶜAttār has said of Rābiᶜa, 'This is not a woman but a man, absorbed as she is by the love of God.'"

You will now, I think, understand how there are women saints in Islām. In the ecstatic religious life only does the difference between the man and the woman drop away; both are simply human beings before their God. In that presence they are equal in virtue of the common human nature, though the woman can inherit only half that a man can, and can never divorce her husband. The distinction even of Roman Christendom, as I have pointed out above, that a woman cannot be a priest, does not exist for Islām. The relation between the princess Fāṭima and Mollā-Shāh was only that between pupil and teacher.

It would be easy to go on almost indefinitely with concrete examples of the mystical life; or, for it is the same thing, the devotional attitude in Islām.

[1] *Qur.* vii, 178.

But I will come down now to quite modern times and to a European observer. Edward William Lane, during his long residence in Cairo, entered as fully as any non-Muslim has ever done into the life and ideas of the people. In one of the notes to his *Arabian Nights*,[1] he gives the following account of a Cairo friend, and it will serve as an example of another type of the Muslim mystic, the wandering ascetic:

One of my friends in Cairo, Abu-l-Ḳásim of Geelán, mentioned in a former note, entertained me with a long relation of the mortifications and other means which he employed to attain the rank of a welee. These were chiefly self-denial and a perfect reliance upon Providence. He left his home in a state of voluntary destitution and complete nudity, to travel through Persia and the surrounding countries, and yet more distant regions if necessary, in search of a spiritual guide. For many days he avoided the habitations of men, fasting from daybreak till sunset, and then eating nothing but a little grass or a few leaves or wild fruits, till by degrees he habituated himself to almost total abstinence from every kind of nourishment. His feet, at first blistered and cut by hard stones, soon became callous; and in proportion to his reduction of food, his frame, contrary to the common course of nature, became (according to his own account) more stout and lusty. Bronzed by the sun, and with his black hair hanging over his shoulders (for he had abjured the use of the razor), he presented, in his nudity, a wild and frightful appearance; and on his first approaching a town, was surrounded and pelted by a crowd of boys; he therefore retreated, and, after the example of our first parents, made

[1] Vol. I, p. 210.

himself a partial covering of leaves; and this he always after did on similar occasions; never remaining long enough in a town for his leafy apron to wither. The abodes of mankind he always passed at a distance, excepting when several days' fast, while traveling an arid desert, compelled him to obtain a morsel of bread or a cup of water from the hand of some charitable fellow-creature. One thing that he particularly dreaded was, to receive relief from a sinful man, or from a demon in the human form. In passing over a parched and desolate tract, where for three days he had found nothing to eat, not even a blade of grass, nor a spring from which to refresh his tongue, he became overpowered with thirst, and prayed that God would send him a messenger with a pitcher of water. "But," said he, "let the water be in a green Baghdádee pitcher, that I may know it [to] be from thee, and not from the devil; and when I ask the bearer to give me to drink, let him pour it over my head, that I may not too much gratify my carnal desire." "I looked behind me," he continued, "and saw a man bearing a green Baghdádee pitcher of water, and said to him, 'Give me to drink;' and he came up to me and poured the contents over my head, and departed! By Allah it was so!" Rejoicing in this miracle, as a proof of his having attained to a degree of *wiláyeh* (or saintship), and refreshed by the water, he continued his way over the desert, more firm than ever in his course of self-denial, which, though imperfectly followed, had been the means of his being thus distinguished. But the burning thirst returned shortly after, and he felt himself sinking under it, when he beheld before him a high hill, with a rivulet running by its base. To the summit of this hill he determined to ascend, by way of mortification, before he would taste the water, and this point, with much difficulty, he reached at the close of the day. Here standing, he saw approaching, below, a troop of horsemen, who paused at the foot of the hill, when their chief, who was foremost, called out to him by name, "O Abu-l-Kásim! O Geelánee! Come down and drink!" but, persuaded by this that he was Iblees with a troop of his sons, the evil genii, he withstood the temptation, and remained stationary until the deceiver with his attendants had passed on, and were out of sight. The sun had then set; his thirst had somewhat abated; and he only drank a few drops. Continuing his wanderings in the desert, he found, upon a pebbly plain, an old man with a long white beard, who accosted him, asking him of what he was in search. "I am seeking," he answered, "a spiritual guide; and my heart tells me that thou art the guide I seek." "My son," said the old man, "thou seest yonder a saint's tomb; it is a place where prayer is answered; go thither, enter it, and seat thyself, neither eat nor drink nor sleep; but occupy thyself solely, day and night, in repeating silently, '*Lá iláha illa-lláh*' [there is no deity but God]; and let not any living creature see thy lips move in doing so; for among the peculiar virtues of these words is this, that they may be uttered without any motion of the lips. Go, and peace be on thee." "Accordingly," said my friend, "I went thither. It was a small square building, crowned by a cupola; and the door was open. I entered, and seated myself, facing the niche, and the oblong monument over the grave. It was evening, and I commenced my silent professions of the Unity, as directed by my guide; and at dusk I saw a white figure seated beside me, as if assisting in my devotional task. I stretched forth my hand to touch it; but found that it was not a material substance, yet there it was; I saw it distinctly. Encouraged by this vision, I continued my task for three nights and days without intermission, neither eating nor drinking, yet increasing in strength both of body and spirit; and on the third day, I saw written upon the whitewashed walls of the tomb, and on the ground, and in the air, wherever I turned my eyes, '*Lá iláha illa-lláh;*' and whenever a fly entered the tomb, it formed these words in its flight. By Allah it was so! My object was now fully attained; I felt myself endowed with supernatural knowledge: thoughts of my friends and acquaintances troubled me not; but I knew where each of them was, in Persia, India, Arabia, and Turkey, and what each was doing. I experienced an indescribable happiness. This state lasted several years; but at length I was insensibly enticed back to worldly objects; I came to this country; my fame as a caligraphist drew me into the service of the government; and now see what I am, decked with pelisses and shawls, and with this thing [a diamond order] on my breast; too old, I fear, to undergo again the self-denial necessary to restore me to true happiness, though I have almost resolved to make the attempt." Soon after this conversation, he was deprived of his office, and died of the plague. He was well known to have passed several years as a wandering devotee; and his sufferings, combined with enthusiasm, perhaps disordered his imagination, and made him believe that he really saw the strange sights which he described to me; for there was an appearance of earnestness and sincerity in his manner, such as I thought could hardly be assumed by a conscious imposter.

Here is, again, another example given by Lane in the same place:

A reputed saint of this description, in Cairo, in whom persons of some education put great faith, affected to have a particular regard for me. He several times accosted me in an abrupt manner, acquainted me with the state of my family in England, and uttered incoherent predictions respecting me, all of which communications, excepting one which he qualified with an "*in shâa-llâh*" [or, "if it be the will of God"], I must confess proved to be true; but I must also state that he was acquainted with two of my friends who might have materially assisted him to frame these predictions, though they protested to me that they had not done so. The following extract from a journal which I kept in Cairo during my second visit to Egypt, will convey some idea of this person, who will serve as a picture of many of his fraternity. Today [November 6, 1834], as I was sitting in the shop of the Báshà's book-sellers, a reputed saint, whom I have often seen here, came and seated himself by me, and began, in a series of abrupt sentences, to relate to me various matters respecting me, past, present, and to come. He is called the sheykh ʿAlee El-Leysee. He is a poor man, supported by alms; tall and thin and very dark, about thirty years of age, and wears nothing at present, but a blue shirt and a girdle, and a padded red cap. "O Effendee" he said, "thou hast been very anxious for some days. There is a grain of anxiety remaining in thee yet. Do not fear. There is a letter coming to thee by sea that will bring thee good news." He then proceeded to tell me of the state of my family, and that all were well excepting one, whom he particularized by description, and who he stated to be then suffering from an intermittent fever. [This proved to be exactly true.] "This affliction," he continued, "may be removed by prayer; and the excellences of the next night, the night of [i. e., preceding] the first Friday of the month of Regeb, of Regeb, the holy Regeb, are very great. I wanted to ask thee for something today; but I feared; I feared greatly. Thou must be invested with the *wiláyeh* [i. e., be made a welee]; the welees love thee; and the Prophet loves thee. Thou must go to the sheykh Muṣṭafa El-Munádee, and the sheykh El-Baháee. Thou must be a welee." He then took my right hand, in a manner commonly practiced in the ceremony which admits a person a darweesh, and repeated the Fáteḥah (commonly pronounced Fát-ḥah); after which he added, "I have admitted thee, my darweesh." Having next told me of several circumstances relating to my family—matters of an unusual nature—with singular minuteness and truth, he added, "Tonight, if it be the will of God, thou shalt see the Prophet in thy sleep, and El-Khiḍr and the seyyid El-Bedawee. This is Regeb, and I wanted to ask of thee,—but I feared—I wanted to ask of thee four piastres, to buy meat and bread and oil and radishes. Regeb! Regeb! I have great offices to do for thee tonight." Less than a shilling for all that he promised was little enough. I gave it him for the trouble he had taken; and he uttered many abrupt prayers for me. In the following night, however, I saw in my sleep neither Mohammed nor El-Khiḍr nor the seyyid El-Bedawee, unless, like Nebuchadnezzar, I was unable, on awaking, to remember my dreams.

I must now draw toward a close on the saintly life. Let me, then, return to the thesis with which I started and sum up our results. These, of necessity, are very fragmentary and very incomplete, and can be regarded only as opening a vista and suggesting its possibilities. Consider that down that vista all the religious life of all the Muslim peoples has poured for thirteen centuries, and you will realize how ridiculously inadequate a few lectures must necessarily be. I believe that, in the broad, I have touched the true keynotes and, in the details, have given what is generally characteristic only, but more I cannot say. Ridiculous inadequacy, I repeat, is the only expression.

But to the results. The reality, for the Muslim, of the background of the Unseen is now before you, of that unknown spiritual order from which his life has come, which it constantly touches, and to which it will return. I have spoken of that background hitherto as the Unseen simply, and have not, so far, taken in its being an unseen *order*, as Mr. William James expresses it. So we must now ask to what extent the Muslim regarded, and regards, that world beyond the pale as an ordered world, a world subject to laws at which he may dimly grasp and a world dependable in its actions and reactions. The Muslim, it is true, takes life bit by bit, but can he be sure that he can take hold of the right bit and in the right way, with regard to this unseen background? He may not have any very definite sense of law; but can he be sure that all his ethical conceptions will not be upset tomorrow, by some voice out of the darkness?

This question tends to be much more one of dogmatic theology than of the religious psychology with which we are now engaged. Yet some attempt at it we must make. First, then, the idea that behind the curtain there is at work an absolute, inflexible law, the same yesterday, today, and for ever, must, for the enormous mass of Islām, be set aside. Only the few scattered, and steadily dwindling philosophers ever held such a view. Their basis was the Aristotelian conception of law, shot, it is true, with warmer fervors from the ecstasies of Plotinus, but still law. Personalities, the Active Intellect and the Spirits of the Spheres were in that law—*were* that law—but dominant, over and through them, was the conception of the great mechanical animal of the universe and its law.

Yet such philosophers and their disciples were a vanishing, and now are a vanished fraction in the Muslim world. At the opposite extreme from them is the old Muslim position—still the half-unconscious view of the great mass—that over all is Allāh, and that all hangs on his personal will. An extreme school of scholastics has reduced this to a theory of the universe, in which the universe, as a whole and in details, is being constantly recreated by Allāh, from moment to moment, as he at such moment wills. It is will and not law that is behind our world. On this view, no ethical theory of science is possible. All that can be sought is the will of Allāh on the case, as it is supernaturally revealed.

Yet it is admitted that there is a certain unity in that so revealed will corresponding to the unity which must lie in the mind of Allāh. We may be fairly sure that our ethical imperatives will stand; they will stand because they are imperatives, commands from the will of Allāh. Between these two dogmatic and rationalistic extremes lie the various mystical conceptions. He who has seen God, he knows him, trusts him, depends on him; and that is enough. He does not reason about law or personality; these have melted together in the vision of the inner life. Order in the unseen world, then, for the mass of Muslims, means either the accepted will of God or the assurance of his personality. In one way or another it is for man to learn that will and to put himself under the control of that personality. In harmonious adjustment thereto lies man's supreme good; his chief end is to glorify God and enjoy him forever.

The pathways to that knowledge and intercourse are now before you. The distrust of reason, save as a tutor to bring the soul to the Prophet or his like; the frank agnosticism, so far as reason is concerned; the equally frank supernaturalism and dependence on extra-rational guides; all these are plain. The prophet, the soothsayer, the dreamer, the wizard, the familiar spirit, the saint, have all their place in the scheme. Prophecy, dreaming, sainthood are the lawful and accepted means by which man may know God. Prophecy is historical. The prophets are all gone, and none will now come until Armageddon and the millenium draw nigh. The guidance of dreaming is open to every man. So, too, the varied ranks of sainthood, from the humblest darwīsh to the Axis himself, the saintly vicegerent of God on earth.

Further, the path of the mystic is the path of the religious life, and to that in detail we must now turn. The preceding narratives must have already suggested to you its course and methods. One inevitable question, however, I must here meet, however briefly. The types of the religious life among us are numerous and among them the ascetic, emotional, ecstatic, play a comparatively small part. Does all the religious life of Islām move in those paths; or are there others which should fairly be taken into account? The reply need not be long. It is true that there are some minor and opposed drifts, but they may fairly be disregarded. First, the canon lawyers still feel that in their studies salvation may be found and, like the Pharisees, they emphasize the importance of a scrupulous observance of the ritual law. But while the masses respect them, the people can hardly be expected to find in legal subtleties satisfaction for their religious cravings. Secondly, the puritan element of the Wahhābites has always denounced the mystical attitudes and the reverence for saints, and has sought to lead Islām back to the supposedly simple monotheism of Muḥammad. But their power is fast waning and has lost the reforming energy which it at first showed. Thirdly, there may be some small remains of philosophical speculation concealing itself behind Ṣūfīism; but that does not affect the masses. Practically, the conception of the mystical, saintly life and the organization of darwīsh fraternities cover all Islām and are the stimulants and vehicles of Muslim piety. The religious institutions tend to foster this. Above all, comes the pilgrimage to Mecca and the many imitation pilgrimages all over the Muslim lands, to the tombs of celebrated saints. These are the scenes of orgasms of ecstatic emotion comparable in many ways to those at negro camp-meetings. Here, for example, is an incident and a meditation thereon from a recent book, *With the Pilgrims to Mecca* (London, 1905), which professes to be written by a Persian Muslim who had been educated in England. I see no reason to doubt that statement, although the pilgrim's Arabic is of the queerest, and he makes distinct slips in his law and theology. The scene itself shows clear marks of psychological truth and autobiographic value:

While I was admiring the unpretentious grace of the holy shrine, and meditating from its threshold on the golden age of Islám, my guide broke in on my thoughts, saying, "You are allowed to make two prostrations at the base of any one of the pillars. Let me advise you, in the welfare of your immortal soul, to choose the one facing the Black Stone outside, which is the most sacred spot under the canopy of heaven." The difficulty was to force my way thither. The whole house was packed with pilgrims. Some were praying, some were weeping, others were groaning or beating their chests, and all—except the Bedouins—were clad in their sacred habits. A great awe fell on me. It was as though the graves had yielded up their dead at the blast of Israfil's trumpet. All eyes were blind, all ears deaf. The thought of home, of country, of wife, and child seemed drowned in a sea of passionate devotion to the creator of those human blessings. And from outside, in the Harem, there arose the chant of the Talbih, which every pilgrim must sing on sighting Mecca, on donning the Ihram, on entering the Harem, on starting for the Valley of Desire and the Mountain of Compassion, and on performing the little pilgrimage of Omreh. I paused in the effort to reach the southern pillar, and listened to the singing from without:

Labbaik, Allahomma, Labbaik!
Labbaik, la Sherika lak Labbaik!
Labbaik, enal-hamda, Vanahmeta lak Labbaik!
Labbaik, la Sherika lak Labbaik!

(Verily, here am I! O Allah, here I am!
Verily, here am I! O Allah, thou hast no mate!
Verily, here am I, O Allah! All praise and glory to thee!
Verily, here am I! O Allah, thou hast no mate!)

On my soul, it was fine! All my senses must have deserted me. I must have lost all consciousness of self suddenly. The burden of existence seemed to be lifted. If I did not actually slip off the slough of the flesh I came to realize in a flash that the soul is immortal. These introspective thoughts were not mine at the moment of the transformation. They were retrospective, forced on me, when, on coming back to a sense of my surroundings, I found myself kneeling at the Door of Repentance, and heard myself crying, "*Labbaik, la Sherika lak Labbaik.*" Yes; there was I—"an agnostic who would like to know"—rubbing my brow on the marble floor of the Kaᶜbah, without the dimmest notion in my mind as to how I came to be there. Only a month before, I had been sipping lemon squash in a London restaurant. Strange. The first thing I did was to look round in search of my guide, as skeptical a rascal as ever breathed. He was on his knees, at my side, his eyes starting out of the sockets. I put my hand on his shoulder. "Come," I said, "let us go out. I am suffocating." He rose to his feet, looking scared and abashed; but his face assumed its usual expression of sunny mirth on reaching the Harem. He put his tongue in his cheek as of yore; then, repenting him of his unregenerate mood, he told the truth. "*Yá-Moulai* (Oh, sir)," said he, "within the house so great reverence fell on me that I did hardly think of the blessed houris and peris promised to me in paradise. The same emotion overmasters me every year on entering the Kaᶜbah of Allāh, and yet what does it all mean? What is the value of this dream which we call life, and which is my true self? Is it the self that inquires, scoffs, doubts, but wants to find the truth? Or is it the self that you discovered a moment ago bereft of every sense save one, namely, that which would seem to have drawn me irresistibly to a power whose will none would seem to be able to dispute? Has that power an existence outside of my emotions, or is it merely the fabric of my senses? You are silent, *Yâ-Moulai.* Well, there are more ways of getting drunk than by drinking of the juice of the forbidden fruit. I escaped from myself, just then, on a spiritual rather than a spirituous fluid. Let us return to our camp."[1]

This last piece of comment, of course, bears signs of manufacture; but the emotional outburst is evidently genuine, and gives a true picture of how the pilgrimage ceremonial, and especially the hoary sanctity of the Kaᶜbah affects the pilgrim. And the same scenes are being repeated at saintly shrines over the Muslim world.

It is, then, as I have already suggested several times, with Roman rather than Protestant christendom that Islām must be compared as to its emotional life. There the likeness is singularly close, reaching down even to the Ghazzālian combination of philosophical agnosticism and supernatural faith. And for this theological likeness there is good ground. Almost certainly, Thomas Aquinas was deeply influ-

[1] Hadji Khan, *With the Pilgrims to Mecca*, p. 170.

enced, though indirectly, by al-Ghazzālī's views; and he, in his turn, has molded the Roman theology. That the rules and attitudes of one order at least, that of the Jesuits, were similarly affected by the Muslim fraternities and especially by the doctrine of the relationship of shaykh and disciple, seems certain. "Let the disciple in the hands of his teacher be like a dead body," is the metaphor used by both.

If you consider, then, how in the Roman communion the religious life, almost necessarily, connects itself in some way or degree with an order, and finds its support in a mystical attitude toward the universe, the overwhelming preponderance of such institutions and attitudes in Islām will not appear so strange. This parallel might be worked out in detail; but that, like so much else, I must now leave with this mere touch.

LECTURE VIII

THE DISCIPLINE OF THE TRAVELER ON HIS WAY TO THE UNSEEN AND THE NATURE, WORKING, AND USE OF THE HEART

I desire now to put before you a sketch of the theory, and, to some extent, the practice of the discipline of the traveler on his way to direct knowledge of the divine and during his life in it. We have already had narratives telling the story of such journeys as made by individuals. Our lack now is of a broad and philosophizing generalized description. For that I turn again to al-Ghazzālī.

The first half of his great work, *The Revivifying of the Sciences of Religion*, is devoted, as he tells us himself,[1] to a consideration of what shows itself externally in the traveler by way of acts of devotion and religious usage. Under these he includes creeds and their bases, religious ritual, and the religious manner of carrying out the ordinary operations of life in the broadest. The second half deals with the internal and hidden side of life, the heart and its workings, good and evil. Under it are considered the lusts and passions, the virtues and perfections. To this second half, then, he prefixes an introduction dealing with the wondrous qualities

[1] *Iḥyā*, edition with commentary of Sayyid Murtaḍà, Vol. VII, pp. 201 ff.

and nature of what is called "the heart," and with the general discipline by which it can be directed and purified. That done, he is free to deal with the lusts and virtues in detail.

But our interest is with the general subject, and I shall therefore now put before you al-Ghazzālī's doctrine of the heart. I translate thus literally the Arabic *qalb*, but it will be well to notice that there is an essential difference of idea in the derived uses of *qalb* and "heart." With the English "heart," when thus used, there goes always, I think, the conception of emotions, affections, desires, sentiments; the emotional nature in general is fundamental and the intellectual has comparatively little part. That cannot be said of the Arabic *qalb*. It is far more the seat of the mind, and it approximates to the English "heart" only in that it suggests the inmost, most secret and genuine thoughts, the very basis of man's intellectual nature. In the words of a Muslim commentator, it is a "transcendental (or theologic) subtlety" (*laṭīfa rabbānīya*); that is, a fine, non-material thing connected with the unseen world. We have, therefore, to dismiss the idea that "heart," so used, implies a blind reaching out of the affections toward the divine and a submergence of the intellectual powers; it is rather the bringing to bear of another and more trustworthy and absolute organ of the mind. But that al-Ghazzālī himself will now make clear.

He opens his statement with an ascription of praise to Allāh involving a declaration that man, physically and mentally, is confused and perturbed if he tries to reach absolute appreciation of God while God himself absolutely apprehends and comprehends everything. What man apprehends of God is that he cannot absolutely apprehend him. So Paul (Phil. 3:2) felt that he had rather been laid hold of than had himself laid hold. But man has a glory and excellency which distinguishes him from all other created beings and equips him for that knowledge of God which in this world is his beauty and perfection and in the world to come his equipment and store. This is his "heart" in the above sense. It knows God and draws near to God and works for God and labors toward God. It reveals what is with God; it is accepted by God when free from aught but him, and is curtained off from God when immersed in aught but him. It is sought and addressed and rebuked and punished. It is happy when near God and prospers when man has purified it, and is disappointed and miserable when man pollutes and corrupts it. At one time it is obedient to God, and then what appears externally by way of acts of piety is from its illumination; and at another time it is rebellious against God and what appears externally by way of corruption and rebellion is an effect from it. As it is dark or bright, vices or virtues appear, for "a vessel drips with what is in it." When a man knows it, he knows himself; and when he knows himself he knows his Lord; and contrariwise, if he is ignorant of it. Whoever is ignorant as to his heart is still more ignorant as to everything else; and most are thus ignorant. For "God intervenes between a man and his heart"[1] in such a way as to hinder him from observing God and knowing his qualities and perceiving how he is turned between two of God's fingers and how, at one time, he lusts toward the lowest things and is depressed to the region of devils and, at another time, is raised to the loftiest things and mounts to the world of those angels who are nearest to God. He who does not know his heart so as to watch it and guard it and observe what shines on it and in it from the treasures of the heavenly kingdom, he is of those concerning whom God has said, "They forget God, so he makes them forget themselves; they are the evil-doers."[2] So knowledge of the heart and its essential qualities is the root of religion and the foundation of the way of travelers thereto.

It is, then, al-Ghazzālī's purpose to expound the wonders of the heart. He will do it by comparisons, because most intelligences are too dull to attain to the spiritual world. By this, I think, he means only that the terms he uses must not be taken in a literal way; there are no absolute terms for the things of

[1] *Qur.* viii, 24.
[2] *Ibid.*, lix, 19.

the heavenly kingdom of which he is going to speak, and human words can only approximate.

But first some terms must be defined: "Heart" (*qalb*) does not mean the heart of flesh but, as we have seen, a certain transcendental (or theologic) spiritual subtlety in some connection with the physical heart. It is the essence of a man, the part which perceives and knows. How it is connected with the physical heart is a very perplexing question. Its connection resembles the connection of accidents with substances, or qualities with things they qualify, or the user of a tool with the tool, or things located with their *locus*. Al-Ghazzālī does not wish to enter farther on this for two reasons: (1) The question belongs to speculative science rather than to practical, which is his present subject. The practice of life requires consideration of the qualities of this "heart," not of its essence. And (2) it is connected with the question of the spirit (*rūḥ*) on which the Prophet kept silence; in this, as in everything, it behooves all Muslims to imitate him. Yet the commentator remarks that this "heart" has been called the rational soul; that the spirit (*rūḥ*) is its inner part and the animal soul is its vehicle.

As to the use of "spirit" (*rūḥ*), the second term, a similar ambiguity exists. On one side it is the subtle substance or vapor issuing from the hollow of the physical heart, being matured by its heat, and spreading by means of the arteries through the whole body. This physiology, of course, is pre-Harveyan. Al-Ghazzālī compares it to a lamp carried about through a house, lighting it up. The spirit is the lamp, and life is the light which it spreads. But, on another side, the term indicates apparently much the same knowing and perceiving subtlety as does "heart." Al-Ghazzālī does not here make clear a distinction. Further, as we have seen, he regards general discussion of the meaning of the term as unsuitable. God himself has told the Prophet in the *Qurʾān* (xvii, 87) to say, "The spirit is my Lord's affair."

This, however, applies only to the masses, those who cannot think except in terms of matter, or, if they have so far freed themselves, cannot clear their minds further of the conception of position in space. Before such the full doctrine of the spirit must not be laid; they would accuse the expounder of it of claiming qualities peculiar to the divine nature. They do not realize that the real essence and *differentia* of the divine nature is aseity, existence through itself; all other things having only an existence borrowed from it. But for those who have realized this the definition of spirit is simple. It exists in itself, being neither an accident, nor a material substance, nor a thing bounded; it is not located in a place or a direction; it is not joined with the human body and the world, nor separated therefrom; it is not within the bodies of the world (*i. e.*, the concentric shells of the universe) and the human body, nor without them. All this is part, also, of the definition of God; but he has aseity as well. Into al-Ghazzālī's arguments and illustrations of the possibility of the existence of such a substance, we need not enter. His method, as always, is to defend logically the possibility of this transcendental fact; to illustrate by physical analogies its workings; to base its actuality upon revelation; it being always understood that the fact itself is transcendental and can be put in human words and presented to human thought only in images.

The spirit further comes into existence through a direct outpouring (*fayḍ*) from God upon the embryo fitted to receive it. Upon an embryo so ready the divine outpouring stamps itself, as an image does in a polished mirror. All Muslim mysticism is ridden by the primitive feeling that there must be some entity in a reflection. It goes with the problem of the metaphysical schoolboy who asked where the figures went when wiped off the slate. But the term "outpouring" must not suggest the pouring of water upon the hand, where there is a separation of part of the water from the pitcher and a joining of it to the hand. Rather, it should be imaged as like the outpouring of the light of the sun upon a wall. In that case there is no separating in the substance of the sun and joining and spreading on the wall. The light of the sun is only the cause why something similar to it in the property of light, although weaker, originates on the illuminated wall. So, too, in a mirror; the only relationship is pure causality. Thus, the divine beneficence is the cause of the origination of the light of being in every entity fitted to receive it. This, in short, is al-Ghazzālī's secret; the very kernel of his doctrine of the nature of man.[1]

That an economy of teaching so plain as this was so openly used and confessed is one of the greatest puzzles in the history of the development of Muslim theology. "Ye cannot bear it," we hear again and again, and no "now" is added. Through Muslim thought runs an intellectual snobbishness, which cannot believe that the masses can ever be taught. And it is so complacent and self-satisfied that it does not hesitate to state itself openly. The people, it is implied, must be quite willing to accept this limitation. With al-Ghazzālī, we have simply an economy of teaching, resulting in several stages of intellectual truth, with absolute certainty attainable in the mystical revelation, open, more or less, to all. But when we come to Averroes, the method has hardened in his hands into the philosophical doctrine of the twofold truth. And there is the additional difference that, for al-Ghazzālī, all methods reached one truth, though with varying degrees of spirituality, while between Averroes' philosophical

[1] *Al-maḍnūn aṣ-ṣaghīr*, edition of Cairo, A. H. 1303, pp. 5,8, 13.

and theological truths, there were flat contradictions. The one could not be called a spiritualizing of the other.

The third term is hardest of all to translate. By a curious accident, the word in Arabic which literally should mean "soul" has come to be the nearest equivalent for our word "flesh" in the theological sense. This word is *nafs*. Etymologically, it is closely connected with the idea of "breath," and is the same as the Hebrew *nêphesh*, frequently translated in our Bible versions "soul," and sometimes "breath," "life," "appetite." The last is primary, for the essential idea of the word is life on the side of its passions and appetites—it is, in a word, the appetitive soul. Of the many meanings, then, which *nafs* can have, al-Ghazzālī says that two are to our purpose. It is used to express the idea which combines the force of anger and fleshly appetite in man. The Arabic word for fleshly appetite (*shahwa*) can be used in either a good or a bad sense. It is "truthful" (*ṣādiqa*) when it indicates a physical need which must be met if the body is to be sound, and "lying" (*kādhiba*) when that is not the case. It is used of desire of food, etc., and of sexual appetite. This usage is the prevailing one among Ṣūfīs, for they mean by the *nafs* that which combines in man his blameworthy qualities, and they say that man must fight against the *nafs* and break it. In this way the Prophet used it when he said, "Thy *nafs*, which is between thy two sides, is thy worst enemy." Here, of course, we have exactly our idea of "the flesh." And ascetics, as Ṣūfīs are generally, would naturally describe all physical appetites as movements of the flesh, and regard as a religious duty their suppression to the limit of possibility.

The second usage is to indicate that same subtlety which has been mentioned already, and which is the verity and soul and essence of a man. It is indicated when a man says, "I," by which he means a spiritual, abiding substance. But this "soul"—if we can so call it—can be described in different ways according as its states are different.

When it is submissive to the command of God and undisturbed by contending lusts, it is called "the soul at rest" (*an-nafs al-muṭmaʾinna*). So God addresses it in the *Qurʾān* (xxxix, 27), "O thou soul at rest, return unto thy Lord, well pleased, accepted!" This, of course, can never be said of the *nafs* of the first usage. Its return to God is inconceivable, for it belongs to the host of the devil. But, secondly, when the state of rest of the soul is incomplete and it is still struggling with the lustful soul, it is called "the upbraiding soul" (*an-nafs al-lawwāma*); of it God speaks in the *Qurʾān* (lxxv, 2), "And nay! I swear by the soul that upbraids." But, thirdly, if the soul ceases to oppose the enticements of the lusts and the summoners of the devil, and yields itself to them, it is called "the soul that commands to evil" (*an-nafs al-ammāra bis-sū᾽*). Thus God puts in the mouth of Joseph in the *Qur᾽ān* (xii, 53), "Verily the soul indeed commands to evil." Yet here, adds al-Ghazzālī, we may perhaps have the soul of the first usage, i. e., that which comprises man's anger and lust; it is altogether blameworthy, while the soul of the second usage is praiseworthy as the very essence of man which knows God and all knowable things.

The fourth term is *ᶜaql*, by which Arabic writers on philosophy have generally rendered the Greek *νοῦς*. For the present purpose it may be rendered "intelligence," and has two usages. It means, in the first instance, knowledge of the true nature of things, and is an expression for the knowledge whose seat is the heart. And in the second instance, it is that which perceives knowledge, thus the heart itself, namely that subtlety of which we have spoken. Thus there stands in a tradition, "The first thing that God created was Intelligence (*al-ᶜaql*)." *ᶜAql*, then, means either the quality of intelligence in one who perceives, or the percipient mind itself in which that quality inheres.

Elsewhere[1] al-Ghazzālī further subdivides the knowledge of the heart into three: (1) axiomatic knọwledge; (2) knowledge from experience; (3) prudence, the last fruit of experience. Thus *ᶜaql* seems to be used both for *ὁ νοῦς* and for *τὸ νοούμενον*.

[1] *Iḥyā*, Vol. I, pp. 458 ff.

These, then, are four terms and behind each lie two ideas. Behind *qalb* there is the physical heart; behind *rūḥ* the physical vapor which issues from the physical heart; behind *nafs* there is the sensual being, the "flesh;" behind *ʿaql* there is knowledge. But there is also a fifth idea, that knowing and perceiving subtlety in man, which lies behind all four, and to which the four terms apply in common. It is called specially the heart, because its first connection is with the heart, though it rules and uses all the body. Its seat is there as the seat of God is on his throne in heaven, while he rules the universe.

But having fixed these terms, the next point is the equipment and working of this "heart." God has said,[1] "And who knoweth the armies of thy Lord save himself?" To God belong in hearts and spirits and in all the worlds serried armies whose nature and number none knoweth save he; the world is full of armies in conflict; but all are his. So in the human heart there are armies, and some are to our present purpose. Of these are two, an army that can be seen with fleshly eyes, and one that only eyes of the spirit can see. Of both the heart is lord, and they to it are servants. The visible are such as the hand, the foot, the eye—all the organs of the body within and without. They are fashioned for obedience to the heart and cannot disobey it, even as the angels are related to God, with the one

[1] *Qur.* lxxiv, 34.

difference that the angels know their own obedience, and the eyelid, for example, has no knowledge of itself when it opens or shuts. Thus we are to understand that all things in earth and heaven, material and spiritual, belong alike to the armies of God. And of these armies the heart has need as a vehicle and as provision on the journey for which it was created, namely, the journey to God. "I created not mankind and Jinn," saith Allāh, "save to serve me."[1] That is the end; the vehicle is the body; the provision is knowledge; and it is not attained and stored save through sound action. Thus the creature cannot reach God except by inhabiting the body; it is a necessary stage on the journey; a seed-field of the world to come; therefore the world is called *ad-Dunyà*, the nearer one, because it is the first of those stages. "A wanderer is man from his birth," quotes the commentator from ᶜAlī; and from an unnamed poet, "He who is in this world, though city-pent, is a traveler, and his journey goes on, though he knows it not."

The body, then, is the vehicle, or boat, by which man reaches this world. So it is his duty to care for it by bringing to it that which it needs by way of food, etc., and by warding off from it what may hurt it or destroy it. The heart, therefore, needs two armies to provide food for the body—an internal, the appetite, and an external, the organs of the body.

[1] *Qur.* li, 56.

The needed appetites are created in the heart; and the needed organs, the instruments of the appetites, are created in the body. Similarly, for driving away destructive things, there is anger in the heart and its instruments in the body. Further, if food were not known, what would avail the appetite for food? The heart has need, therefore, of two other armies—one internal, perceptions of hearing, seeing, smelling, etc., and one external, the eye, the ear, the nose, etc. This could be developed at great length, as al-Ghazzālī does in his *Book of Thanksgiving*. But, in short, the armies of the heart can be divided into three classes: a class which excites either to the obtaining of that which is necessary, or to the repelling of that which is hurtful and which is often called the will; a class which moves the limbs, scattered equally through them, often called power; and thirdly, a class which perceives and recognizes, being settled in the individual organs of sense, and which is often called knowledge and perception. Corresponding to each of these is an external army, organs of flesh and blood, adapted to be their instruments. But this last, which belongs to the physical, sensible world, is not our subject now.

Further, this third class divides, on one hand, into the five senses inhabiting the five external organs of sense and on another, into five internal senses which inhabit the hollows of the brain. Thus, if a man closes his eyes after seeing something, he perceives the image of it in himself; this is the picturing power. Then this image remains with him by reason of something that preserves it; this is the memory. Then he reflects on what he remembers and makes of it new combinations. Then he recalls to memory what he has forgotten. Then he gathers into a compound the ideas of the sensuous impressions on his imagination through the "general sense." Thus, within the brain are this "general sense," the imaginative power, the reflective power, the recollective power, and the memory.[1]

This psychological scheme al-Ghazzālī goes on to expand and apply in a series of allegories. The armies of anger and fleshly appetite are sometimes completely submissive to the heart, and that submission aids it on its way to eternal felicity; and sometimes they revolt and even overcome it and subdue it, and thus destroy it and its success. The heart, too, has yet another army, knowledge and wisdom and reflection—the host of God—and this army assists it against the other two armies which sometimes join the hosts of the devil. If the heart then does not seek such assistance but gives up the struggle, it perishes of a certainty. Such is the state of most men; their intelligence is so subdued by their appetites that it is devoted to devising ways of satisfying these appetites. The soul of man, then,

[1] On this psychological scheme cf. above pp. 72 ff.

in his body, may be likened to a king in his kingdom. The members and powers of the body are like the artisans and laborers; the intelligent reflective power is like the wise wazīr; the physical appetites are like the evil slave who brings provisions; and anger and indignation are like the police force. The purveying slave is a liar, deceitful, guileful, vile, who poses as a sincere adviser. His custom is to set himself against the true wazīr at every moment, but the safety of the kingdom lies in the rejection of his advice and in the keeping of him and the police force in their fit places. The slave, especially, can be subdued by subjecting him to the admonitions and rule of the police. But each in turn can be played off against the other. So, exactly, the fleshly appetites and the power of indignation can be used to subject one another.

But the body of man can also be likened to a city, and the intellect to its king. The senses, within and without, are the people. Against it wars the "soul commanding to evil" (the fleshly lusts and anger) and strives to destroy the people. We have the leaguer of Mansoul in Bunyan's *Holy War*. So the body is like a castle on a hostile frontier, and the soul as its keeper must ever be on guard against the forces of evil. God will take account with it at the last day for the folk that have been in its charge. This is the truest *jihād*, or "holy warfare," and so Muḥammad said, "We return from the lesser *jihād* to the greater," from contending with unbelievers to contending with ourselves.

Or man's intellect can be likened to a horseman who has gone a hunting with his fleshly appetite as his horse and his anger as his dog. If then the horseman be skilled, and his horse trained and his dog broken and accustomed, his hunting will prosper. But if he be awkward and his horse restive and his dog vicious, then he can neither rule his horse nor guide his dog, and he himself is rather worthy of blame than of success in his hunting. And what this means in the regimen of the soul is plain.

In these three allegories the whole structure of man is reckoned with and used. Everything, from the lowest appetites, has its place and purpose. The scheme is not one of absolute asceticism, but of balanced development of all man's being. Nor does this so far hold of man alone. Up to this point it might apply to all animals, for all have these appetites and senses, internal and external. Even a sheep sees a wolf coming and has an inward sense of fear and flees from it. Apparently al-Ghazzālī would assign to the lower animals some power, even, of reflection, of making combinations, but at that his commentator protests.

What in man, however, distinguishes him from the lower animals and makes possible his approach to God is a particular kind of knowledge and of will. The knowledge is that about religion and the world to come and about the intellectual essences; these all lie behind the objects of sense, and are metaphysical. To this belongs, also, necessary universal knowledge, as when a man judges by his intellect that an individual cannot be in two places at one time, even though he has not observed this of all individuals. And the will is that produced when a man observes by his intellect the consequences of an act and how to reach what is really best. A desire for that is then aroused in him, and he gives himself to it and wills it. This, too, the lower animals know nothing of; they seek the immediate, sensuous good and are heedless of consequences.

This kind of knowledge, then, and this kind of will distinguish man from the other animals. Yet even he must grow up to these things; the child at first is as the beasts that perish. He gains them in two steps. The first is that he grasps in an external fashion all that axiomatic, necessary knowledge which is intuitively perceived, such as the impossibility of this and the possibility of that; but of speculative knowledge he has only, so far, the near possibility and not the actuality. It is as though he knew the elements of writing but could not put together words which would convey a meaning. Then, secondly, there comes to him knowledge acquired by experience and reflection, and he has a store of it on which he can draw when he wills. Now he knows all about writing and can write what he pleases. In this stage there are all manner of degrees, reaching through the ordinary experiences of men to the direct vision of saints, and finally to the divine revelation to prophets. To some, the ascent is slow; to others fast; but to the knowledge concerning God there are no bounds. Each knows his own degree, but cannot know the essence of that which is beyond him. He may believe in prophecy and be certain that there are prophets; but unless he is a prophet, he cannot know the essence of prophetship. All this comes freely of the grace and bounty of God, who is ever ready to hear and answer. If the pure yearn to meet him, he yearns more grievously still to meet them. If they advance to him a span, he advances a cubit. There is no niggardliness on his part, nothing hinders men but the darkness of their own hearts and the curtains which the cares of this world draw.

Man, therefore, is between the beasts and the angels. But his true "differentia" is his knowledge of the essences of things. He, then, who employs all his members and powers by seeking aid from them in the attaining of knowledge and well-executed labor, he has become like the angels and worthy to be joined with them and called one of them. But if he turn to the body and its appetites, then he will become stupid as an ox, greedy as a pig, fawning as a dog or a cat, malicious as a camel, insolent as a leopard, or shifty as a fox. Or he may join all together and become a very devil. In a word, all his members and senses can be used either to bring him to God and his eternal salvation, or to plunge him in destruction. He must walk the way of the world as a passer-by, not as a dweller; this world is a bridge to the next.

Thus, there mingle in every man four properties, and he can be described in four ways. He may show the qualities of ravenous beasts, or of the lower animals, or of devils, or of sages. There are in him anger, physical appetites, deviltry, and lordship. The first two have already been sufficiently explained; on the two latter al-Ghazzālī dwells with a whimsical humor which suggests large experience. In the soul of man there is a certain lordly part. This belongs apparently to the *rūḥ* of man, for, in explanation, *Qurʾān*, xvii, 87, is again quoted: "Say, 'The spirit (*rūḥ*) is of the affair of my Lord.' " This is because he claims for himself lordship, and loves rule and superiority and distinction and exclusiveness in all things, and being single in rule and removed from servileness and humbleness. And he longs to learn all sciences; claims for himself science and knowledge and comprehension of the true natures of things; and rejoices when thought wise and sorrows when thought ignorant. Comprehension of all verities and seeking of rule by force over all creatures describe the quality, lordship; for that man's desire is strong.

There we have evidently a fundamental analysis

of the absolute sage, as al-Ghazzālī had known him—an outgrowth of the spirit of rule, developed through lust of knowledge.[1] But here is the other, the Satanic side. It is in man through his having, besides the physical appetites and anger, a quality of distinguishing which is not in the lower animals. So he becomes peculiarly evil, through using this quality of discriminative rationality to search out fashions of wickedness, and attains his evil ends by guile and deceit.

Under the hide of every man, therefore—such is al-Ghazzālī's phrase—there is a pig, a dog, a devil, and a sage; and it is his problem to see to it that the sage exposes the wiles of the devil, and keeps the pig and the dog in subjection by playing them off, one against the other. So everything may go smoothly, and the wrath of man be made to praise God. The quality of lordship, thus fulfilling its best purpose, will turn to wisdom, knowledge, insight, and have a true claim to precedence; the pig quality will turn to chastity, patience, temperance, gentleness, reverence; the dog quality to courage, generosity, clemency, dignity. But most frequently this does not happen, and the strange thing is how men will blame the worshipers of idols, and yet if the veil were removed from them and their essential state revealed, they would see themselves bowing down to pigs and dogs.

[1] Cf. "Life," *Journal of American Oriental Society*, Vol. XX, p. 105, and p. 194 above.

Another allegory describing the heart as a mirror exposed to all manner of influences follows in detail. But I need not give it here, though there is an interesting passage describing how the thought (*dhikr*) of God "rests the heart,"[1] and leads to the unveiling which leads to the great felicity, the meeting with God himself. So Augustine said, "Our hearts are restless till they rest in thee."

But when, in his next section, al-Ghazzālī comes to consider the heart as the instrument of knowledge, he makes more elaborate use of the same allegory. This heart, which controls all the members, is the *locus* of knowledge as to the essences of known things. Its relation to them is that of a mirror to the changing forms of the material world. In the one case, you have the mirror, the form of the thing to be reflected and the reflection; in the other, the heart, the form of the essence of the thing perceived and the production and presence of the latter in the heart. "Knower" is an expression for the heart in which is the likeness of these perceived essences. "Known" is an expression for the likeness which results in the heart. But five reasons may prevent a mirror reflecting: It may be unformed and unpolished; it may be dirty; it may be turned away from the thing to be reflected; there may be a curtain over it; there may be ignorance as to the direction of the thing to be reflected. So, too, the mirror of the

[1] *Qur.* xiii, 28.

heart. It may be unformed and incapable, like the heart of a child. It may be soiled by sin. This is a stain that can never be perfectly done away with; subsequent good deeds may remove it, but even then, without it, the heart would have been still brighter. Thirdly, the heart may be formed and capable; it may be pure and bright; but it may not be turned in the direction of the truth which it should reflect, because it is immersed in the details of actions of piety and obedience and in zeal for its own purification. Thus the heart is not really occupied with God, but with the means of reaching him, and by these means it is defeated of the end. Fourthly, the heart may be veiled by some inveterate prejudice of traditional faith. This is the case with most scholastic theologians and those who zealously uphold definite schools. Even many of the pious, when they think of heavenly things, are limited by their early training and do not reach unveiled, direct vision. Fifthly, there may be ignorance as to the direction in which the desired vision must be sought. No knowledge, except that which is innate, is gained save through combining such preceding knowledge as is of the same nature. Ignorance, then, as to this preceding knowledge and how to use it is a fatal but common defect. We must always put together two pieces of knowledge to gain a third. Here the syllogism is evidently thought of, but al-Ghazzālī illustrates with the, for us, odd but, in Arabic, common illustration that you must use two mirrors if you want to see the back of your head. Just as devious and seemingly perplexed ways must be followed in gaining any knowledge, even that of the truth.

Without these five hindrances, then, the heart attains to knowledge of the essences of things, for it, by its created nature (*fiṭra*) is adapted thereto. It is a divine and noble thing, differing from all other substances of the world in this peculiarity and nobility. Of it God has said, "We offered the trust to the heavens and the earth and the mountains, then they refused to bear it and feared it; but man bore it."[1] Thus the heart of man is different from the heavens and the earth, in that it can bear the burden of God's trust, that is knowledge of and unity with God. The heart of every human being is, in its origin, fitted for and equal to that, but often hindered by these five causes. Muḥammad said "Every child is born according to God's plan (*ᶜalà-l-fiṭra*); it is only the parents who make it a Jew or a Christian or a Magian." And again he said, "If it were not that the devils were hovering round the hearts of men, verily they would behold the heavenly kingdom (*al-malakūt*)." So, too, he was asked, "Where is God? in the earth or the heavens?" He replied, "In the hearts of his believing creatures." And a tradition represents God as saying,

[1] *Qur.* xxxiii, 72.

"My earth cannot contain me, nor my heaven, but the tender and tranquil heart of my believing creature contains me."

In this vision, then, all things are revealed. ᶜUmar said, "My heart saw my Lord, when he had raised the veil through godly fear." For whomsoever the veil rises between him and God, to him the form of the world of sense and of the heavenly kingdom appear in his heart, and he sees a paradise, the breadth of but part of which is as the heavens and the earth. This is simple, for "the heavens and the earth" is only an expression for the world of the senses, and it, wide as it is, is finite. But the world of the heavenly kingdom consists of those secrets which are hidden from the sight of the eyes and are perceived by spiritual vision only. It is true that that of it which shines in the heart is a limited amount; but it, in itself, and in relation to the knowledge of God, has no limit. The worlds, then, of sense and the kingdom, taken together, are called the Divine Presence, because that Presence encompasses all existing things. Nothing exists except God and his works and his realm, and his creatures are part of his works. Further, what appears of this to the heart is Paradise itself, according to some; this is the basis of the claim to Paradise by those who see it.

In this way, then, knowledge and purification of the heart and vision are bound together. "Whom

God wills to guide," says the *Qur'ān* (vi, 125), "he opens his breast to Islām." And again (xxxix, 23), "Shall he, then, whose breast God has opened to Islām, and he then follows a light from his Lord . . . . ?" The beginning is with God and his beneficence. Thence come increase of faith, light, knowledge, and comprehension of and in God, nearness to God, who is near to all, a proportioned amount of certainty and assurance in order; of these each has his share, reaching to the point where there is clear knowledge that naught exists but God, and that "Everything is perishing save his face."[1] It is, therefore, natural that to this revelation and faith there should be degrees. These are three: (1) the faith of the populace, a purely traditional faith; (2) the faith of scholastics, which is partly deductive and not far removed from that of the populace; (3) the faith of those who know by experience and have seen for themselves in the light of certainty.

But the commentator further subdivides these on the basis of al-Ghazzālī's statements elsewhere. Under (1) come three others: (*a*) Faith because of absolute trust in the narrator, as of children in their parents or teachers; (*b*) Faith because of accompanying circumstances which are not really decisive; (*c*) Faith because the belief appeals to and corresponds with the nature of the believer. Under (2)

[1] *Qur*. xxviii, 88.

come also three others; (*a*) Faith because of exhaustive and complete proof, worked out step by step in detail to the very roots; (*b*) Faith because of verbal, descriptive proofs, based upon concessions believed in because generally accepted by the greatest scholars and because there would be disgrace in rejecting them; (*c*) Faith on mere rhetorical proofs, commonly used and accepted.

Finally, under (3), come also three subdivisions: (*a*) Belief that all besides God, whenever its essence is considered, *qua* its essence, has no existence, nay its existence is borrowed from something; and that this borrowed existence has no subsistence in itself but in something else, and that this relation of borrowing is a pure metaphor; whenever this verity is revealed to a creature in the light of certainty, he knows that it is a possession to its possessor, for him alone; no one partakes with him in it. (*b*) They mount from the level of metaphor to the peak of reality and complete their ascent and see with vision of their eyes that there is nought in existence except God, and that "Everything is perishing save his face."[1] This does not mean that it comes to perish at some time or other, but that it is perishing from eternity and to eternity and cannot be otherwise thought of; further, that everything except him, when its essence is considered, *qua* essence, is

[1] *Qur.* xxviii, 88; *wajh*="face," "aspect," "direction;" in what follows there is a play on the two meanings "face" and "direction."

a pure nonentity. And whenever it is considered from the aspect which brings it into existence at first, it is seen to exist, not in its essence but from the aspect which appertains to that which brings it into existence. So that which exists is only the aspect of God. Everything has two aspects, one to itself and one to its Lord. As regards the aspect to itself, it is a nonentity; but as regards the aspect of God it is an entity. Then since nothing exists except God, and his aspect, and since everything is perishing save his aspect from eternity to eternity, those who know this stand in no need of the coming of the day of resurrection to hear the cry of the creator. "Whose is the rule to-day? It is Allāh's, the One, the Conqueror!"[1] Nay, that cry is never out of their ears.

There follows an explanation on the basis of this, of the Muslim war-cry *Allāhu akbar*, "Allāh is greater," i. e., than any other, a cry derived probably from pre-Muslim times and a constant stumbling block to Muslim exegetes. Here it is said that it means that he is greater than that "greater" can be said of him in any sense of relationship or comparison.

Lastly, (*c*) after they have ascended to the heaven of reality, they agree that they have not seen in existence aught but the One, the Real (*al-ḥaqq*). To some this state is knowledge, both experimental

[1] *Qur.* xl, 16.

and scientific (*ʿirfān* and *ʿilm*), while to others it is a passing taste. Multiplicity is driven from them in totality, and they are plunged in absolute solitariness. Their reason is absorbed completely and they become bewildered; no capacity remaining for the thought of aught but God; or for the thought, even, of themselves. So there is nothing with them but God, and they are drunken with a drunkenness which rules in place of reason. Then one of them may say, "I am the Real (*al-ḥaqq*)," and another, "The praise is mine, how mighty am I!" and another, "There is nothing in this cloak but God." But the speech of lovers in a state of drunkenness hides and does not narrate. So when their drunkenness has passed from them, and they have returned to the rule of reason—God's weighing balance upon earth—they recognize that that was not real union (*ittiḥād*) but only resembled union. When, then, this state prevails, it is called, in relation to him under it, "passing away" (*fanā*), or rather, the passing away of passing away. For the subject passes away from himself, and passes away from his passing away; he does not feel himself nor the lack of feeling himself. If he felt the lack of his feeling, he would feel himself. This state, in relation to him who is plunged in it, is called, metaphorically, "union" (*ittiḥād*), but its real name is "unifying" (*tawḥīd*; i. e., perception of and belief in God's unity).

So far the commentator, following al-Ghazzālī's tabulation elsewhere. I now return to the simpler division. An illustration of it, says al-Ghazzālī, may be drawn from the degrees of your knowledge that such and such a man is in his house. First, some one in whom you have absolute trust may tell you so; you believe it on his authority. The like of this in religion is a saving faith, but it will not assure a place near to God in Paradise. This, I may add, is a very vexed point in Islām. Some have even held that no faith can save which is not based on elaborate proof.[1] But, secondly, you may hear the voice of that person in his house, and may deduce from that his presence there. This is more personal and certain, but even in this case, you may have mistaken the voice. But thirdly, when you enter his house and see him there, you know assuredly his presence. This is like the religious knowledge of angels and saints; yet it, too, has degrees, for you may see this man with greater or less distinctness according to the light and other conditions.

The knowledge, then, that is in the heart may be subdivided in different ways: first, into intellectual and religious; the religious comes by tradition from prophets, but the intellectual is either axiomatic or acquired through study and deduction; the acquired knowledge, finally, is either of the things of this

[1] Cf. Macdonald, *Development of Muslim Theology*, etc., pp. 316, 318.

world or of those of the world to come. But it must not be thought that intellectual and religious knowledge, or that the intellect as an organ and tradition as a source of knowledge, are opposed to one another. Each stands in need of the other; and the wise man is he who combines both. Intellectual knowledge may be regarded as food, and religious knowledge as medicine; each has its place, and only the intellectually or the religiously blind is ignorant of this. It is true that the two kinds of acquired knowledge—that of this world and that of the world to come—are mutually opposed. He who devotes himself to the one is generally ignorant of the other. The power of the intellect cannot in general extend equally over both. Only the prophets whom God has sent to instruct men as to gaining their subsistence in this world and their happiness in the world to come can cover all knowledge. For this God assists them with the Holy Spirit and with divine power.

Here, again, is made very plain that the unity of Islām is absolute. All spheres of knowledge are controlled by the Prophet, and he is the guider and instructor of men in every department. There can be no rendering to Caesar and to God, nor could Muḥammad ever have said, "Who hath made me a ruler and divider over you?" That, in Islām, is precisely what the Prophet is for.

It is natural, then, that all processes of revelation—of a forcible breaking in from the Unseen—should be of the first importance, not only for the devotional life, but for the theory and practice of knowledge. To such violent in-breakings we shall turn in the next lecture.

LECTURE IX

THE MYSTERY OF MAN'S BODY AND MIND AND THE TWO SOURCES OF KNOWLEDGE

Knowledge which is not axiomatic but is in the mind at one time and not at another comes in al-Ghazzālī's classification in two ways. One is by study and deduction. It is called reflection and meditation, and is the method of the ʿUlamā, the formal authorities on theology and law in general. The other comes with a sudden attack upon the heart, as though something were cast (*qadhafa*) into the heart without its knowledge. The creature does not know how it comes to him, or whence, or the reason why that knowledge is granted to him. It is simply a contemplation of the world of angels which he finds in his heart. The name given to this form of revelation when it is granted to saints is *ilhām*, which means literally "a causing to swallow or gulp down." Once it is used in the *Qurʾān* (xci, 8), but whether in the primitive or the theological sense is obscure. The earliest exegetes take it in both (Ṭabarī, *Tafsīr*, Vol. XXX, pp. 115 f.), and in later Muslim usage the word came to indicate, normally, the minor inspiration of *walīs*, or saints. It is significant for the external violence with which this knowledge is supposed to be given. The major inspiration, that of prophets, is called *waḥy*, (literally "sending," "writing" a message)—fixed already in that theological sense in the *Qur'ān*—but the phenomenon itself is felt to be essentially the same.

The result, then, is that we have the heart of man so equipped that the essence of all things can be disclosed in it as in a mirror. Over against it is the Preserved Tablet (*al-lawḥ al-maḥfūẓ*) on which is engraved all that God has decreed until the day of resurrection. This would be reflected in man's heart, if it were not for the veils of sense which hang between. Yet these may be moved aside, as it were, either by the hand or blown by the wind of God's favor. When that happens, part of what is written on the tablet is disclosed. Sometimes this takes place in sleep when the future is revealed; the process is complete only at death. And sometimes, during waking life, the veil is lifted by secret favor from God, and there shine on the heart from behind it some of the hidden things. At one time this happens in a single flash and at another continuously to a certain degree; but this last is very rare. The difference between knowledge acquired by study and deduction and this *ilhām* knowledge lies purely in the removing of the veil—a matter outside of man's will; the nature, the place, and the cause of the knowledge are the same in both cases. Between *ilhām* and *waḥy* the only difference is that the angel messenger, who casts the knowledge into the heart, can be seen by the prophet. In all cases the knowledge is given by angels. So God said, "And it is not for a human being that God should speak with him save by revelation (*waḥy*), or from behind the veil, or [save] that he should send a messenger and so reveal in his ear what he wills."[1]

The commentator adds a brief statement of the kinds of knowledge: (1) knowledge axiomatic or directly from impact on the senses; (2) knowledge by consideration of premises, either intellectual or of the senses; (3) knowledge from the report of men, either by hearing or reading; (4) knowledge from inspiration (*waḥy*) either by the tongue of an angel who is seen, or by hearing his speech without seeing him, or by having it cast into the mind while awake or in dream.[2]

[1] *Qur.* xlii, 50.

[2] The following table may perhaps make al-Ghazzālī's epistemology somewhat clearer:

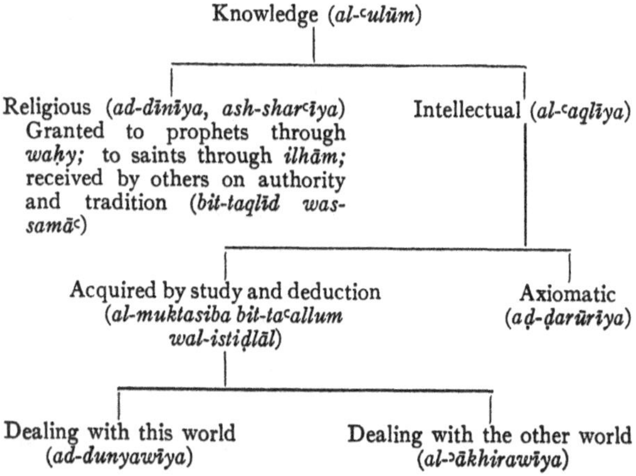

The Ṣūfīs, then, turn rather to knowledge gained by *ilhām* than to that acquired by study. Books and proofs they shun. Their path (*ṭarīq*), rather, is to cleave to spiritual striving, to remove blameworthy qualities, to sever all ties, to advance with the utmost zeal toward God. Whenever these things take place, God takes charge of the heart of his creature, and illumines it with knowledge, and opens the breast of the seeker so that he accepts guidance and trusts God; there is revealed to him the secret of the heavenly kingdom (*al-malakūt*), and there is cleared away from the surface of his heart the veil of error, and so the essences of divine things shine in it. All that he has to do is to prepare himself by simple purifying, by showing zeal joined to pure will, by thirsting and watching and expecting. If any turn thus to God, God will turn to him.

Practically, the course which is advised is as follows. Let the seeker sever all the ties of this world and empty it from his heart. Let him cut away all anxiety for family, wealth, children, home; for knowledge, rule, ambition. Let him reduce his heart to a state in which the existence of anything and its non-existence are the same to him. Then let him sit alone in some corner, limiting his religious duties to what are absolutely incumbent, and not occupying himself either with reciting the *Qur'ān* or considering its meaning or with books of religious traditions or anything of the like. And let him see to it that nothing save God most High enters his mind. Then as he sits alone in solitude, let him not cease saying continuously with his tongue, "*Allāh, Allāh,*" keeping his thought on it. At last he will reach a state when the motion of his tongue will cease, and it will seem as though the word flowed from it. Let him persevere in this until all trace of motion is removed from his tongue, and he finds his heart persevering in the thought. Let him still persevere until the form of the word, its letters and shape, is removed from his heart, and there remain the idea alone, as though clinging to his heart, inseparable from it. So far all is dependent on his will and choice; his continuance, too, in this state and his warding off the whisperings of Satan are also thus dependent; but to bring the mercy of God does not stand in his will or choice. He has now laid himself bare to the breathings of that mercy, and nothing now remains but to await what God will open to him, as God has done after this manner to prophets and saints. If he follows the above course, he may be sure that the light of the real will shine out in his heart. At first unstable, like a flash of lightning, it turns and returns; though sometimes it hangs back. And if it returns, sometimes it abides and sometimes it is momentary. And if it abides, sometimes its abiding is long, and sometimes short. And sometimes appearances like to the first show themselves, coming one after the other, and sometimes all is of one kind. The attainments of the saints of God in this respect cannot be reckoned, just as their differences of character cannot be reckoned.

That a state of auto-hypnosis, with very curious consequences, could be produced by the abstraction, physical and mental, above described and by the mechanical repetition of a single phrase seems tolerably certain. There is the case on record of Tennyson who, by the repetition of his own name, could bring himself into a similar dreamy state with resultant ideas which he regarded as veridical.[1] The like performance, also, of Mr. Kipling's "Kim" is undoubtedly a fair representation of Indian practice.[2] That the boy of Indian training and the Englishman should endeavor to reach the Unseen through emphasis on their own personalities, while the Muslim does the same by the name of Allāh, is certainly significant. The first probably connects with the pantheism which sees the All as God, and the other with that which sees God as the All.

We have already had another example of this in Lane's Persian friend (p. 208 above). He used as his formula not *Allāh*, but *Lā ilāha illā-llāh*, "There is no God but Allāh." The Sayyid Murtaḍà, al-Ghazzālī's commentator, here remarks upon the different value of these two phrases.

[1] James, *Varieties of Religious Experience*, pp. 383 f.; Tenny son, *Memoirs*, Vol. II, p. 473.

[2] *Kim*, chap. xi.

Allāh is the formula used by those with whom drawing (*jadhba*) on God's side predominates, while the longer phrase is used by those with whom their own journeying (*sulūk*) toward God comes first. In the later development of the darwīsh fraternities this distinction between *jadhba* and *sulūk* went much farther. Those who preferred orderly progress under definite law were *sāliks*, "journeyers," while those who embarked without restraint on the broad sea of their feeling of God's drawing them and attracting them to himself were *majdhūbs*, "attracted." The one party held fast to a theological statement—half of the fundamental Muslim creed—while the other plunged into those subjective dreamings of Allāh which his name alone might provoke. It is to be remembered that Allāh, for Muslims, is the proper name of God like Jehovah, and not a common noun like the word God. In the end, the distinctions issued in the now primary division between the darwīshes who observe the outward usages of the Muslim faith and those who have dropped all such observance, although they continue to call themselves Muslims. The one class is called, in the Persian phrase, *bā-sharᶜ*, "with law," and the other, *bī-sharᶜ*, "without law." Those *bī-sharᶜ* not only reject the ritual law, considering themselves raised above such requirements, but are also, in teaching and practice, simple antinomians. This, of course, was very far from al-Ghazzālī's teaching, nor, certainly, has his commentator any such distinction here in mind.

The commentator now enters upon some further details of interest. The method (*ṭarīqa*) here laid down by al-Ghazzālī is traced back on two lines of teaching descent to the Prophet himself. It had also reached the commentator in a similar way from one of al-Ghazzālī's contemporaries. But the name by which it is known is the Naqshbandite method, from a certain much later Muḥammad an-Naqshbandī, who founded the order of Naqshbandite darwīshes, with this as their rule, and died in A. H. 791 (A. D. 1389). It was not until more than fifty years after al-Ghazzālī's death that any still existent darwīsh fraternities were founded as continuous corporations.

These authorities all agree that the essence of the method is that the aspirant should abide in thought continuously in the presence of the Reality (*al-ḥaqq*, meaning Allāh), without perception of anything else and heedless, through the existence of Allāh, of being in his presence. This can happen only through operation of the divine drawing and is most powerfully aided by companionship with a shaykh who is drawn in the same way. They say, also, that it can be attained either by this companionship alone, or by thought (*dhikr*) of Allāh, or by contemplation (*murāqaba*).

1. The thought of God (*dhikr*) is expressed by

the phrase *Lā ilāha illā-llāh*, "There is no God but Allāh," and its effect is part denial and part assertion. The first phrase is denial, and with it there is banished the existence of humanity; the second phrase is assertion, and there appears with it one of the effects worked by the divine drawing. This effect differs according to the preparation. In the case of some the first effect to appear is distance (*ghayba*) from all but God; in the case of others the result is "thankful praise" (*shukr*) and distance and, thereafter, the existence of non-existence is assured to him, and, finally, he is ennobled with complete "passing away" (*fanā*). Another expounder took *Qur.*, xviii, 23, "And remember thy Lord when thou forgettest," and explained, "when thou forgettest other than him; then thou forgettest thyself; then thou forgettest thy remembering in thy remembering; then thou forgettest in Allāh's remembering thee, all thy remembering." The loftiest and most complete of the stages is "passing away" (*fanā*), when there does not remain to the traveler information concerning anything save Allāh. The object of this school is the beholding of Allāh—the reality—just as though you saw him; the habit of being present with him is called "beholding" (*mushāhada*), and this takes place through the heart.

2. "Contemplation" is the easiest of the methods and leads most directly to God. It is scrutiny of the

holy idea, lofty beyond limit and without like, which is understood from the blessed name Allāh without the intermediary of any expressions, Arabic or Persian or otherwise. After the understanding comes the holding of that idea in the imagination and the facing with all the forces and perceptions toward the physical heart and continuing that and taking pains in clinging to it until the taking of pains departs, and that becomes a habit. If this is difficult, let the seeker image that idea as a wide light encompassing all existences, seen and known. Then let him set this over against his inner eye and, holding it fast, turn with all his forces and perceptions to the physical heart, until the inner eye be strengthened and the form depart; and the appearance of the sought-for idea thereupon be firm. On account of the greater ease and immediacy of this method al-Ghazzālī limited himself to describing it above. It leads, also, directly to the miraculous powers of *walīs* as God's representatives. By it, too, is made possible the control of thoughts and, by divine gift, the power of looking into others and illuminating their inner being. When it is a habit, there results continuance of union with God and receiving of his speech; this is the idea behind the words, "joining" (*jam*ᶜ) and "receiving" (*qabūl*).

3. The method connected with a shaykh has the same advantage as lies in (1), that of the "thought" (*dhikr*) of God, only companionship with the shaykh

helps to bring forth companionship with God, who is "thought of." The seeker ought, as much as possible, to preserve the effect which he perceives to result from his companionship with his shaykh. If there is any break, he returns to that companionship until the effect returns. This he does, time after time, until that mode becomes a habit. Sometimes there results from this companionship such love and attraction that the figure of the shaykh is held in the imagination, and there is a turning to the physical heart with it until distance (*ghayba*) and passing away from the self (*fanā*) result.

To this method one of the later shaykhs made an addition which he said had been taught him and urged upon him by al-Khaḍir. This was the restraining of the breath in the course of "remembering" and "contemplation." He made it one of the fundamentals of the method and said that labor should be given to a certain constraint between two breaths so that the breath should not go in or out without attention. This became a usage generally followed and an addition of which the commentator approved. Whether al-Ghazzālī would have approved is another matter. Some very singular mechanical aids came later to be in more or less repute. Undoubtedly, suggestive usages and the association of certain ideas with them would go far to help the self-hypnotizing process. With the views stated here of the value of a shaykh, the experience of Tawakkul Beg should be compared.[1]

We can now return to al-Ghazzālī himself. As might be expected, the speculative theologians objected to the general use of this method of reaching religious truth. They admitted its existence and that it was the method of prophets, but it was difficult and slow, and its conditions were hard to combine. The propitious state of insight lasted only a moment; a breath from the outside destroyed it. The heart, too, was essentially mobile and uncertain. It was easily affected by physical conditions, and, under these, pathological and destructive imaginings might arise, which might then be trusted and followed with disastrous results. These we should now call non-veridical hallucinations, and al-Ghazzālī, too, was well aware of their possibility. Finally, a prophet might become a canon lawyer by inspiration, but for ordinary men there was no way except study; any other course was like exchanging farming for treasure-digging.

But the essential difference between the two methods—insight by the heart and study—must now be made clear. Al-Ghazzālī does it again by means of two illustrations. One is a really startling anticipation of Wordsworth's "eternal deep, haunted forever by the eternal mind," and of the still more recent conception of a subliminal consciousness in

[1] See above, pp. 195 ff.

direct touch with the infinite. Let there be imagined a pond into which water flows in streams from the higher-lying ground. And let, also, the bed of the pond be dug up until there rises into it, from the springs of the earth, water purer and more abundant than that which the streams afford. Then, if the streams are closed up, the water will still rise in the pond, and will do so even more spontaneously and steadily. This pond is the heart; the water which pours in from the streams is knowledge coming by way of the five senses; the water which rises from the springs is the knowledge which comes directly to the heart. When the paths of the senses are closed, from the depths of the heart there will rise knowledge still purer and more abundant.

But it may be said, "There are veins of water in the earth which thus rise, but whence does knowledge flow directly into the heart?" The answer comes by asking another question. How does knowledge come to the heart in any case? Al-Ghazzālī views it thus. For all that is, or is done in the world, God has written on the Preserved Tablet (*al-lawḥ al-maḥfūẓ*) something that can be compared to an architect's plan for a house. Of course this is only using the qurʾānic expression to say that all earthly things and doings exist and have always existed definitely registered in the spiritual world. According to this plan, then, the world has been created and is being conducted. It has now become material (*jismānī*) and factual (*ḥaqīqī*). From this second is derived a third corresponding existence in the senses and in the imagination, or picturing power of the mind (*al-khayāl*). Thence, finally, comes a fourth, an intellectual form of existence (*ʿaqlī*), in the heart. Thus things have four existences, and in this way comes our ordinary knowledge of the outside world. But is it so ordinary? How can the eye take in the unbounded universe, or the mind know that which is outside itself, or retain the knowledge of that which has passed away? It can be only by an act of beneficence of the divine wisdom that there can come these existences in the senses, in the imagination and in the heart. We could never perceive a thing that did not reach us, and unless there were something in our being corresponding to the world, we could never retain any knowledge of what had gone by. That means that the human body is a mysterious structure, combining relationships with the material and with the spiritual worlds. Al-Ghazzālī, in short, forces us back on the primary mystery of the relation of mind and body. Man's body is the link, but it and its operations are, none the less, perpetual miracles.

If, then, we are asked how the heart sees, the answering question is pertinent, How do the eye, the imagination, the mind see, retain, know? No more nor less miraculous is the vision which the heart has directly of the plans on the Preserved Tablet. The evidence for this as fact is the evidence of those who have attained to such knowledge; it is the same in kind, though not so large in amount, as the evidence for the fact of vision. Direct heart-vision is a permanent property belonging to the nature of man, but the hearts of most God has blinded so that they cannot see. If they can, by suitable meditations and exercises, raise the veils, then they will see and know. Every man is potentially a seer and a saint.

The heart, then, has two doorways; one opening on the spiritual world, and the other on the five senses which take hold of the world of sense. And the one of these worlds corresponds after a fashion to the other world. How the door is opened to knowledge through the senses is already plain. Certainty as to the other can be acquired through considering the marvels of vision and how the heart is instructed as to the future or the past in sleep. That doorway is opened only to one who has given himself up to the thought of God and keeps himself aloof, through that thought, from everything else.

But, turning from the two means of access, al-Ghazzālī propounds another parable to explain the different methods of working of the Ṣūfīs and of the speculative students of theology. The people of China and the people of Byzantium once competed before one of the kings as to their respective abilities in decorating. So the king gave over a vestibule to be adorned by them; one side by the people of China, and the other by the people of Byzantium. A curtain was let down between, and none knew what the other was doing. The people of Byzantium set to work with all manner of strange paints and dyes. But the people of China took nothing behind their side of the curtain and simply smoothed and polished their wall. So all men wondered what they could be doing without any paint or materials. But when the curtain was removed, their wall shone like a mirror and reflected all the beautiful work of the Byzantine artists, with the added glory of brilliancy and clearness.

Such is the manner of working of God's saints. They strive only to polish and purify the soul, until it may reflect clearly the spiritual world. But speculative theologians, like the people of Byzantium, try to adorn it with all manner of knowledge and science. Each has his method. But however that may be, rank in the world to come will depend upon knowledge of divine things. Both purity of heart and knowledge in the heart persist there with the hearts to which they belong. "The dust cannot devour the abode of faith," said a saint, and that faith is a means of access and nearness to God; there can never be more than enough of it. It is true that there are all manner of grades of spiritual experience and faith; but all count. A man who has a little money is independent (*ghanī*) to that extent, and so far is in the same class with the very wealthy man (*al-ghanī*). So with faith, and spiritual knowledge; these are as lights (so spoken of in the *Qurʾān*) leading to God; but they may be mere tapers, and they may be as the sun.

This affects the doctrine of the faith that is to salvation. He who has over a grain of faith will never enter the Fire; he who has a grain or less, if he has any, will not abide in the Fire. It is certain, from the teaching of the *Qurʾān*, that there are many stations in the Garden just as there are divisions in knowledge, ranging from the most ignorant believer on authority (*muqallad*) to the most experienced saint (*ʿārif*).

But a proof may still be needed that this is legally a sound method. To such a proof al-Ghazzālī now turns. This section is, naturally, not of the same importance to us, and I give only so much here as may be of value for our knowledge of the spiritual life of Islām. Ibn Khaldūn's argument, on pp. 165 ff. above, should be compared. No one, says al-Ghazzālī, who has had any experience, however slight, of such falling of knowledge into the heart, he knew not whence, will ask for any other proof that he is within the law. As for him who has had no such personal experience, let him consider the following proofs. These divide into passages in the *Qurʾān*, traditions from the Prophet, experiences and stories from the saints. The first are all somewhat general and deal with turning, striving, pressing towards God, elaborate developments of the metaphor of "light," promises of aid toward the understanding of the *Qur'ān*. Nothing seems to go beyond the devout life, seeking support and guidance from its Lord. One somewhat famous text is *Qur.* xviii, 64: "And we taught him some knowledge of our own (*min ladunnā*)." All knowledge is of God, but transcendental knowledge (*al-ʿilm ar-rabbānī, al-ladunī*) is that which is given directly to the heart without passing through human teaching. So the true scholar (*ʿālim*) is not he who learns a book by heart, which he may forget, but he who takes knowledge from his Lord (*min rabbihi*) at what time he wills, without learning by heart or studying.

The stories of saints given are largely of the nature of thought-transference, and very simple cases at that. One of the more picturesque is as follows: Someone went in one day to ash-Shiblī, a celebrated mystic and ascetic who died A. H. 334 (A. D. 945–46), and ash-Shiblī said to him, "Tested! Aḥmad." Said Aḥmad to him, "How was that?" "I was sitting," he answered, "and there suddenly came into my mind, 'You are a miser.' I said, 'I am not a miser,' but the thought kept coming back to me and saying, 'Nay, but you are a miser.' So I said, 'Whatever God sends me today I will give to the first poor man I meet.' My thought was hardly complete when there came to me a friend of Muʾnis, the

Khādim, and brought me fifty dīnārs, saying, 'Use them for your affairs.' So I rose and went out and there was a poor blind man, sitting before a barber, who was shaving his head. I went to him and offered to him the dīnārs, but he said, 'Give them to the barber.' I said, 'But they amount to such and such.' He said, 'Have we not said to you that you are a miser?' So I offered them to the barber, but he said, 'When this poor man sat down before me I determined not to take anything on his account.' "So," finishes ash-Shiblī, "I cast the dīnārs into the Tigris and said, 'None honoreth thee but God abaseth him.'" Here ash-Shiblī had a flash of insight into himself, which he would not at first believe, but which was justified by his protest to the poor man; and the poor man read from the mind of ash-Shiblī his previous experience. So he comments upon himself in bitter humor that he must be so low that no one can honor him with a present without being dishonored by the throwing away of his present. His trial had shown him that no one could come to any good through him.

The following are of a different kind and humor. The commentator tells them from al-Qushayrī, a Ṣūfī writer who died in A. H. 465 (A. D. 1072–3): Sufyān ath-Thawrī once pilgrimaged along with Shaybān ar-Rāʿī, and a lion encountered them. Then said Sufyān to Shaybān, "Don't you see this lion?" But Shaybān said, "Don't be afraid," and he took hold of the lion's ears and rubbed them, and the lion wagged his tail and moved his ears. Then Sufyān said, "What kind of showing off is this?" But Shaybān replied, "If it were not for the fear of showing off, I would set my provender upon his back until I came to Mecca." The miraculous power of *walīs* should be concealed by them and never turned to a show or a boast. The miracle of a prophet, on the other hand, is always a public sign. Another story is that Ibrāhīm ibn Adham was in a traveling company and a lion encountered them. But Ibrāhīm went to it and said, "O lion! if thou hast been commanded anything against us, execute it; and if not, depart!" And the lion departed. Another narrator says, "I was with Ibrāhīm al-Khawwāṣ in open field, and when we were beside a tree a lion came. So I climbed the tree and remained there, unsleeping, until the morning. But al-Khawwāṣ lay down and slept, and the lion sniffed him all over from head to foot and went away. The second night we passed in a mosque in a village, and a bug fell upon his face and bit him, and he moaned and cried out. So I said, 'This is a wonder! Yesternight you were not troubled at the lion, and tonight you cry out for a bug.' But he said, 'As for yesterday, that was a state in which I was with God most high; but as for tonight, this is a state in which I am with myself.'" For such minor miracles (*karāmāt*) parallel testimony can be found, not only in the hagiology, but in the psychology, abnormal and normal, of all peoples. The lion stories, for example, are of exactly the same type as the case reported by Dr. Weir Mitchell,[1] of a woman who, in a secondary state of personality, wandered in the woods and treated with similar familiarity the bears which she met. St. Francis, too, appears to have had like powers.

But al-Ghazzālī, like our present day psychical investigators, knew very well that any number of such stories could force no conviction on the deniers who had themselves experienced nothing of the kind. They had not met al-Khaḍir face to face, or heard the bodiless voice of a *hātif*, the *bath qôl* of the Hebrews, the *δαίμων* of Socrates and the auditory hallucination[2] of modern psychology, and they were very sure that no one else had. So he falls back on two points which even they could not deny. The first is the marvel of a veridical dreaming (cf. above pp. 70 ff.). If that is possible in sleep, it should not be impossible in waking; for the only difference between the two states is the slumber of

[1] *Transactions of College of Physicians of Philadelphia*, April 4, 1888; quoted in James, *Psychology*, Vol. II, pp. 381–84, and Myers, *Human Personality*, Vol. I, pp. 336, 337; also the story of the saint and the tiger in Swynnerton, *Indian Nights' Entertainment*, pp. 32 f.

[2] There are curious cases, also, of visual hallucination. Ash-Shādhilī (d. A. H. 654 = A. D. 1256) said, "They sometimes ask me a question to which I do not know the answer, and lo! there it is written in the corner on the reed-mat or the wall."

the senses and the lack of occupation with sensuous percepts. In this distinction, of course, our psychology will hardly bear him out. The second is the fact that a prophet gives information about the unseen world and future things; that all admitted. But a prophet is simply a man to whom the essential natures of things have been revealed, and who is occupied with the improvement of mankind. The existence, therefore, is not impossible of others, possessing the first characteristic but having nothing to do with the second. These are the *walīs*, saints, who have no commission to preach, but only to cultivate their own souls. This is another example of the argument from classification noticed above, pp. 63 and 152.

Anyone, then, who admits these two things, must admit the two gateways of the heart, an external one through the senses and an internal one, opening directly on the heavenly kingdom. Through both knowledge must come, mediate and immediate, and the truth of the description of the heart as swaying between the world of the senses and the Unseen is evident. How great a thing this is must also be plain. Through the heart man can come into direct and intimate association with God and know what angels know not. They cannot see what is in the heart, and the heart of the man of spiritual experience (*ᶜārif*) can tell him things which they cannot. For the Muslim, man is higher than the angels.

LECTURE X

THE TEMPTATIONS OF THE HEART AND THE NATURE OF EVIL SPIRITS

We pass now to the temptations which assail the heart. The fundamental conception here is the whispering (*waswās*) of the devil to the heart. Twice in the *Qur'ān* the expression is used distinctly of the devil (vii, 19; xx, 118); once uncertainly, but of something evil (cxiv, 4, 5) and once (l. 15) of the soul (*nafs*), evidently as inciting to evil. In Muslim theological and ethical works the word has come to be normal for such satanic incitation.

Al-Ghazzālī divides this subject into five sections: (1) how the devil gains rule over the heart by "whispering" and the meaning of "whispering" generally; (2) the different modes of the approach of the devil to the heart; (3) what "whisperings" in the heart the creature is punished for and for what he is forgiven; (4) is it conceivable that "whisperings" can be cut off entirely at times of the thought (*dhikr*) of God? (5) with what speed the heart turns and changes, and how hearts differ in this respect.

I. The heart is like a round building with doors open on all sides, or a target struck by arrows from all directions, or a mirror over which forms are continually passing, or a pond into which waters are constantly flowing; ever-renewed and ever-changing impressions are being produced upon it.

They come through the senses externally, and internally through the imagination, the fleshly appetite, anger—the complex nature of man in general. Whenever he perceives anything by the senses, an effect is produced on his heart. So, too, when the fleshly appetite is moved by overfeeding. And even if the senses are closed the imagination moves from thing to thing and the heart with it from state to state. So it is in constant change on account of these causes. The most specific of these impressions are the ideas which occur to the mind (*khawāṭir;* literally *Einfälle*), coming from thoughts and recollections. These move operations of the will; for a thing must be thought of before it can be intended or willed; then the will moves the body. Next, these ideas can be divided into those which summon to good and those which summon to evil. The first are called *ilhām* and the second *waswās*, "whispering." The causer of the first is called an angel, and the causer of the second a devil (*shayṭān*). The divine benignity by which the heart is prepared to receive ideas inciting to good is called "help" (*tawfīq*) and the opposite is "seduction" and "desertion." "Angel," then, is an expression for one of God's creations whose business is the urging of good and adding of knowledge and unveiling of the truth and promising of good and commanding kindness; "the devil" is an expression for a creature whose business is the opposite of that, promising evil and commanding vileness and scaring by the threat of poverty when there is solicitude for the good.[1] So "whispering" is over against *ilhām* and the devil against the angel and "help" against "desertion." As has been said in the *Qur'ān* (li, 49), "Of every thing we have created a pair," and all things are coupled in apposition except God himself.

So the heart is pulled about between the devil and the angel. It has two traveling companions, as Muḥammad has said; for the one, God should be praised; and against the other, his aid should be sought. This, too, is the meaning of his saying that the heart of the believer is between two of God's fingers. It is a metaphorical expression for God's working upon it through the angel and the devil. By its created nature the heart is equally fitted to be affected by either. Passion (*hawā*) may be followed or opposed. In the one case, the devil settles in the heart and rules it; in the other case, the angels. But no heart is free from fleshly appetite and anger and desire, and therefore the devil and his whisperings always haunt it. The Prophet said, "There is not one of you who has not a devil." They said to him, "Even thou, O apostle of God?" He replied, "Even I; only God aided me against him, and he gave it up and commands only good,"

[1] *Qur.* ii, 271.

the meaning of which is that when the fleshly appetite keeps within due measure, the devil who has clothed himself in it can command good only. And, on the other hand, those in whose hearts passion and the lusts are strong come to be ruled by the devil, who becomes their real god. The cure is to empty the heart; but more curious prescriptions are sometimes given. One complained to the Prophet that the devil came between him and his prayers. "That is a devil," said Muḥammad, "who is called Khinzib. Whenever you feel him, seek refuge with God from him and spit thrice on your left." But the thought of God in general is the most effective means. To destroy the whisperings of the devil another thought must be put in the mind. That of God and of the things connected with him should therefore be used, for in it the devil never can find room. Hence, the virtue of such phrases as, "I seek refuge with God from the stoned devil," and "There is no strength or power save in God, the High, the Mighty."

The lusts, then, so run in the flesh and blood of men, and the rule of the devil over them is, in consequence, so normal that at all points the devil lies in wait for them. Even in their embracing of Islām, in their migrating with the Prophet to al-Madīna, in their fighting in the path of God, the devil has been able to suggest evil. He has also the art to suggest things praiseworthy in themselves and yet so to develop them that they lead to destruction. A description is given, for example, how a man can be led into preaching and through it brought into spiritual pride, love of popularity and ambition. This, with little doubt, is autobiographic; al-Ghazzālī preached at one time and gave it up for the sake of his own soul.[1] Another example is that Satan (Iblīs) appeared once to Jesus and said to him, "Say, 'There is no God save Allāh.'" Jesus replied, "That is a true word, but I will not say it for thy saying." Under its good are implications. It is the duty, then, of the creature to watch every solicitude that runs in his mind and test it whence it comes. Absolutely to cut off these things there is only one way. Let him retire into solitude in a darkened house—this will block the senses, the avenues outward; let him strip himself of family and fortune—this will diminish the avenues of whisperings from within; let him occupy himself with the thought of God—this will keep off the imaginations which flow into the heart; let him constantly draw his heart Godward and strive on in this way—the striving will last his life. The gates of the devil to the heart cannot be finally locked; they must always be watched. The devil never sleeps; "Then we should rest!" said one saint. Yet he can be worn out for a time, as a wayfaring man wears out his beast in travel.

[1] "Life," *Journal of American Oriental Society*, Vol. XX, pp. 101 ff.

And, again, while the devil has many gates there is but one by which the angels come. So, while he has many paths to which he calls men, there is but one true path. The Prophet once drew a line upon the ground. "That is the path of God," he said, Then he drew many lines to right and left. "On each of these," he said, "stands a devil calling you." Finding his way here man is like a traveler on a dark night in a desert crossed by innumerable trails A discerning eye and the morning light from the Book of God and the usage of the Prophet alone can guide him.

In what has preceded, concerning the relation of man to his fleshly nature, a curious contradiction has ruled—a reflection, perhaps, of the unresolved paradox of man's nature. At one time al-Ghazzālī recognizes the necessary part which the fleshly appetites and emotions play in the maintenance of human life; he even reckons Satan into this and finds him a creation of God for God's purposes, a necessary balance to the angels. But at another, the absolute ascetic note is struck; all sensuous life must be excluded; existence must be the contemplation of God; Satan is the accursed One. How this develops will appear. Al-Ghazzālī's sense of humanity rose above his theories.

2. But a knowledge of the avenues of approach of the devil is also necessary and is as absolute a duty of the individual as warding them off. These

avenues of approach are human qualities, and are very many. Here al-Ghazzālī can give only the most important; as it were the great gates only of the City of Mansoul: (*a*) anger and fleshly lust. Of these he tells this legend. It should be remembered that the cause of the fall of Satan from his angelic state was his refusal to adore Adam:[1]

Satan met Moses and said "Thou art he whom Allāh has chosen to be his Apostle and with whom he has spoken[2] and I am one of his creatures. I have sinned and desire to repent; so intercede for me with my Lord, that he accept my repentance." To this Moses agreed. Then when he had gone up into the mountain and spoken with his Lord, and was about to descend, his Lord said to him, "Deliver that intrusted to thee." So Moses said, "Thy creature, Satan, desires to repent." And Allāh revealed to Moses, "O Moses, thy request is granted; command him that he adore the grave of Adam, that his repentance may be accepted." Then Moses met Satan and said to him, "Thy request is granted; thou art commanded to adore the grave of Adam that thy repentance may be accepted." But he was angry and proud, and said, "I did not adore him living, and shall I adore him dead?" Therefore he said, "O Moses, thou hast a right against me, because thou didst intercede for me with thy Lord. If thou remember me, then, on three occasions, I shall not destroy thee. Remember me when thou art angry, for my spirit is in thy heart and my eye is in thy eye and I affect thee as does thy blood, and whenever a man is angry I blow in his nostrils, and he knows not what he does. And remember me when thou meetest an army in array, for when one of mankind meets an army in array I make him to remember wife and child and

1 *Qur*. vii, 10 ff.

2 *Ibid*., iv, 162.

folk, and he turns aside. And beware thou that thou sit with a woman who is not of near kin, for I am her messenger to thee and thy messenger to her."

This story is regarded as a warning against anger, desire of the world and fleshly lust. It is a curious and distinctive feature of Muslim hortatory legend that the warning is so often put into the mouth of Satan himself. (*b*) Envy and cupidity, too, have their tale. It is narrated that—

when Noah entered the ark, he took into it a pair of every kind, as Allāh had commanded him. Then he saw in the ark an old man whom he did not know; and he said to him, "What brought thee in?" He replied, "I came in that I might reach the hearts of thy comrades, that their hearts might be with me and their bodies with thee." Said Noah to him, "Go forth from here, O enemy of Allāh! for thou art accursed." But Satan said to him, "There be five things by which I destroy mankind. Shall I tell thee of three of them or of two?" And Allāh revealed to Noah, "Thou hast no need of the three; let him tell thee of the two." So Noah said, "What are the two?" And he said, "They are the two which give me not the lie; they are the two which fail me not; by them I destroy mankind; they are envy and cupidity. For by envy was I accursed, and became a pelted devil."

(*c*) Fullness of food, even though it be lawful and pure. It is narrated—

that Satan appeared to John, son of Zacharias, and he saw upon him thongs or straps for every purpose. So he said, "O Satan, what are those thongs?" And Satan said, "These are the lusts by which I reach men." He said, "And have I anything among them?" Satan replied. "Sometimes thou art full of food, and we make thee too heavy to pray and think of God." He said, "Is there aught else?" Satan replied, "Nay." Then he said, "I make my vow to God that I will never fill my belly with food again." Then said Satan, "And I make my vow to God that I will never give sound counsel to a Muslim again."

(*d*) Love of adornment in furniture and clothing and house. When that begins there is no end except death. The devil need only start it, and it will go of itself.

(*e*) Importuning men for aught. This because the man importuned becomes, as it were, an object of worship, and to insinuate one's self with him hypocrisy and false carriage are used. Ask naught of any but God.

(*f*) Haste and abandoning of steadiness in affairs. The Prophet said, "Haste is of the devil and patience of Allāh." And there stands in the *Qur'ān* (xxi, 38), "Man was created out of haste," and (xvii, 12) "Man was a hastener." The Muslim version of "The oracles are dumb" is brought to bear on this as follows:

When Jesus, son of Mary, was born, the devils came to Satan and said, "The idols have hung down their heads." He said, "This is something which must have happened; remain ye." So he flew until he had gone to the east and the west of the world, and found naught. Thereafter he found Jesus; he had been born, and lo! the angels surrounded him. So he said, "Lo! a prophet was born yesternight. Until this, a woman never conceived nor bore but I was present. So despair ye that the idols will be worshiped after this night;

but approach ye the sons of men on the side of haste and levity."

(*g*) Money and all kinds of wealth. That is everything above what is absolutely necessary. The heart of him who has only so much is at leisure; with more, desires arise. This is illustrated oddly. If a man finds one hundred dīnārs on the road, ten desires spring up, each of which to accomplish would need a hundred dīnārs. So the man is now really in need of nine hundred dīnārs instead of having a hundred to the good. It is related that Jesus once used a stone as a pillow. Satan passed and said, "O Jesus, thou hast desire of the world!" But Jesus took the stone from under his head and cast it away, and said, "Take it along with the world!" So even a stone may do mischief. A devotee who has one is tempted by it as he stands in prayer; the thought that he could use it as a pillow, and lie down and sleep is in his mind, and disturbs his devotions. How much more, then, the apparatus of luxury!

(*h*) Miserliness and the fear of poverty. There is much in the *Qur'ān* bearing on these, for it constantly exhorts to alms and the expending of money generously and to trust in God. Fear of poverty is thus almost unbelief. It drives, too, to the frequenting of market-places which are the especial abodes of devils.

(*i*) Partisanship for schools and leaders in theology and law. On the hatred, envy, and malice, slighting, contempt, and open hostility to which that leads, al-Ghazzālī has much to say. He had known it himself and seen it around him. It was lip-devotion, too. He who professed to follow one of the great Imāms should imitate his life and deeds. Otherwise that Imām would be his enemy on the day of resurrection.[1]

(*j*) That the masses try to study the problem of the nature and attributes of God. It is the devil who leads them to this, and involves them in vain imaginings and finally makes them unbelievers. For the stupidest of men are those who believe most fixedly in their own reasoning powers, and the most rational of men are most full of suspicion of themselves The Prophet said, "The devil comes to one of you and says, 'Who created you?' then that one says, 'Allāh, who is blessed and exalted in himself.' Then he asks, 'But who created Allāh?'[2] When that, then, comes to one of you, let him say, 'I believe in Allāh and in his apostle;' then that will pass from him." So the Prophet did not command that this "whispering" of the devil should be investigated and disputed, for it comes to the masses rather than to the ʿUlamā. It is the duty, rather, of the masses that

[1] On al-Ghazzāli's own experiences of this kind, in his unregenerate days, see the "Life" of him in the *Journal of the American Oriental Society*, Vol. XX, pp. 74, 104, 107.

[2] Cf. Professor J. B. Pratt's *Psychology of Religious Belief*, p. 203.

they should believe and be submissive and occupy themselves with worship and the gaining of their daily bread, and leave knowledge to the ᶜUlamā. It were better for such an one to commit adultery or steal than to busy himself with theological knowledge, for he who without sure foundations does so, comes to unbelief, he knows not how.

(*k*) Evil suspicion of Muslims. There stands in the *Qurʾān* (xlix, 12), "Avoid ye carefully suspicion; some suspicion is a sin." By it the devil gets hold of a man, and leads him round until he thinks himself better than others. But giving occasion of suspicion should also be avoided. Even the Prophet guarded not himself, but others, by carefulness there. So no one should think that he need not be careful in this way, however high and unshakable his repute. The evil think evil of all. Whenever a man has evil suspicions of men in general and seeks faults in them, know that he is vile within and that that is his vileness oozing out of him.

Such are some of the avenues of approach of the devil; to give them all were impossible.

How, then, can we guard these? Is the thought (*dhikr*) of God enough?

In answer: The treatment is to close these avenues by purifying the heart from evil qualities. This is a long matter, but in sum, when these qualities have been rooted out from the heart, the devil has left to him only transient passage through it;

he can throw ideas into it, but has no fixed abode there. Then the thought of God hinders him, for it is of the essence of that thought to be fixed in the heart only after it has been equipped with piety and purity. Otherwise this thought is mere talk (*ḥadīth nafs*), does not rule the heart and cannot prevent the rule of the devil. He is like a hungry dog who comes to you. If you have anything to eat in your hand, you cannot drive him off; but if you have nothing, a word is enough. If there are lusts in the heart, the thought of God remains without, and cannot pierce to the interior where the devil sits. On the other hand, he can work against the saints only when they are careless for a moment.

There follows a number of formulae used in such "thoughts" of God, the repeating of which drives the devil away. Stories, too, come of how he even confessed their efficiency and tried to bribe saints not to teach them to others. They had, evidently, in themselves a magical value. There used to come to the Prophet himself, at his prayers, and disturb him, a devil carrying in his hand a firebrand. He would station himself before the Prophet and could not be driven away by any formula. So Gabriel came and taught the following, to which this devil yielded: "I take refuge in the perfect words of Allāh, which neither pure nor impure can ever pass, from the evil of that which comes forth from the earth and enters into it, of that which descends from the heavens and ascends into them, from the temptations of the night and the day, from the accidents of the night and the day, save an accident that brings good, O Merciful One!" On another occasion he had a personal struggle with the devil, and the traditions about it seem to be the confused and contradictory record of an actual episode in his pathological development. He took the devil by the throat, and choked him, "and I did not let him go until I had felt the cold of his tongue upon my hand. And I thought of tying him to a pillar [of the mosque] until you could come in the morning and see him, but I remembered how Solomon had asked[1] of God that he would give him such rule as would not belong to any after him."

But these formulae are of value only when used by the saintly. Let none think that by reciting them at any time—an *opus operatum*—he can drive away the devil. That is as absurd as to imagine that a medicine will take effect when the stomach is burdened with food. So, "remembering" (*dhikr*) is a medicine, and piety (*taqwā*) is abstinence from food; apply piety first to the heart, empty it of fleshly lusts, and these formulae will drive the devil from you.

But all this leads naturally to a weighty question: This inciter to different acts of rebellion, is he one devil or are there different devils? Al-Ghazzālī

[1] *Qur.* xxxviii, 34.

does not approve of this question here. For practical purposes (*fī-l-muᶜāmala*) it is enough to drive the enemy away; "Eat the vegetable, wherever it may come from, and ask not about the garden." What is plain in the light of reflection on the evidence given by tradition is that there are armies of devils, and each kind of sin has a devil of its own. This would be plain of itself; the variety of effects leads back to variety of causes.

As for the armies, many differing accounts are given of their origin. But they all spring from Satan who is their father. He has especially five sons, each with his *métier:* Thabr, al-Aᶜwar, Miswāṭ, Dāsim, and Zalanbūr. Thabr stirs up trouble; he brings tearing of garments and slapping of cheeks. Al-Aᶜwar's department is fornication; Miswāṭ's is lying; Dāsim makes a husband reproach his wife and be angry with her; Zalanbūr is in charge of markets—hence the continual wrangling and striving there. Khinzib interferes with prayer and Walahān with ritual ablution. These are the best-known names, but other writers enter into greater detail.

So, too, there are armies of angels, and each specializes in the same way. Every believer, says one authority, has one hundred and sixty as a guard; if he were left to himself for an instant, the devils would snatch him away. The relations of men, devils and angels are described thus curiously:

After Adam had fallen to earth—the Muslim Fall was literal, from the top of the mountain of the Earthly Paradise—he said, "O my Lord! if thou dost not aid me against this one between whom and myself Thou hast put hostility, I shall not be strong enough for him." The Lord said, "A son will not be born to thee without an angel being put in charge of him." But he said, "O my Lord! give me more." And the Lord said, "I will requite an evil deed once, and a good deed tenfold, besides what I increase." But he said, "O my Lord! give me more!" The Lord said, "The gate of repentance is open so long as the spirit is in the body." But Satan said, "O my Lord! if Thou dost not aid me against this creature whom thou hast honored over me, I shall not be strong enough for him." The Lord said, "There shall not be born to him a child, but one shall be born to thee also." But Satan said, "O my Lord! give me more." The Lord said, "Thou shalt flow in them as their blood, and take their bosoms for your abodes." But Satan said, "O my Lord! give me more." The Lord said, "Assemble upon them with thy horse and thy foot, and share with them wealth and children, and promise them—and the devil promises them naught except deceit."[1]

On such easy terms are the Lord and Satan in Islām, much as in the Book of Job. Emphasis on the absolute sovereignty of Allāh naturally negates the independence of an evil power, and the sense of Allāh's immediate working negates Satan's isolation. He no longer, it is true, appears in the court of heaven, but he says, "My Lord," and regards himself as part of the necessary apparatus of things.[2]

[1] *Qur.* xvii, 66.

[2] Compare generally with this the chapter above on the Jinn, and especially pp. 139 ff.

But the question is bound to come up: How does the devil appear to some and not to others; and when anyone sees a form, is that the veritable form (*ṣūra*) or only a symbol (*mithāl*)? If it is his veritable form, how is he seen in different forms, or at one time in two different places and in two forms? The answer is that angels and devils have, it is true, each a form which is their real form; but it cannot be seen by the eye, and only in the light of the prophetic gift. Even the Prophet saw Gabriel only twice in his true form, once when he stood up before him blocking all the horizon from east to west, and again on the night of the ascent to heaven (*al-Miʿrāj*) beside the lote-tree of the extremity.[1] Apart from these occasions he mostly saw him in a human form.

So with Satan. By far the most frequent case is that those who have attained the power to see him when awake, see him in a form which is a symbol or likeness of his veritable form. There are many tales of this. And this takes the place of seeing his veritable form. The heart is of such a nature that there must needs appear in it a verity which comes on the side which is over against the world of the heavenly kingdom. Then an effect from that flashes out on the side over against the world of sense; because the two are joined. What so appears is only a construction of the imagination (*mutakhayyila*), as are all things in the world of sense. In that world the

[1] *Qur.* liii.

outside, only, is reached by the senses, and the imagination taking that result is sometimes led entirely astray; the world of sense is a world of much equivocation. But what comes to the imagination by the flashing out of the world of the kingdom upon the secret heart is like to and corresponds to the quality itself, for the form in the kingdom follows the quality, and assuredly a vile conception there is not seen except in a vile form.

The result, then, is that the devil is seen sometimes by way of symbolization and likeness, and sometimes, but very much more rarely, in his true form. He who sees him by a symbol differs from the dreamer only in the fact of actual beholding with the eye.

The commentator adds a very interesting note from Ibn ʿArabī, asserting the same thing of the Jinn, whom he joins with the angels under the one name "spiritual being" (*rūḥānī*). One curious further detail may be worth giving as it agrees exactly with Irish folk-lore. So long as a spiritual being is looked at fixedly in one of its forms by the human eye, it cannot change that form, but is, as it were, fettered by it. The *rūḥānī* must then use a strategem which seems not to have occurred to the Irish leprechaun. He produces a form before himself like a screen and then causes this screen to move away to one side; the eye of his observer follows it involuntarily and he escapes.[1]

[1] *Iḥyā*, Vol. VII, p. 272; Keightley, *Fairy Mythology*, pp. 372 ff.; compare the case of an apparently veridical hallucination

But though al-Ghazzālī declined to go farther on this subject to his present audience, it may be in place for me here to introduce a statement of his philosophy of spirits. I extract it from his *Maḍnūn*, a book containing developments of his teaching which he considered suited for specialist students only. There he continues the subject thus:[1]

Angels, Jinn, and devils are substances existing in themselves, and differing in essence in the same way as do species. An example of that is "power," for it differs from "knowledge," and "knowledge" differs from "power" and both differ from "color." So "power" and "knowledge" and "color" are accidents, existing in something that is not themselves. Similarly, between angel and devil and Jinn there is a difference, and yet each of these has a nature of its own. That there is a difference between Jinn and angels is certain, but it is not known whether it is a difference between two species, like that between "horse" and "man," or whether the difference is in accidents like that between "man complete" and "incomplete." Similarly, the difference between angel and devil. There—if the species is one, and the difference applies to accidents—it is like that between a good man and a bad man, or between a prophet and a saint. To all appearance, the difference is that of species; but knowledge as to this is with God only.

The above-mentioned beings are indivisible. I mean that the *locus* of knowledge of God is one and indivisible, for unitary knowledge is not located save in one *locus*. So, too,

in the *Journal of the Society for Psychical Research* for February, 1907, where "a big bumble bee whirled right through" the phantasm and made it disappear.

[1] Pp. 23 ff., edition of Cairo 1303.

the essence of man. Knowledge and ignorance of one thing, when situated in one *locus* are contradictory, and when in two *loci* are not contradictory. And with respect to the indivisibility of this substance and the question as to whether it is limited or not, the consideration of these questions goes back to our opinion as to the existence of units that can not be further divided [the indestructible atom]. If an indivisible unit is an impossibility [if there are no atoms], then this substance is undivided and unlimited, and if the existence of an indivisible unit is not impossible, then it is possible that this substance is limited. And some have said that it is not allowable that it should be either undivided or unlimited, for God is both, and what then would separate this from him? But that does not necessarily follow, because perhaps they differ in the essence of their individuality; and if there are stripped from both of them their divisibility and limitedness and space conditions—which is simply removing from God qualities belonging to human beings (*sulūb*)—then there remains only the consideration of the essences, because that which is stripped from the essences is like the two accidents differing in definition and nature and located in the same *locus*, for the assertion of their need of a *locus* and of their being in the same *locus* does not mean that they are like one another. So, similarly, stripping away the need of *locus* and place does not mean that this stripping is common to these two things.

And it is possible that these substances, I mean the substances of angels, may be seen, although they are non-sensible. This seeing is of two kinds, either by way of taking a semblance, as Allāh said, "And he took for her the semblance of a well-formed man."[1] and as the Prophet saw Gabriel in the form of Diḥya al-Kalbi. And the second kind is that some angels have a sensible body, just as our souls are non-sensible but have a sensible body, which is the *locus* of their

[1] *Qur.* xix, 17, of Gabriel appearing to Mary.

control and their peculiar world. So it is with some angels. And perhaps this sensible body is dependent upon the illumination of the light of the prophetic gift, just as the sensible things of this world of ours are dependent for perception upon the illumination of the light of the sun. The case is similar with the Jinn and devils.

3. The references in the *Qurʾān* and in the traditions from Muḥammad to the culpability of evil thoughts in the heart are contradictory to a degree. Some statements make such thoughts punishable and others let them go free. But al-Ghazzālī believed that he could clear up the confusion by a fourfold analysis. First, he says, there comes the idea thrown into the mind; second, an inclination of the nature toward the thing thus suggested; third, a decision or conviction of the heart in favor of the thing; fourth, a determination and purpose to do the thing. Then comes the actual doing which, of course, is punishable.

The first two stages are to be accounted guiltless; they come from the nature of man. As to the third, all depends upon whether the decision is voluntary or not. The fourth is plainly culpable, but if it does not pass into action, the guilt may be wiped out. It may have been only a moment's heedlessness, and in the books of the recording angels good is entered at ten times the value of evil. Yet if anyone dies in the purpose of mortal sin, he goes to the Fire. By intentions, deeds are judged. When Muslims fight together, both the slayer and the slain are guilty;

the one because he has slain his brother; the other, though dying wronged, because he had purposed the slaying of his brother. The doctrine of intention (*nīya*) in Muslim ethics plays a large part. Ignorance as to an essential fact may make a man guilty or innocent, but the law itself is unaffected. If, as in the case above, a man willingly slays a brother Muslim, he is guilty; if he slays him, believing him not a Muslim, he is innocent; if he slays a non-Muslim, believing him a Muslim, he is guilty.

4. As to whether the "whisperings" of the devil can be entirely cut off by the thought of God, those who have studied and know the human heart are of five different opinions. Some say flatly that they can, and base this on the saying of the Prophet, "Whenever God is remembered, the devil retires." This they take absolutely. A second party teaches that they cannot be utterly destroyed. They remain in the heart but produce no effect; the heart is too much occupied by the thought of God. A third party holds that their effect also remains; there are still the "whisperings," but they are as from a distance and weak. A fourth, that they are destroyed when God is remembered, but only for a moment; then the "remembering" is destroyed for a moment; and so the two follow at such close intervals that they seem to be competing, and the effect is like a row of dots round a ball; if you make it rotate rapidly

they become a circle. So the withdrawal of the devil really takes place, but we see his "whisperings" along with our "remembering." A fifth holds that the "whisperings" and "remembering" compete continuously in abiding in the heart, as a man can see two things at one time.

But the fact, in al-Ghazzālī's opinion, is that all these views are sound; only each does not cover all the phases of "whispering." He would divide these phases as follows. First, there is a kind that is mixed up with the truth. The devil says to a man, "Do not abandon the pleasures of life; life is long, and patience from the lusts of the body all one's life is a grievous burden." Then if the man remembers the great fact of God and of reward and punishment, and says to himself that patience from the lusts is grievous, but patience in the Fire more grievous, and that one of these must be, the devil turns and flees; for he cannot say that the Fire is easier than patience from sin, or that sin will not bring to the Fire. So his whispering is cut off by the man's faith in the Book of God. And so, too, if he whisper wondering admiration and say, "What creature knows God like thee, or serves him as thou dost, and how great is thy standing with God!" The man remembers that his knowledge and heart and limbs with which he knows and works are of God's creation; and how, then, should he be admired? So the devil must needs retire. This kind of "whispering" can be completely cut off in the case of those who know and see in the light of faith.

The second phase of "whispering" is that which rouses and moves lust, and it is either of a kind which the creature recognizes certainly as sin, or suspects vehemently. It he knows it certainly, the devil retires from the kind of rousing which actually results in moving lust, but not from simple rousing. And if it is only a suspected kind, it often remains at work so as to call for vigorous treatment in repelling it. So this "whispering" exists but is repelled and does not have the upper hand.

The third phase is that it should be a "whispering" of ideas (*khawāṭir; Einfälle*) only, and reminding of past states and a thinking of something else than prayer, for example. Then when the man turns to "remembering," it is conceivable that the whispering should be repelled at one time and return at another; so the two things keep alternating in the heart. So it is conceivable that they should compete with one another until the understanding embraces an understanding of the sense of what is recited and of those ideas, as though they were in two different places in the heart. And it is hardly conceivable that this kind can be repelled completely; yet it is not impossible, since the Prophet said, "He who prays a two-bow prayer without his soul bringing into it something of the world, all his sins that have gone before are forgiven to him."[1] If this were not conceivable the Prophet would not have mentioned it; but it can be looked for only in a heart that love has so mastered that it is infatuated. We sometimes see, in the case of a man whose heart is so occupied with an enemy who has injured him, that he will think, not for two bows but for many, about disputing with him, without another thing than thought of his enemy coming into his head. So, too, with one who is deeply in love and thinks of his beloved; he neither hears nor sees aught else. How, then, may not the same be looked for from fear of the Fire and desire of the Garden? Yet it is rare, for faith in God and the last day is weak.

All the views, then, that have been held as to the possibility of repelling the whisperings of the devil are possible as applied to the different kinds and phases of that whispering. Safety from it, too, for a short period of time is possible; but continuance in safety for a whole life is highly improbable; even, as things are, impossible. The Prophet himself was distracted from prayer by the border of his own robe and by a gold ring on his finger. So the slightest possession, beyond absolute necessity,—a single *dīnār*—will distract and bring thoughts of the world. There can be no compromise. He who

[1] Compare the story of S. Bernard and the man and the horse and the saddle in the *Golden Legend*, Vol. V, p. 23, Temple edition.

holds the world fast with his claws and yet desires to be free from the devil is like one who has been plunged in honey and thinks that flies will not light on him. The world is an enormous gateway for the devil; or rather, a multitude of gateways. First, he approaches a man through his sins; if he is repelled, then through advice, until he makes him fall into some innovation (*bidʿa*); if he is repelled in that, he leads him into abstinence until he regards something as unlawful that is not so; if he is repelled in that, he raises doubts as to whether his ablution or his prayer have been legally sound; and if he is repelled in that, he makes his deeds of piety easy for him, so that men regard him as most abstinent and patient; their hearts turn to him; he admires himself and perishes. This is the last stage of temptation; the saint who escapes self-admiration is safe of the Garden.

4. To illustrate the quickness of change in the heart and its sensitiveness to influence, the Prophet compared it to a sparrow, turning at every moment; to a pot boiling up all together; and to a feather blown on the surface of the desert. But it is always in the hand of God. Thus the Prophet was fond of using as an oath or form of address the title of God, "Turner of Hearts."

From the point of view of stability in good or evil, or swaying between the two, hearts are of three kinds: First, the fixedly good, however the devil may assail it;

to such a heart God turns his face; it is the heart at rest as in the *Qur'ān* (xiii, 28), "Do not hearts rest in the thought of Allāh!" Second is the hopelessly bad heart. In it black smoke rises from passion, fills it and extinguishes its light; reason cannot see to guide and is subdued by the lusts. But third is the heart in which there is constant swaying and contest between good and evil. The devil urges upon it the pleasures of the world and the example of learned theologians; but the angel, the abiding joys of heaven and pains of hell. The position is frankly otherworldly, and the fear of the Fire is the great motive urged. "If it were a hot summer day, and all mankind were standing out in the sun, while you had a cool house, would you stand by them, or would you not rather seek safety for yourself? How, then would you oppose them out of fear of the heat of the sun and not out of fear of the heat of the Fire?"

According, then, as the satanic qualities or the angelic qualities in each heart are predominant, will the issue be; and all that will happen will be in agreement with the decree of God. To him who is created for the Garden, the causes of obedience will be made easy; and to him who is created for the Fire, the causes of rebellion are made easy.

He whom Allāh wills to guide, he opens his breast to Islām; and he whom he wills to lead astray he narrows his breast.[1] He is the guider aright and the leader astray; he does what

[1] *Qur.* vi, 125.

he wills, and decides what he wishes; there is no opposer of his decision and no repeller of his decree. He created the Garden and created for it a people, then used them in obedience; and he created the Fire, and created for it a people, then used them in rebellion. And he informed his creation of the sign of the people of the Garden and of the sign of the people of the Fire; then said, "The pure are in pleasure and the impure are in Jaḥīm"[1] ["blazing fire," i. e., hell]. Then he said, as has been handed down from the Prophet, "These are in the Garden, and I care not; and these are in the Fire, and I care not." So he is Allāh Most High, the King, the Reality; "He is not asked concerning what he does; but they are asked."[2]

This is the end of the whole matter, and to this must return the vision of the Muslim mystic and the ecstasy of the Muslim saint; the dreams of a lover and a beloved, and the groanings and travailings of creation. Whenever the devout life, with its spiritual aspirations and fervent longings, touches the scheme of Muslim theology, it must thus bend and break. For it, within Islām itself, there is no place. The enormous handicap of the dogmatic system is too great; and if it would live its life, it must wander out into the heresies either of the mystic or the philosopher. Safety and dignity for the individual must be sought in some pantheistic scheme, starting either from God or from man. The darwīshes "without law" (*bī-sharᶜ*) are the legitimate outcome of this paradox of al-Ghazzālī.

[1] *Qur.* lxxxii, 13, 14. [2] *Ibid.*, xxi, 23.

Al-Ghazzālī's general introduction to the internal and hidden side of life has now been put before you, and the nature and working of that organ of communication with the spiritual world which he calls the "heart" should now be tolerably clear. Clear, also, in the broad, I trust, are the religious attitude and the religious life of Muslims—the general development for Islām of the text, or thesis, which I borrowed from Mr. William James. You have seen how real to Muslims is that invisible world; you have seen in what ways they think of it and turn toward it; and you have seen how they try to adjust themselves to it and live into it. The general drift is now before you.

Yet it would be easy to outline further and certainly fruitful lines of investigation. The precise pathology of Muḥammad's psychology is one. Another would be the history of the pantheistic development in the later Ṣūfī schools, under Buddhistic and Vedantic influence—a wide field. A third would be as wide and still more weighty—the present religious attitudes and movements of the Muslim peoples. That there are in them stirrings of new life, born of many causes, there can be no question. But these for the present must remain untouched.

INDEX

INDEX[1]

A

ᶜAbd al-Qādir al-Jīlānī, 145, 162, 199.
ᶜAbd ar-Razzāḳ, 170.
Abel, 139.
Aboo'l Ḥasan, 149, 150.
Abū Bakr, the Khalīfa, 204.
Abū Bakr ash-Shāshī, 93.
Abū Ḥanīfa, Code of, 143.
Abu-l-Kásim of Geelán, 206-8.
Abū Nuwās, 85.
Abū Shujāᶜ, 153.
Abū Sufyān, 48.
Active Intellect, 212.
Adam, 136, 141, 280, 289.
—*Aghānī*, 22, 31, 36.
ᶜĀʾisha, sayings of, 44, 60, 113.
—*Ākhirawīya, al-ᶜulūm*, 254.
—Akhṭal, 23.
ᶜ*Alā-l-fiṭra*, 243.
ᶜ*Ālam al-ḥaqq*, 72.
Alaeddin, Payne's trans. of, 105.
Alee El-Leysee, the Shaykh, 210.
Alexandria, 143.
ᶜAlī, 204; sayings of, 91, 232.
ᶜ*Ālim*, 264.
Allāh (*see also* God), 129, 135; his sovereignty, 37; his unity, 38; creation an aspect of him, 38; throned afar, 79; seen in dreams, 80; his daughters, 134; his immanence in the world, 159; Allah and not-Allah, 159; a concealed treasure, 170; Great Name of, 197; his personal will, 213; his aseity, 225; his armies, 231; his presence, 244; "Everything is perishing save his face," 245; *Allāhu akbar*, 247; *Allāh-Allāh*, 256; "All is God;" "God is all," 257; *Lā-ilāha illā-llāh*, 208, 257, 260; contemplation (*mushāhada*) of him, 260; "Turner of hearts," 299; his absolute guidance aright and astray, 300; "These are in the Fire and I care not," 301.
Almsgiving, 37.
Amalek, 28.
Amicable Numbers, 115.
Āmina, 22.
Amos, the Prophet, 14, 37.
Angels, 275, 276, 292, 294, 300; of revelation, 59; at Babel, Hārūt and Mārūt, 113; armies of, 288.

[1] The Arabic article, (*al*, etc.) is omitted when it would occur at the beginning of any of these entries; in its place a—is inserted.

Animal Spirit, 72.
Antichrist, Jewish, 35.
Apuleius, *Golden Ass* of, compared with *Arabian Nights*, 128, 129.
ᶜ*Aql* = ὁ νοῦς and τὸ νοούμενον 230, 231.
ᶜ*Aqlī*, 265.
—ᶜ*Aqlīya, al-ᶜulūm*, 254.
Aquinas, Thomas, 218.
Arabia, poets in ancient, 16, 18; *kāhin* of, 49.
Arabian Nights, 126, 128, 141–43; "Story of Sūl and Shumūl, 141; "Story of Hārūn ar-Rashīd and Tūḥfat al-Qulūb," 141; "History of the Forty Vizirs," 141; "Story of Abdullah and his Brothers," 141; "Story of the Fisherman and the Jinnī," 151.
Arabs, 17, 24; skepticism of, 4; soothsaying among, 9; inspiration of their poets, 19.
ᶜ*Ārif*, 268, 273.
—Arim, breaking of dam of, 21.
Aristotle, 53; "common sense" of, 56, 67, 78.
Aristotelian philosophers in Islām, 42, 51, 151, 158.
Armenians, 106.
ᶜ*Arrāf*, 25, 99.
Artemidorus (oneirocritic), 77.
—Ashᶜarī, 91, 92; his visions of Muḥammad, 89 ff.
ᶜAttār, 205.
Augustine, 14.
Aurangzib, 195, 196, 202, 203.
Auto-hypnosis, 257, 262.
Automatic speech, 99.
Automatic writers' formulae, 76.
Auto-suggestion common in the East, 156.
Averroes, position of, 125; two-fold truth of, 227.
Avicenna, 56, 152.
Aᶜwar, 288.
Awliyā, 136.
—*Azhar*, University of, 152.

B

Balaam, 17, 26, 27.
Babel, people of, 108, 113.
Badakhshān, 195.
Badger, Dr. G. P., *English-Arabic Lexicon* of, 121.
Baghdād, 145, 162.
—Baháee, the Shaykh, 210.
—Bājūrī, canon lawyer, 138, 153.
Bā-sharᶜ Darwīshes, 258.
Bath qôl, 272.
—Bedawee, the Sayyid, 211.
Bedawis, 11.
Benê Elôhîm, 38.
—Bērūnī, dream of, 86.
Berkeley, Bishop,—"The esse is the percipi," 170.
Bidᶜa, 299.
Bī-sharᶜ Darwīshes, 258, 301.
Bit-taqlīd was-samāᶜ, al-ᶜulūm, 254.

Body, a vehicle, 232; needs of, 232; likened to a king in his kingdom, 235; and mind, 252, 265.
Black Stone at Mecca, 216.
Bland, N., reference to, 77.
Breath, constraint of, in religious exercises, 262.
Brockelmann, Prof. Carl, 101.
Browne, Prof. E. S., quoted, 86, 127, 153.
—Bukhārī, *Ṣaḥīḥ* of, 35.
Bunyan, *Holy War* of, 235.
Burdon, Major Alder, reference to, 162.
Burton, Sir Richard, quoted, 91, 142.
Byzantium, 267.

C

Cain, 139.
Cairo, 126, 143, 148, 153, 206.
Canon lawyers of Islām, 215.
Caper plant, virtues of, 150.
Carmen, 28.
Chaldeans, 108, 113.
Chauvin, Professor Victor, reference to, 143.
Chillê, 153.
China, 267.
"Christian Science," 117.
Colored photisms, 201.
"Comforters, the," 72.
Companionship with a shaykh, 261.
Copts, 106.
Crystal gazing, 97, 126.

D

—Damīrī, quoted, 22, 23, 148, 151.
Dārā Shukōh, 202.
—*Darūrīya, al-ᶜulūm*, 254.
Darwish fraternities, 162 ff., 210, 301; place of, in Islām, 163; religious exercises of, 14; *bā-sharᶜ-bī-sharᶜ*, 258; Naqshbandite, 259; Qādirite, 195.
Dāsim, 288.
David, 29.
Death, artificial, by asceticism, 100.
Decorated vestibule, parable of, 266.
Defrémery, reference to, 94.
De Slane, references to, 84, 105, 110, 113, 124, 132, 142, 165.
Deuteronomy, Book of, 22.
Devil, devils, 284, 296, 300; never sleeps, 278; form of, 290; Devil or devils? 287; nature of, 292–94; pelting of, 65, 136.
Dhawq, 182, 187, 190.
Dhikr, 161, 259, 261, 274, 284–87.
Dieterici, Professor Fr., 152.
Diḥya al-Kalbī, 293.
—*Dīnīya, al-ᶜulūm*, 254.
Discipline of the Traveler, 220.
Divination through the insane, 98.
Dominicans, 164.
Dreams, books of, 77, 80; "bundles of dreams," 73;

interpretation of, 77; seeing Muḥammad or God in dream, 93; access to Unseen in dream, 214; veridical dreams, 272.
Duldul, 91.
Du Maurier's "dreaming true," 83.
—*Dunyā*, 232.
—*Dunyawiya, al-ʿulūm*, 254.
Dupont and Cappolani's *Confréries religieuses Musulmanes*, 165.
—*Dukhān* (chap. of Qur.), 35.

E

Earthly Paradise, the, 289.
Ecclesiastes, 8.
Economy of teaching in Islām, 227, 284.
Ego in Islām, 229.
Egypt and its magicians, 108, 113.
Eli, 29.
Elijah, 11.
Eve, 141.
Evil Eye, the, 119.

F

Fall, the, 139, 289.
Fanā, 248, 260, 262.
—Fārābī's definition of the Jinn, 151.
Fātiḥa, the, 210.
Fāṭima, sister of Dārā Shukōh, 203.
—Farazdaq, 36.
Fayd, 226.
Fetish power in poetry, 26.
Fez, 94.
Fī-faḍli-l-ʿilm, 120.
Fihrist, the, 77, 144.
Fi-l-istinjā, 138.
Fi-l-muʿāmala, 288.
Fire, the, fear of, in Islām, 123.
Fleischer on colored photisms, 201.
"Flesh," 228.
Flint, Robert, reference to, 41.
Franciscans, 164.
Freemasons, lodges of, comparison with, 164
Fulani Emirates of northern Nigeria, 162.

G

Gabriel, Archangel, 19, 20, 38, 287, 293.
Galen, 72.
Galland's MS of *Arabian Nights*, 151.
Geber, 109, 110.
"General sense," 74, 234.
Geomancy, 105.
Ghanī, 267, 268.
Ghayba, 260, 262.
—Ghazzālī, Abū Ḥāmid, 6, 14 82, 83, 91–93, 131, 144, 145, 150, 220, 223–28, 230, 236, 239, 240–42, 245, 249, 252, 258, 261–65, 268, 272, 274, 278–80, 284, 287, 292, 294, 296, 301, 302; on dreaming, 80; dreams of, 92; conversion of, 123; his Jinn-raising, 144; as a Ṣūfī, 174–219; anecdotes about, 193; philo-

sophical agnosticism and faith in the supernatural, 218; *Iḥyā* of, 220, 291; doctrine of the "heart," 221; —"*Maḍnūn aṣ-ṣaghīr*" of (quoted), 227, 292; *Book of Thanksgiving* of, 233; psychology of, 234; allegories of life of man of, 234; epistemology of, 254.
Gibb, E. J. W. "Story of Khannās," quoted, 140.
God, fatherhood of, 39; suffering, 39.
Golden Legend, 298.
Goldziher, Prof. Ignaz, quoted; *Arab. Philol.*, 16, 23, 28, 34, 139, 160; *Muhammedanische Studien*, 160, 161.
Goliath, 28.
Greeks, oracles of, 29.

H

Hadīth nafs, 286.
Hadji Khan, *With the Pilgrims to Mecca*, quoted, 216–18.
Hāgâ, 30.
Ḥāl, 182.
Hallucinations, non-veridical, 263; auditory, 272; visual, 272.
Ḥălōm, 75.
"Ḥalūma of the perfect nature," 75.
—*Ḥalūmīya*, 75.
Ḥêrēph, 28.
Holy Spirit, 188.
Holy Ghost, the, 39.
Hosea, the Prophet, 14, 37.
Hughes, *Dictionary of Islam*, reference to, 161.
Ḥulūl, 187.
Hypnosis, 67, 196; "Suggestion" in, 200.
—*Ḥaqq*, the Reality, 247, 248, 259.
Ḥaqīqī, 265.
Harem, the, at Mecca, 216, 217.
Ḥarrān, 100.
Hārūn ar-Rashīd, marriage to a Jinnī of, 143.
Hārūt, 113.
Ḥassān ibn Thābit, initiation of, 18, 19.
Hātif, 25, 272.
Hawā, 276.

I

Iblīs, 135, 136, 139, 141, 208, 278.
Ibn ᶜAbd Rabbihi, *Iqd* of, 84, 85.
Ibn ᶜArabī and the sea monster, 147; on knowledge, 188.
Ibn Baṭūṭa, 94, 101.
Ibn Khaldūn, 40–45, 47–49, 52 ff., 76, 79, 83, 93, 104–16, 119, 120, 131, 133, 150, 166, 169, 170, 173, 189, 203, 268. *Muqaddima* of, 40; on inspiration, 42; his definition of prophecy, 42; on signs of the prophets, 44; on mission of prophets, 53 ff., on verses

of Qurʾān on angels, Jinn, etc., 61 ff., 130; on dreaming, 69; on Ṣūfīs, 101, 166; on idiot-saints, 104; on magic and talismans, 108, 117; his experiences of magic, 113, 114; his philosophy of miracles, etc., 117; on miracles of saints, 118; his utilitarianism, 119, 122; on the evil eye, 119; on mysticism, 123; on the Divine Unity, 124; on the Jinn, 130; his pragmatic position, 131; on soothsaying, 162.
Ibn Khallikān, 142; dream of, 84–86.
Ibn Qāsim, 138, 153.
Ibn Ṣayyād, 34–36, 64, 66.
Ibn Shaddād, Qāḍī Bahā ad-dīn, College of, 84.
Ibn Sīnā, see Avicenna.
Ibn al-Waḥshīya, 110.
Ibrāhīm al-Khawwāṣ, 271.
Ibrāhīm ibn Adham, 271.
Idea, devotion of orientals to single, 10.
ʿIfrīts (*see also* Jinn), 155.
Ilhām, 252, 254, 255, 275, 276.
ʿIlm, 288.
—*ʿIlm ar-rabbānī, al-ladunī*, 269.
Imr al-Qays, 31.
Intellect, like a hunter with horse and dog, 236.
Intention, doctrine of, 295.
"Interesting," 120–22.
Iqtibās, 1.
ʿIrfān, 248.
Isaiah, 13, 14, 37.
Isaiah, Book of (8:19), 29.
Islām, religious attitude in, 2, 14; future life in, 15; Holy Spirit in, 19, 37, 62; inspiration of poets in, 25; pantheism in, 39; dualistic mysticism in, 39; shell of law in, 42; Aristotelianism in, 53; Neoplatonism in, 51, 53, 77, 124; dream-books in, 77; stories of dreams in, 83; dreaming in, 94; alchemy in, 110; fear of the Fire in, 123; magic in modern, 126; the Fall and original sin in, 139; saints in, 157; ascetic-ecstatic life in, 157; mystical faith in, 159; communities of begging friars in, 161; monasteries in, 161; darwīsh fraternities in, 163; tertiaries in, 164; women saints in, 165; pathways to reality in, 214; final pantheism in, 301.
Ismāʿīlite influence on Ṣūfīs, 171.
Ispahan, 153, 154.
Isrāfīl, 216.
Ittiḥād, 187, 248.

J

Jacob, blessing of, 22.
Jacobus a Voragine, *Legenda Aurea* of, 5, 298.

Jadhba, 258.
Jaḥīm, 301.
Jamᶜ, 261.
James, Professor William, references to, 1, 175, 201, 212, 257, 272, 302.
Jeremiah, the Prophet, 14, 37.
Jesuits, order of, 219.
Jesus, 139, 278, 282.
Jethro, 29.
Jihād, lesser and greater, 235, 236.
Jinn, the, 11, 17, 26, 29, 44, 62, 116, 127–37, 141, 149, 150, 153, 154, 289, 291–94; in Islām, 130 ff., Robertson Smith on, 133 ff.; Muḥammad and the J., 135 ff.; Jinn of Naṣībīn, 138; salvability of, 139; Hārūn ar-Rashīd and the, 142; can they be seen? 142; marriages with men, 143; loves of, 144; al-Ghazzālī's raising of, 144; in folk-lore, 145; Jinn of China, 146; devotees and students of, 149; have they reason? 151; al-Fārābī's definition of, 151; Avicenna's definition of, 152; speech of, 152; whistling of, 152; how to control, 153.
Jinnī, a, 18, 20, 33, 37, 45.
Jismānī, 265.
Job, Book of (10:30), 289.
Judah, 14.
Jūkīya, i.e. yogis, 101.

K

Kaᶜba, 218.
Kāhin, *kāhina*, 22, 25, 29, 30–34, 37, 49, 64, 67, 98, 99, 135.
Karāma, *karāmāt*, miracles of saints, 50, 95.
Keightley's *Fairy Mythology* referred to, 291.
Khawāṭir, 275, 297.
Khayāl, 265.
—Khaḍir, el Khidr, 211, 262.
Khinzib, 277, 288.
Kipling's, Mr. Rudyard, *Kim* referred to, 257.
Kôhēn see *Kāhin*, 25, 29.

L

Labbayka yā rabbanā, 32, 217.
Lane, E. W., on magic mirror, 126; his trans. of *Arabian Nights*, 139, 143, 153, 163, 206, 209; his *Modern Egyptians*, 139, 163.
Lang's, Mr. Andrew, *Making of Religion*, reference to, 97.
Laṭīfa rabbānīya, 221.
—*Lawḥ al-maḥfūẓ*, 253, 264.
Legenda Aurea, 5, 298.
Leprechaun, 291.
Law, attitude to in East and West, 6 ff.; Ottoman, 143, 153; Shāfiᶜite, 153; shell of, in East and West, 8 ff.

M

—Madīna, 18, 34, 36, 61, 80, 137, 277; chapters and verses of, 61.

—*Maḍnūn* of al-Ghazzālī, quoted, 80, 190.
Magic, theory of, 51; three kinds of, 112; slitters, 114–16; magicians in modern Islām, 126 f.; black, 128.
Majdhūbs, 258.
—*Malakūt*, 243, 245.
Man, between the beasts and the angels, 237; his knowledge and will, 237; four properties in, 240; what "under his hide," 240; higher than the angels, 273; all his knowledge ultimately inspirational, 250.
Mandal, magic figure, 153.
Mansoul, leaguer of, 235; City of, 280.
Margoliouth, Professor, *Life of Muḥammad*, referred to, 46.
Marco Polo, 94.
Mar'ī basīṭ, 98.
Mārūt, 113.
Maṣābīḥ, 36.
Maslama ibn Aḥmad of Madrid, 109, 110.
Maxwell, Dr., 117, 200; his *Metapsychical Phenomena* referred to, 127.
Mecca, 45, 61, 91, 197, 203; chapters and verses of, 61; Meccan period of Muḥammad, 68; pilgrimage to, 86, 88, 215.
"Mental Science," 117, 200.
Merv, 87, 88.
"Metapsychical," 117.
Myers', F. W. H., *Human Personality*, reference to, 272.
Min ladunnā, 269.
Min rabbihi, 269.
—*Mi'rāj*, 290.
Miswāṭ, 288.
Mitchell, Dr. Weir, reference to, 272.
Mithāl, *mithl*, 81, 82, 290.
Molla Shāh, 195, 199, 202–4.
Morocco, saints of, 149.
Moses, 1, 21, 22, 28, 108, 113, 280.
Môshēl, 15, 17.
—Mubarrad, *Kāmil* and *Rawḍa* of, 84, 85.
—*Mubashshirāt*, 72.
Muḥammad, the Prophet, 1, 10, 14, 18, 19, 22, 31, 33–42, 45–49, 65, 67, 69, 72, 80, 135, 204, 210, 225, 277, 290, 292; sayings of, 19, 43, 44, 59, 60, 64, 72, 74, 81, 124, 136, 137, 139, 175, 178, 179, 199, 214, 228, 235, 241, 276, 277, 279, 281, 284, 294, 295, 297, 299; inspiration of, 19; inspirational seizures of, 33, 44, 59 ff.; two ideas of, 37; miracles of, 49; auto-hypnosis of, 68; M. seen in dreams, 77, 80; M. and the Jinn, 135 ff.; at Mt. Ḥīra, 187; usage (*sunna*) of, 279; psychological experiences of, 298.
Muḥammad ibn Ahmad at-Tabasī, 144.
Muḥammad al-Andalusī, 149.

Muʿjiza, 49.
—*Muktāsiba bit-ta ʿallum wal-istiḍlāl, al-ʿulūm*, 259.
—*Munqidh* of al-Ghazzālī, quoted, 170.
Murāqaba, 259.
Murtaḍà, the Sayyid, 220, 257.
Musaylima, 66.
Mushāhada, 260.
Muṣṭafa al-Munádee, 210.
Mutakhayyila, 290.
Mutashābihāt, 113.
Muttaḥid, 169.
Muʿtazilites, 49–51, 87, 89, 91, 150.

N

Nabateans, 108, 113.
Nabatean Agriculture, Book of, 108, 109.
Nafatha, 19.
Nafs, 228, 229, 231, 274.
—*Nafs al-mutmaʾinna*, 229.
—*Nafs al-lawwāma*, 229.
—*Nafs al-ammāra bis-sūʾ*, 230.
Nāṣir ibn Khusraw, dream and conversion of, 86–88.
—*Nawawi*, 36.
Nebhīʾīm, 13, 16, 37.
Neoplatonism in Islām, 51, 53, 77, 124.
Nephesh, 228.
New Testament, 49.
Nīya, 295.
Noah, 281.
Numbers, Book of, 20.

O

Occam, 158; nominalism of, 172.
"Odysseus," *Turkey in Europe* of, quoted, 122.
Old Testament, 11, 15, 29, 49, 160.
Omreh, 216.
Original sin in Islām, doctrine of, 139.
Ottoman law, 143.
"Outpouring," 226.

P

Paul, 222.
Payne, Mr. John, on geomancy, 105; transl. of *Arabian Nights*, 141, 142.
"People of the upper region," 70.
Pepys, 94.
Perinde ac si cadaver, 219.
Peter the Cruel, 40.
Piper, Mrs., 46, 47, 64.
Plotinian pantheism, 151, 159, 170.
Poet in ancient Arabia, 16 ff.; as leader of Arabs, 21; inspiration of poets in Islām, 25.
Porphyry, the oneirocritic, 77.
"Possession" in abnormal psychology, 99.
Potiphar, 29.
Powers of numbers and letters, 106.
Pratt, Professor J. B., 203.
Preserved Tablet, the, 253, 264, 265.
Prophecy, 214.
Prophets, sons of, 11; schools of, 16; miracles of, 5; soul

of, 52, 58; inspirational nature of, 58.
Prophetism; 37, soil of, 12 ff.
Proverbs, Book of (chap. 31), 30.

Q

Qabas, 1.
Qabūl, 261.
Qādirites, 162, 195.
Qadhafa, 252.
—Qādisīya, 119.
Qā'id, 22.
Qalb, 221, 231.
Qārib ibn al-Aswad, 66.
Qarīn, 19.
—Qazwīnī, 145.
Qur'ān, 30, 60–62, 65, 67, 74, 113, 137, 138, 143, 151, 172, 253, 255, 268, 269, 274, 283, 294; revelation of, 18; creation of, 26; Q. of the devil, 26; a miracle, 52; in *saj'*, 67; "clear" and "obscure" verses in, 133; references to —ii, 271, p. 276; iv, 162, p. 280; v. 4, p. 61; vi, 125, pp. 179, 245, 300; vii, 10 ff., p. 280; vii, 19, p. 274; vii, 171, p. 92; vii, 178, p. 205; viii, 24, p. 223; xii, 44, p. 74; xii, 53, p. 230; xiii, 28, pp. 241, 300; xiii, 33, p. 45; xv, 18, p. 65; xvi, 74, p. 143; xvii, 12, p. 282; xvii, 66, p. 289; xvii, 87, pp. 225, 239; xviii, 23, p. 260; xviii, 48, p. 136; xviii, 64, p. 269; xix, 17, p. 293; xx, 10, p. 1; xx, 110, p. 47; xx, 118, p. 274; xxi, 5, p. 74; xxi, 23, p. 301; xxi, 38, p. 282; xxvi, 89, p. 190; xxvii, 7, p. 1; xxvii, 63, p. 184; xxviii, 30, p. 93; xxviii, 88, pp. 245, 246; xxxiii, 41, p. 161; xxxiii, 72, p. 243; xxxvii, 8, p. 57; xxxviii, 34, p. 287; xxxix, 23, p. 245; xxxix, 27, p. 229; xl, 9, p. 143; xl, 16, p. 247; xlii, 50, p. 254; xliv, p. 35; xlvi, 28 ff., p. 136; xlix, 12, p. 285; l, 15, p. 274; l, 21, p. 178; li, 49, p. 276; li, 56, p. 232; liii, p. 290; lix, 19, p. 223; lxxii, p. 135; lxxiii, pp. 34, 44; lxxiii, 5, p. 60; lxxiv, p. 34; lxxiv, 34, p. 231; lxxv, 2, p. 229; lxxv, 16, p. 47; lxxxii, 13, 14, p. 301; xci, 8, p. 252; cxii, p. 197; cxiii, p. 113; cxiv, 4, 5, p. 274.
Quraysh, tribe of, 22.
—Qushayrī, 270.
Quṭb or "axis," 171.

R

Rābi'a, 205.
Rāhib, 161.
—Rāzī, *Mafātīḥ al-ghayb* of, 152.
Reality, the, 259, 301; pathways to, 214.
"Remembering" God, 161, 295.
Renan, reference to, 125.
Robertson, W. F., quoted, 1.

Romans, Epistle to (8:22), 66.
Rūḥ, 224, 231, 239.
Rūḥānī, 291.

S

Sā'iḥ, 161.
Saints, 70, 103 ff.; fastidiousness of, as to burial, 5; in East and West, 5; examples of miracles of, 49, 103, 172, 269; of Morocco, 149; hierarchy of Muslim, 158; as ascetics, 160; as teachers, 160; hypnotic and antinomian, 195; stories of, 269.
Sainthood, 214.
Saj', 22, 29–32, 64, 67.
Ṣāliḥ Beg, 197.
Sālik, 259.
Samuel, 13, 23, 25, 29.
Sanguinetti, reference to, 94.
Sanūsites, 162.
Satan, 92, 140, 141, 290; his family, 288.
Sawdā bint Zuhra, 22.
Selves, subliminal, 42.
Sensuous-ascetic paradox of man's nature, 197.
Seville, 40.
Scroll of the seven stars, 109.
Scrying in Islām, 97.
—Shādhilī, 272.
Shah Jahān, 202, 203.
Shahwa kādhiba, ṣādiqa, 228.
Shā'ir, 17, 21, 25.
Shakhṣ, 81.
—Sha'rānī, 147, 149.
—*Shar'īya, al-'ulūm*, 254.
Shaṭaḥāt, 173.
Shaybān ar-Rā'ī, 270, 271.
Shayṭān (*see also* Satan, devil), 26, 56, 275.
Schefer, reference to, 86.
—Shiblī, 269, 270.
Shī'ite, 171.
Shiloh, 29.
Shi'r, 31.
Shukr, 260.
Smith, W. Robertson, quoted, 133, 139.
Snobbishness in Muslim thought, 227.
Signatures, doctrine of, 107.
Ṣirāṭ, 204.
Society for Psychical Research, 36, 84, 155, 156, 201, 292.
Socrates, δαίμων of, 24, 272.
Solomon, 287.
Soothsaying, nature of, 62.
Soul and body, 55, 116, 228, tendency upwards, 55; three kinds of, 57; apprehension by, 73; rational soul, 76–78; nature of, 96; child's rational soul, 96; rational soul of magicians, 111, 112.
Speaking head, the, 100.
Speaking with tongues, 172.
Spirits of the spheres, 212.
Spitta Bey, reference to, 89.
Sprenger, Alois, references to, 44, 46.
St. Bernard, 298.
St. Francis, 272.
St. John, Bayle, *Two Years in*

a Levantine Family, references to, 143, 155, 156.
Subliminal consciousness, 42, 263.
Ṣūfīs, derivation of name, 161, 166; Muslim view of origin, 165; dictionaries of biography, 165; ladder of "states," 167, 173, 174, 188, 189; books of, 167; methods of rending veil of sense, 168; metaphysics, 169; discipline of the soul, 171; unveiling of the unseen world, 171; control of material things, 171; path of, 181, 255, 256; view of *nafs*, 229.
Sufyān ath-Thawrī, 270, 271.
Sulūb, 293.
Sulūk, 258.
Ṣūra, 290.
Surayj, 85.
Swinnerton's *Indian Nights' Entertainments*, reference to, 272.
Syrians, 108, 113.

T

—Ṭabarī, Qurʾān commentary of, references to, 47, 252.
Tajallà, 170.
Takahhana, 32.
Talismans, 11, 117, 216.
Taqwa, 287.
Tabūk, Raid of, 61.
Ṭarīq, *ṭarīqa*, 255, 259.
Tawakkul Beg, 195–98, 200, 202, 203, 263.
Tawfīq, 275.
Tawḥīd, 248.
Tennyson, auto-hypnosis of, 257.
Thabr, 288.
Theologians, speculative, 118, 266.
Thomas, Mr. N.W., on crystal-gazing, 126.
"Thought" (*dhikr*) of God, 259, 277, 286.
Ṭimṭim the Indian, Book of, 109.
Timur, 40.
Trinity, doctrine of, 19.
Ṭulayḥa al-Asadī, 66.

U

—ʿ*Ulūm*, 254.
—ʿ*Ulūm al-maḥmūda wal-madhmūma*, 120.
ʿUmar, the Khalīfa, 101, 204, 244.
Unity and multiplicity, 170.
Unseen, reality of, to orientals, 2 ff.
Urim and Thummim, 25.
ʿUthmān, the Khalīfa, 204.

V

Van Vloten, reference to, 139.
Van Dyck, Dr. E. A., reference to, 56.
Vates, 28.
Verne, Jules, 126.
"Verse of the Religion," 61.
Vision, 70 ff.; from God, 74; from angels, 74; from the

devil, 74; of God and of Muḥammad in dream, 80.
Vollers, Professor Karl, reference to, 163.
Von Kremer, quoted, 163, 195, 202.

W

Wahhābites, 215.
Waḥy, 59, 252–54.
Walahān, 288.
Walī, awliyā, 161, 252, 261, 271, 273.
Waswās, 274, 275.
Wellhausen, Professor Julius, references to, 25, 139.
Wells, Mr. H. G., 126.
Weil, Gustav, reference to, 46.
Weir, Mr. T. H., *The Shaikhs of Morocco*, quoted, 149.
"Whisperings" of the devil, 274, 278, 296, 298.
Wilāyeh, 207, 210.
Wizards, 95, 99.
World of the elements, 54; of becoming, 54; of animals, 54; of angels, 55; of reality, 72.
Wordsworth, quoted, 12, 13; his "eternal deep" referred to, 263.
Women in religious Islām, 205.
Wuṣūl, 187.
Wüstenfeld, references to, 84, 85, 142, 145.

Y

Yahwé, 21.
Yiddiᶜônî, 17, 29.
Yogis, 101.
Young, Mr. George, *Corps de Droit Ottoman*, references to, 143.

Z

Zāhid, 161.
Zalanbūr, 288.
Zeller's *Aristotle and the Earlier Peripatetics*, reference to, 56.
—Zubayr ibn al-ᶜAwwām, 137.
Zuhayr ibn Janāb, 21.

www.ingramcontent.com/pod-product-compliance
Lightning Source LLC
Chambersburg PA
CBHW021819300426
44114CB00009BA/232
9781850770503